Theory and Concepts of English for Academic Purposes

Also by Ian Bruce

ACADEMIC WRITING AND GENRE: A SYSTEMATIC ANALYSIS

Theory and Concepts of English For Academic Purposes

Ian Bruce
University of Waikato, New Zealand

palgrave
macmillan

No portion of this publication may be reproduced, copied or transmitted save with written permission or in accordance with the provisions of the Copyright, Designs and Patents Act 1988, or under the terms of any licence permitting limited copying issued by the Copyright Licensing Agency, Saffron House, 6–10 Kirby Street, London EC1N 8TS.

Any person who does any unauthorized act in relation to this publication may be liable to criminal prosecution and civil claims for damages.

The author has asserted his right to be identified as the author of this work in accordance with the Copyright, Designs and Patents Act 1988.

First published 2011 by
PALGRAVE MACMILLAN

Palgrave Macmillan in the UK is an imprint of Macmillan Publishers Limited, registered in England, company number 785998, of Houndmills, Basingstoke, Hampshire RG21 6XS.

Palgrave Macmillan in the US is a division of St Martin's Press LLC, 175 Fifth Avenue, New York, NY 10010.

Palgrave Macmillan is the global academic imprint of the above companies and has companies and representatives throughout the world.

Palgrave® and Macmillan® are registered trademarks in the United States, the United Kingdom, Europe and other countries

ISBN 978–0–230–24974–5   hardback

This book is printed on paper suitable for recycling and made from fully managed and sustained forest sources. Logging, pulping and manufacturing processes are expected to conform to the environmental regulations of the country of origin.

A catalogue record for this book is available from the British Library.

Library of Congress Cataloging-in-Publication Data

Bruce, Ian, 1953–
Theory and concepts of English for academic purposes / Ian Bruce.
   p. cm.
  Includes index.
  ISBN 978-0-230-24974-5 (hardback)
1. Academic writing—Study and teaching (Higher)   2. English
  language—Study and teaching (Higher)   3. Language and education.
  I. Title.
  P301.5.A27B78 2011
  428.2′4–dc22   2011001473

10   9   8   7   6   5   4   3   2   1
20 19 18 17 16 15 14 13 12 11

Printed and bound in Great Britain by
CPI Antony Rowe, Chippenham and Eastbourne

To the BALEAP community

Contents

List of Tables and Figure   viii

Acknowledgements   x

Part I   A Theoretical Basis for English for Academic Purposes

1   Introduction to EAP: Key Issues and Concepts   3

2   Investigating the Academic World   15

3   Students' Needs and EAP Course Design   36

Part II   The Design of EAP Courses

4   Developing an EAP Syllabus: Approaches and Models   53

5   EAP Courses and Subject Discipline Knowledge   66

6   EAP Courses and Language Knowledge   83

Part III   The Implementation of EAP Courses

7   EAP and Teacher Competencies   103

8   EAP and Teaching the Writing Skill   118

9   EAP and Teaching the Reading Skill   140

10   EAP and Teaching the Listening Skill   154

11   EAP and Teaching the Speaking Skill:
     Teaching Critical Thinking   177

12   EAP and Assessment   196

References   210
Index   225

List of Tables and Figure

Tables

3.1	Needs analysis	39
3.2	Present situation analysis	40
3.3	Target situation analysis: pre-sessional EAP courses	42
3.4	Target situation analysis: in-sessional EAP courses	43
3.5	Target situation analysis: postgraduate EAP courses	44
4.1	Goals for two courses	60
4.2	Course goal and overall objectives of the reading and writing course	62
4.3	Course goal and overall objectives of the listening and speaking course	62
4.4	Sample general EAP writing syllabus unit objective	64
4.5	Sample general EAP writing syllabus unit	65
5.1	Approaches to text classification	77
6.1	Data commentary text (Report cognitive genre)	85
6.2	Analysis of the data commentary text	86
6.3	Five uses of *the* for defining or specifying nouns	87
6.4	Use of *the* in the data commentary text	88
6.5	Contrastive argument text (Discussion cognitive genre)	88
6.6	Analysis of the contrastive argument text	90
6.7	Mark-up of the contrastive argument text	91
6.8	Markers of purpose	92
6.9	Hyland's interpersonal model of metadiscourse	94
6.10	Metadiscourse features in the contrastive argument text	95
6.11	Word networks	100

8.1   Proposal for a general EAP writing course syllabus   134

8.2   Studies of Results sections   136

8.3   Findings of Results section study: sociology
      and organic chemistry articles   138

Figure

3.1   Needs analysis and EAP course design   37

Acknowledgements

The author and the publisher wish to express thanks to the following for the use of copyright materials: The British Association of Lecturers in English for Academic Purposes (BALEAP) for permission to quote the 11 competency statements from the *Competency Framework for Teachers of English for Academic Purposes* (2008) document, along with the list of elements of *knowledge and understanding* that relate to each statement; Cambridge University Press for permission to quote the sections 'A Target Situation Analysis' (pp. 59–60) and 'A Framework for Analysing Learner Needs' (pp. 62–3) in Tom Hutchinson and Alan Waters' book, *English for Specific Purposes* (1987); and the Continuum International Publishing Group Ltd for permission to reproduce the Table (3.1) entitled 'Metadiscourse' from Ken Hyland's book *Metadiscourse* (2005).

If any copyright holders have inadvertently been overlooked, the author and publisher will be pleased to make amends.

Part I

A Theoretical Basis for English for Academic Purposes

1
Introduction to EAP: Key Issues and Concepts

1. Introduction

During the last two decades, *English for Academic Purposes* (hereafter EAP) courses have grown exponentially around the world. These are courses that either prepare non-native speaker students for English-medium academic study or support such students who are already taking courses in universities or some other branch of higher education. Section 2 of this chapter presents a discussion of what constitutes EAP and how it differs from other areas of English language teaching. Given the current growth in this relatively new area of English language teaching, this book aims to theorize the activity of EAP and to propose a basis for the systematic planning and implementation of this type of course. To realize these aims, the book is divided into three parts, following a general to specific principle. Part I proposes a theoretical basis for the teaching of EAP, and consists of three chapters. The present chapter introduces and defines key terms and concepts central to EAP; the second chapter reviews approaches to researching the academic world in order to inform EAP courses; and the third chapter considers issues of student needs as a basis for EAP. Part II focuses on the design of EAP courses. Here, three chapters relate EAP courses to disciplinary knowledge, strategic or organizational knowledge and language knowledge. Principles are then proposed for the development of syllabuses that are able to integrate these knowledge types in ways that support a systematic pedagogy. Part III of the book is concerned with the specifics of the implementation of EAP courses. This part focuses on a number of areas, including EAP teacher competencies, teaching the four skills of reading, listening, speaking and writing within an EAP context, and assessment, particularly of the productive skills in the EAP context.

2.   Defining EAP

EAP has grown out of, and is a branch of, a slightly older field of language teaching – that of *English for Specific Purposes* (hereafter ESP). Richards and Schmidt (2002: 181) define the parent discipline of ESP as 'the role of English in a language course or programme of instruction in which the *content* and *aims* of the course are fixed by the specific needs of a particular group of learners'. For example, an ESP course may be tailored to meet the English needs of a particular professional or voca-tional group, such as lawyers, engineers, medical workers or air traffic controllers. Widdowson (1983), when describing ESP courses, considers types of course aim, and distinguishes between what he terms *narrow angle* and *wide angle* ESP courses, depending on the degree of specificity of the aims of the course: '[b]y aims I mean the purposes to which learn-ing will be put after the end of the course' (p. 7). Widdowson proposes that narrow angle ESP courses are essentially a training exercise designed to 'provide learners with a restricted competence to enable them to cope with clearly defined tasks' (p. 6). The specific types of language use required to fulfil the tasks become the aims of the course. Thus, for example, a narrow angle ESP course could be English for air traffic controllers, which focuses on the specific instructions and interactions of that occupation. On the other hand, Widdowson proposes that wide angle ESP courses are closer to general-purpose English courses, which 'seek to provide learners with a general capacity to enable them to cope with undefined eventualities in the future' (p. 6).

In describing the underlying types of knowledge and skills that are the focus of ESP courses, Widdowson (1983) makes a distinction between what he calls *competence* and *capacity*.

> *competence* – 'the speaker's knowledge of the language system . . . his knowledge also of social rules which determine the appropriate use of linguistic forms' (p. 7).
> *capacity* – 'the ability to create meanings by exploiting the potential inherent in the language for continual modification in response to change' (p. 8).

Widdowson suggests that, at one extreme, narrow angle ESP courses that require a more restricted repertoire of language are essentially a training exercise in developing a competence in the use of relatively formulaic language to perform specific-purpose tasks, as in the case, for example, of the use of English by air traffic controllers. In contrast, wide angle courses give more attention to developing a capacity to exploit the social and linguistic aspects of language competence in ways that cannot be specifically identified in the aims of the course:

> The purposes in ESP are arranged along a scale of specificity with training at one end and education at the other. As one moves along the scale in the direction of education, one has to account increasingly for the development of capacity, and at the same time, one has to take into consideration the pedagogic problem of establishing objectives which are projections of final aims. At the training end of the scale, objectives and aims will converge into close correspondence and will seek to impart restricted competence. At the education end of the scale will cluster courses of *English for academic purposes* [emphasis added] which require the development of communicative capacity and which will call for pedagogic decisions in the formulation of objectives. At this end of the scale, ESP shades into GPE [general purpose English: I.B.] (Widdowson, 1983: 10–11).

Thus on the narrow to wide angle continuum for categorizing ESP courses, Widdowson locates EAP courses at the wide angle end where future academic language needs of students relate to development of 'capacity' as well as 'competence'. However, since Widdowson's (1983) proposal for EAP as a more open-ended, less specific activity, other writers and theorists (Blue, 1988; Coffey, 1984; Jordan, 1989) have emphasized that EAP also needs to focus on the specific characteristics of particular academic disciplines. In order to reconcile the two viewpoints, Jordan (1997) proposes that, depending on the needs of students, EAP courses may be more general, which he terms *English for General Academic Purposes* (EGAP), or relate more closely to the needs of studying in a specific discipline, which he terms *English for Specific Academic Purposes* (ESAP). However, Hyland (2002b) suggests that there needs to be a greater focus on disciplinary specificity in academic English courses and actually challenges both the validity and usefulness of more general EAP courses.

Similarly, in the editorial of the inaugural issue of the *Journal of English for Academic Purposes*, the editors when defining EAP initially refer to Flowerdew and Peacock (2001) who state that EAP is 'the teaching of English with the specific aim of helping learners to study, conduct research or teach in that language' (p. 8). However, as part of their definition of the field, the editors also appear to support the idea that EAP should have a specific, disciplinary focus, stating that it refers to language research and instruction that focuses on the specific communicative needs and practices of particular groups in academic contexts. It means grounding instruction in an understanding of the cognitive, social and linguistic demands of *specific academic disciplines* [emphasis added] (Hyland & Hamp-Lyons, 2002: 2).

More recently, Hyland (2009a) has continued to argue the case for specificity in EAP, citing quantitative findings from corpus studies that have compared the use of linguistic features in different subject disciplines, features such as the use of cautious language (termed *hedges*), author self-mention (the use of 'I' or 'we' when writing), transitions and citations. Hyland's studies show that academic texts from different subject areas differ in the use of these linguistic or citational features. However, the strength of his argument for specificity rests on the extent to which these researched features of academic texts, of themselves, can be said to operationalize the wider phenomenon of academic subject discourses realized in texts. While the range of elements investigated in such studies is probably too small to achieve this operationalization, this research, nevertheless, appears to provide partial evidence for the case for disciplinary specificity.

Thus, even if we continue to locate EAP at the wide end of Widdowson's (1983) 'wide angle/narrow angle' continuum, it would be misleading, for example, to propose that EAP is concerned with teaching one single register of academic English (defined in terms of a single set of linguistic features) that can be used in all disciplines. On the contrary, it is acknowledged that each academic discipline will vary greatly in terms of its values, assumptions and communicative purposes, some of the consequences of which will be evident in the linguistic and citational differences of its texts, such as those shown in the studies to which Hyland (2009a) refers. However, if EAP courses are to employ aims and objectives that relate to discipline-specific communicative outcomes (that differ from more narrow angle ESP courses), they will need to focus on the range of language- and knowledge-organizing resources that *may* be drawn upon as a response to the disciplinary, communicative requirements of specific subject areas, or, as Hyland and Hamp-Lyons, in their inaugural editorial, expressed it succinctly, 'the cognitive, social and linguistic demands of specific academic disciplines' (2002: 2).

EAP, therefore, is the study of English for the purpose of participating in higher education. This study will be centred on the texts (spoken and written) that occur in academic contexts and will include the discourses and practices that surround and give rise to such texts. The focus, therefore, of EAP courses will be on a range of types of *knowledge*, including social, cognitive and linguistic knowledge, acknowledging that within each of these areas there will be considerable variation across particular subject disciplines. As a consequence, the challenge facing the EAP course designer and teacher is to equip students with the tools to deconstruct and make sense of the texts and related discourses of their particular discipline (present or future). In effect, this involves equipping students with the tools of discourse analysis, tools that they can meaningfully apply in present or future study within their chosen discipline.

3. Learner need and EAP

The previous section has established that EAP is a needs-driven activity, involving courses that attempt to meet the needs of students preparing for, or already participating in, higher education (typically at university level). This section begins to consider the issue of learner need and specifically, the needs of students at different stages of their study careers. The issue of learner need as a key background element that drives the design of EAP courses is addressed in Chapter 3, where approaches to performing a *needs analysis* and then relating learner need to the design of courses will be considered. This section merely provides a brief overview of issues that will be unpacked later and in greater detail.

As we saw in the earlier definitions of ESP and EAP, learner need is central to defining both of these approaches to language teaching and learning. However, deconstructing learner need in relation to academic skills and competencies is complex and multi-faceted. Effectively, EAP practitioners have to take two types of situation into account when performing a needs analysis: the students' *present situation* (the knowledge and practices that students bring from their prior educational experiences) and *the target situation*, where the learner needs to get to in order to participate in their chosen subject area (Hutchinson & Waters, 1987). Understanding both of these aspects of need is a key element that will guide the planning of a course and the thinking that governs the selection of the content, processes and activities of the course.

Also, in relation to learner need, it is important to consider the stage or level of academic education at which the EAP course is located. EAP courses are either preparatory, occurring before the student enters their chosen area of study (often called *pre-sessional*) or they take place at the same time as students are engaged in academic study (often called *in-sessional*).

3.1   Pre-sessional EAP courses

Pre-sessional courses may occur at a number of levels: pre-university foundation courses that prepare students for undergraduate study, pre-postgraduate courses that prepare students who already have a first degree for postgraduate study in a particular field. The amount of subject discipline specificity that can be incorporated into any pre-sessional EAP course depends on the level of the course and the intended areas of study of its participants. For example, if all of the participants intend to study in one subject discipline, such as engineering, obviously the pre-sessional EAP course can draw heavily on the texts and discourses of that discipline.

However, in other teaching situations it may not be possible to relate the aims and content of a course to one specific disciplinary context. For example, in the case of a course for a pre-sessional group of students who individually aim to study in a diverse range of academic disciplines, it is not feasible to orientate the EAP course aims and content towards each student's university subject. Thus, a pre-sessional course cannot focus exclusively on the texts and practices of business, or humanities or social sciences – unless it is known that all of the students within the group will be studying in only one of those subject areas. Also, in relation to their language development and their performance of certain types of task, it is proposed here that students in pre-university, pre-sessional EAP courses need to be gaining transferable procedural knowledge rather than topic-connected, discipline-specific knowledge – they need to be developing what Widdowson (1983) refers to as *capacity* as well as *competence*. In designing syllabuses and courses for this group, the key issue is to formulate course aims that develop both capacity and competence.

3.2   In-sessional EAP courses

The other category of EAP courses are in-sessional courses, for example for students already engaged in undergraduate or postgraduate study. Here, meeting the students' target needs usually involves further addressing the language needs (and most urgently, the writing needs) of students at either level. In relation to writing, undergraduate students need to develop the means to interrogate and respond to the requirements of undergraduate assignment genres, which is not a straightforward issue. As Ann Johns (1997: 23) says: '[s]ome genres, particularly in pedagogical contexts, are loosely, and almost casually, named'. According to theorists and researchers in the academic literacies movement, undergraduate assignments, even though they may share a common nomenclature (such as *essay*), will vary greatly in their expectations because of the particular epistemologies of the different subject areas (Lea & Street, 1998: 5). Students at this level, therefore, need to understand the types of orientation, identity and discoursal resources that the assignments of different disciplines require. This issue is multiplied in the case of under- graduates who are taking broad-based degrees and facing courses and assignments in a variety of subject areas. In relation to in-sessional EAP courses, an important design consideration is whether the courses are discipline-specific support courses or interdisciplinary courses that are credit-bearing, as in EAP as a support subject within a degree structure. The approach to the design of such courses will vary considerably in the case of these two different types of course context.

At postgraduate level, in-sessional courses will usually focus on the written and spoken genres used to report research. In some ways this area of EAP is the one that is informed by the most extensive body of research. However, at this level, EAP courses will often still be inter-disciplinary – that is, taken by students from different subject areas. Therefore, they need to provide opportunities to examine disciplinary differences in the research-reporting genres.

4.   Metaphorical descriptions of the roles of EAP: a bridge and a path

Among the metaphors used to describe the role of EAP courses, are those of a 'bridge' or a 'path'. EAP and other such courses are often called *bridging courses*, the underlying idea being that the course forms a metaphorical bridge over which the students can get from where they are, in terms of their current knowledge, skills and educational devel-opment, to where they need to be in order to participate fully in the discipline-specific courses of the university. Similarly, the metaphor of 'path' or 'pathway' is also used to describe an EAP course, in that such a course provides access or a way into an academic course.

Having undertaken a *needs analysis*, teachers are able to identify the prior learning, expectations and values that the students bring from their source learning culture. The teachers' complementary analysis of the target learning situation reveals the language knowledge, edu-cational values, identities and roles that the students need to acquire in order to enter the target learning culture. (Target situation analy-sis that provides a basis for the design of EAP courses needs to draw on comprehensive and inclusive theoretical approaches to analysing academic communities.) Thus, once they have identified the educational 'gap', teachers will then focus on EAP curriculum content and skills development that will assist the students in achieving their goal and in 'bridging the gap'.

Another important part of this 'bridging' role of EAP courses is that they have the capacity to develop effective intercultural communication between students and subject discipline staff, with the EAP teacher playing a mediator role in helping students to understand and adjust to the target learning culture. Also, EAP classes must be places that also encourage effective intercultural communication among the students themselves, who typically come from a variety of cultural backgrounds.

Thus, the content and processes of the EAP course must provide access into the target learning culture by developing students' understanding of its tasks, processes and values. Selection of teaching methods and learning tasks play an important part in this 'bridging' role of leading the students into the target learning culture. Such methods and tasks should take account of the present learning styles of learners as well as the environments and tasks into which the learners must become acculturated.

5.   EAP: accommodationist or critical?

I conclude this chapter by addressing an important, ongoing debate among theorists and second language teachers that concerns whether the teaching of second language (hereafter L2) knowledge, as in an EAP course, should proceed on the basis of an *accommodationist* (sometimes referred to as *assimilative* or *pragmatic*) pedagogy, which assists students to master the conventions and values of academic language in an uncritical way, or whether it should follow the course of a *critical* pedagogy that encourages the questioning and challenging of such norms and values (see Benesch, 2001). This debate relates principally to the teaching of academic writing, since writing tends to be regarded as the core skill in EAP courses. However, although my aim in this book is to theorize the wider activity of EAP instruction, it is important to address this debate from the outset and to state the position on which the chapters that follow are based.

First it must be noted that this debate originated in North America, surfacing in the inaugural issues of the *Journal of Second Language Writing* where Santos (1992) laid out what she saw as the differences between L1 writing pedagogy (North American) and the teaching of L2 writing.

Santos suggested that L1 compositionists, drawing on the fields of literature, literary criticism and rhetoric, have traditionally tackled complex
ideological issues, while on the other hand, L2 teachers of writing draw
on research in applied linguistics, text linguistics and other branches of
the social sciences, and have been more concerned with assisting their
students to master the more technical, linguistic and discoursal aspects
of the writing skill. However, in relation to the context of this debate, it
is important to note that the writing and rhetoric tradition of the North
American compositionists does not exist in the same form in other
countries where English is the heritage language, although the debate
has internationalized somewhat with contributors from other national
contexts (see, for example, Pennycook, 1997, 1999).

In challenging Santos's viewpoint, and in promoting what she terms
a 'critical' EAP pedagogy, Benesch (1993) proposes that 'L2 composition, like all teaching and research is ideological whether or not we are
conscious of the political implications' (p. 106). She therefore proposes
that EAP classes should 'embrace an ideology of resistance . . . and a
pedagogy of critical academic ESL' (p. 716). In expounding this position
again some years later, Benesch (2001) proposes that the EAP classes
'should offer flexibility about topic selection, leaving room for a variety
of possibilities: teacher choice, student choice and whole-class choice'
(p. 84). She proposes that EAP classes, as well as being based on 'needs
analysis', should also take account of *rights analysis*, which is seen as
a 'framework for understanding and responding to power relations'
(p. 108), relations such as those that students will encounter in academic
courses. As the result of the 'rights analysis' of an educational context,
EAP teachers will assist students in acquiring the capacity to identify the
power relations that operate in their courses and to question and resist
both the content and method of delivery of courses. Following such an
approach, the classroom is seen as a site of struggle where students are
involved in shaping what takes place by their active participation. In
describing a particular psychology course where Benesch, as an adjunct
EAP teacher, facilitated the students' resistance to certain aspects of the
course, she states '[f]ormalizing their resistance was the critical work. It
may encourage them to challenge other unfavourable situations inside
or outside of classrooms' (p. 120).

Counter-arguments to the critical view have been put forward by
Santos (1992, 2001) and Allison (Allison & Benesch, 1994). In reviewing
the theoretical origins of critical EAP, Santos (2001) considers its basis in
the critical theory approach to research, incorporating the ideas of post-
structuralism and post-modernism. She traces the filtering of these ideas

into EAP by way of critical pedagogy and critical applied linguistics, ideas which lead to the view that 'EAP and L2 writing courses should challenge and deconstruct academic discourses (of science, technology, and any other subject) rather than encouraging students to accept and practice them' (2001: 178) . In challenging the critical theory approach to EAP, Santos (2001), while accepting that 'education and human relations have a political dimension', questions the critical theory 'premise that everything is ideological and political' (pp. 180–1), arguing that education can proceed on a largely non-ideological basis. However, a somewhat contradictory element of this 'non-ideological' position in relation to this branch of education is her assertion that it originates from 'American values' based on:

> the historical rejection of socialism, the distaste for radical politics (and in the current climate, for any politics), the embrace of pragmatism, the emphasis on individualism and socioeconomic mobility, the principle of the separation of church and state extended to overt politics in the schools – in sum, the weight of US political and cultural tradition – all work against the acceptance of critical theory and the implementation of critical pedagogy on any but a small scale. (Santos, 2000: 188)

In relation to the *critical* versus *accommodationist* debate, this book takes the position that educational debates carried out in terms of such simple binaries can be problematic, resulting in polarized and partial perspectives on what are complex and multi-faceted issues, and this is particularly the case in the area of EAP pedagogy. As a result, such polarities may not necessarily lead to practical solutions to the multiplicity of issues faced by teachers in everyday classroom situations – situations where teachers are required to tailor pedagogy to student need as well as to meet the expectations of a range of other stakeholders in the teaching and learning process. The view taken in this book is that an effective EAP course has to be both accommodationist and critical at the same time, a view that I articulated in an earlier work in relation to student writing:

> *Accommodationist* here is taken to mean exercising a discourse competence by being able to understand and draw appropriately upon the various types of systemic knowledge necessary for producing discoursal outputs. *Critical* here is taken to mean a novice writer being able to exercise an authorial voice by individuated and innovative

use of the various aspects of discourse knowledge that are at his/ her disposal as the member of a particular disciplinary, discourse community. (Bruce, 2008a: 10)

In adopting this synthetic view, it needs to be stated that two key aspects of the critical EAP position largely locate that approach outside of the theoretical frameworks and concepts of EAP that are proposed here. First, while not discounting some role for the 'rights analysis' that Benesch proposes, the theory of EAP proposed in this book *privileges needs analysis over rights analysis*. As a consequence, a greater responsibility is placed on the EAP teacher-practitioner to ascertain student academic needs in systematic ways (through present and target situation analyses), and to address those needs by delivering courses that implement a research-informed and research-led pedagogy. Second, critical EAP differs from the approach taken here in relation to student voice. Critical EAP, in advancing students' rights appropriation, proposes the development of a political voice that is able to challenge and resist the power relations that operate in teaching and learning contexts. In contrast, the focus in this volume is on providing students with the means to develop a 'voice' within their particular *discourse community* (an issue that is addressed in considerably more detail in Chapter 8). At the core of this, students need to develop a *discourse competence* in their subject discipline that incorporates knowledge of the identities, values, attitudes, texts and discourses of their particular discourse community. This position accords with the approach of Johns (1997, 2001), Alexander, Argent and Spencer (2008) and Benson (2001), who advocate training students as discourse analysts in order that they have the means to deconstruct, master and participate in the discourses of the particular academic community that they aim to join. Then, as developing insiders, students will exercise their own voice in individuated and innovative ways. Such participation does not necessarily preclude the type of more radical resistance to the knowledge, identities and practices of their academic discourse community that Benesch proposes.

Neither does such a synthesizing approach to EAP completely preclude a focus on the type of rights analysis that Benesch (2001) proposes. For example, in examining particular disciplinary situations, e.g. when performing a target situation analysis, it may be entirely appropriate for the EAP teacher/researcher to carry out a critical ethnographic study in order to uncover the power relations that operate within a specific disciplinary teaching and learning situation, especially if it is considered that such knowledge will inform and facilitate EAP students' eventual effective participation in that subject context. For example, such an approach may be used to examine certain business courses (e.g. MBA programmes) that require the student to adopt overt roles and show evidence of strong participation in a range of discipline-specific, discoursal situations. Nevertheless, it is suggested that a good deal of research that informs EAP target situation analyses will also draw on research approaches other than that of critical theory. As in any social science research design, the analysis of target situations will involve selection of research approach, style and methods (see Cohen, Manion & Morrison, 2007) that are most appropriate to the research question under investigation.

Thus, overall this book takes a synthesizing approach towards the polarities of the critical/accommodationist debate, noting that a wide range of pedagogic and research orientations and devices need to be drawn upon in so complex an endeavour as the deconstruction and pedagogic reconstruction of academic texts and their surrounding subject discourses to enable students of EAP courses to participate fully in the academic discourse communities they want to join.

2
Investigating the Academic World

1. Introduction

Chapter 1 introduced some of the key concepts relating to EAP courses and discussed the role that such courses play in preparing students to undertake study in higher education. A core concept established in Chapter 1 is that EAP is a needs-driven activity; that is, EAP courses, in their design and implementation, aim to address the future academic and language needs of their participant students. Identifying student need involves a systematic process, termed *needs analysis*, and information uncovered by this process informs the design and implementation of EAP courses. (Chapter 3 will examine specific approaches to performing needs analysis in local contexts.) However, it is argued here that the two pragmatic activities of analysing needs and implementing the findings in the design of courses need to be framed by theory and supported by evidence from research. Thus, in order to establish frameworks within which the activity of needs analysis may be performed, Chapter 2 considers approaches to the research of academic contexts. Specifically, this chapter lays the foundations for the second stage of needs analysis, termed *target situation analysis*, which refers to EAP practitioners' investigations of the target academic communities that their students aspire to join. This involves reviewing approaches to researching:

- academic communities, including their practices and organization
- the discipline-specific subject knowledge of such communities (and its communication)
- the meta-knowledge of academic subjects, including such aspects as course organization, teaching methods, staff/student communication and assessment.

Following the order of this hierarchy, Section 2 reviews three approaches to theorizing community that may potentially be used as frameworks for researching academic subject communities. They are: *speech communities, discourse communities* and *communities of practice*. Section 3 considers approaches to examining subject knowledge and its communication, taking account of the influences of the theoretical values, processes and activities of particular academic subject communities. Section 4 considers the meta-knowledge and day-to-day practices of academic courses, e.g. within a university context. Finally, Section 5 considers three research styles and data collection methods that have been used to investigate these different aspects of academic disciplines. Consideration of these potential approaches to framing investigations of academic disciplines is essential for EAP course designers and teachers, since it is the findings of this type of research that provide an informed basis for needs analyses, as well as for EAP teaching practice and learning.

2.   Investigating academic communities: selecting a framework

In developing and delivering EAP courses, designers and teachers will research target learning situations in terms of the disciplinary, academic communities of which EAP students are 'bidding for membership' (Widdowson, 1998: 10). (As mentioned in the introductory section of this chapter, such research is not a substitute for the activity of local needs analysis, which is described in Chapter 3, but rather supports and informs the local target situation analysis.) To begin examining disciplinary subjects within universities, researchers need to consider possible theoretical frameworks that can be used to conceptualize the particular academic subject community that they wish to investigate. This section briefly discusses three theoretical approaches that may be used for describing and analysing the activities of organized communities, such as an academic community within a university. These approaches are: *speech communities, discourse communities* and *communities of practice*. Each approach is considered in terms of its theoretical basis, the types of knowledge on which it focuses and its potential strengths and limitations in relation to conceptualizing a community for EAP-related research purposes.

2.1   Speech communities

The concept of 'speech community' is central to the sociolinguistic approach to analysing the use of language in context called *ethnography of communication.* Speech communities are defined in the following ways:

- 'a community sharing rules for the conduct and interpretation of speech, and rules for the interpretation of at least one linguistic variety' (Hymes, 1972: 54)
- 'to the extent that speakers share knowledge of the communicative constraints and options governing a significant number of social situations, they can be said to be members of the same *speech community*' (Gumperz, 1972: 16)

Defining a group as a 'speech community' is not merely a question of noting shared use of a particular language. For example, speakers who share the same language may have different norms for the appropriate use and interpretation of language. A common language on its own, therefore, cannot be the only way of identifying such a group. In proposing criteria for identifying a speech community, Saville-Troike (1989: 18) suggests that it may include:

- any group in society which has anything significant in common (including occupation)
- a physically bounded group of people having a full range of role opportunities
- a collection of similarly situated entities that have something in common.

Other considerations may include social, historical and political factors as well as religion, ethnicity and race. Furthermore, people may be members of more than one speech community. For example, they may interact in different speech communities in their private and professional lives as well as in a number of different groups within each of these areas. These groups may have some degree of overlap or they may be completely separate from each other. The notion of speech community, therefore, is a complex one and cannot be defined by language use alone, but rather by the use of language in a social setting (Paltridge, 2000: 63–4).

Thus the investigation of a group of people as a speech community involves close examination of the contexts in which the group functions, including its interactions, relationships and contextualized uses of language. In relation to examining a target academic community for the purpose of informing EAP courses, the notion of a speech community potentially provides a basis for a fine-grained study of the context-specific use of language by a particular academic community:

> Observed behaviour is now recognized as a manifestation of a deeper set of codes and rules, and the task of ethnography is seen as the discovery and explication of the rules of contextually appropriate behaviour in a community or a group; in other words, what the individual needs to know to be a functional member of the community. (Saville-Troike, 1989: 107–8)

For example, a study of a particular academic context that uses an interpretive (naturalistic) approach to research along with an ethnographic research style would commence with few assumptions, and theory will be derived from examining 'thick' (detailed) descriptive data (Geertz, 1973: 6). This type of detailed data gathered from a social context usually involves *triangulation* (a combination) of data-collection methods, such as detailed observational field notes, transcriptions of speech events and semi-structured interviews about such events. Saville-Troike (1989) suggests that information about a speech community can be gathered from background information, material artefacts, social organization, legal information, artistic data, common knowledge, beliefs about language use, and linguistic data.

Despite its potential for providing fine-grained detail about a particular community, it seems that the concept of speech community as part of an ethnography of communication approach has been used less frequently to investigate academic and professional contexts than the concept of *discourse community* (described in the following section). However, an example of a study that draws principally on interpretative ethnography is Smart's (1998) insider study of the institutional practices of economists at the Bank of Canada. This study is an example of detailed research where ethnographic methods were applied to gain an in-depth understanding of the discourses and language practices of a large organization and its professional communities:

> What I've gradually come to see is a world in which the economists employ a distinctive discourse combining language, statistics, and mathematics to create specialized knowledge about the Canadian economy, knowledge used by the Bank's executives to make decisions about monetary policy. (Smart, 1998: 117)

For the purpose of informing ESP and EAP, the focus of research has often been on the genres (categories of texts) of academic communities, since it is mastery of their written forms of communication that is usually an essential requirement for membership of such communities. Thus, this aspect of writing is usually one of the central goals of EAP students. However, some genre theorists (see, for example, Bhatia, 2004; Swales, 1998) now propose that ethnographic investigation may also be an important part of the process of fully understanding genre knowledge. As an example of understanding the contextual knowledge that surrounds a written genre, Smart's (1998) study examined the genre of the *QPM* (the Bank's *Quarterly Projection Model*) in terms of the beliefs of the people who shaped it and the diverse communicative purposes that it fulfils.

2.2 Discourse communities

In their work *New Rhetoric*, Perelman and Olbrechts-Tyteca (1969) discuss the concept of discipline-specific language that, although inaccessible to an outsider, 'summarizes the aggregate of acquired knowledge, rules and conventions' (p. 99). To account for this phenomenon of language that is specific to practitioners of a discipline, the sociolinguist Nystrand (1982) coined the term *discourse community*, a term that has been developed and used extensively in the field of *English for Specific Purposes* (ESP). In defining the characteristics of discourse communities, Swales, (1988: 212–13, 1990: 24–7) proposes that a discourse community:

1. has a broadly agreed set of common public goals
2. has mechanisms for communication among its members
3. uses its participatory mechanisms primarily to provide information and feedback
4. utilizes and hence possesses one or more genres in the communicative furtherance of its aims
5. in addition to owning genres, has acquired some specific lexis
6. has a threshold level of members with [the knowledge of] a suitable degree of relevant content and discoursal expertise.

Thus, according to Swales (1990), a discourse community is a socio-rhetorical network that exists to achieve certain goals. To achieve these goals, it has certain commonly used and understood configurations of language (genres), which may involve some specialized vocabulary. The communicative acts that are meaningful within this discourse community do not have the same currency or meaning among non-members, who are not required to perform the same occupational tasks nor thereby communicate to achieve the same purposes. Swales' (1990) proposal for discourse communities has been subsequently challenged in a number of areas (see Borg, 2003). Issues that have been raised include: how large a discourse community might be; whether spoken language should also be a necessary defining element; the role of purpose as a defining element; and the degree of stability a discourse community ought to have.

. In a later work, Swales (1998: 204) distinguishes between the broader concept of a discourse community which may not be physically connected, and which communicates with itself through written communication, and *place discourse communities*, which use both written and spoken communication. Thus, discourse communities may involve face-to-face, personal interactions (such as in the workplace or at conferences) but potentially they can be disparate and rely mainly on written genres for communications among members.

Generally, researchers using the concept of discourse community to investigate academic communities have tended to focus less on the face-to-face social interactions among members of a community, as seen in Smart's study of the economists at the Bank of Canada, than on its tools of formal communication, such as the particular written genres that are employed. Examples of genres that have been analysed for ESP purposes are introductions to research articles (Swales, 1981, 1990), science dissertations (Dudley-Evans, 1986, 1989; Hopkins & Dudley-Evans, 1988), popularized medical texts (Nwogu, 1991), job applications, sales promotion letters and legal case studies (Bhatia, 1993), grant proposals for European Union research grants (Connor & Mauranen, 1999) and conference abstracts in applied mathematics (Yakhontova, 2002).

Research into disciplinary discourse communities, therefore, tends to focus mainly on the genres (mainly written) that are used for communication between members of the community. Rater analysis of a small sample of texts belonging to a specific genre category, or a corpus analysis of a larger sample of texts, tend to be the research methods used. Originally, genres were conceptualized in terms of the staging or organization of their content and related linguistic resources; however, more recently the ESP genre theorists have acknowledged the importance of ethnographic as well as textual knowledge (Bhatia, 2004; Swales, 1998).

2.3 Communities of practice

In yet another approach that has been applied to examining communities, sociologists Lave and Wenger (1991) and Wenger (1998) have proposed the concept of *community of practice* (sometimes abbreviated to CoP). This term refers to a group of people (such as an occupational or professional group) who have common goals, and who interact as they strive towards the achievement of those goals. Wenger (1998) says that it is participation (practice) within an 'historical and social context that gives structure and meaning to what we do' (p. 47). Achieving the goals of the group gives rise to a process of social learning and the emergence and evolution of shared socio-cultural practices.

In an attempt to 'rethink learning' and to account for the ways in which it takes place in occupational, professional or academic contexts, Lave and Wenger (1991) describe the type of learning that occurs in a CoP as *situated learning*. They propose that 'the practice of the community creates the potential "curriculum" in the broadest sense – that which may be learned by newcomers with legitimate peripheral access' (p. 93). Different communities have different ways of granting access to or admitting novice members. For example, in an academic context, this could involve a student meeting the academic requirements to be able to study within a university or to gain admission to a particular disciplinary programme of the university, such as admission to a law school. Central to the notion of situated learning is the concept of *legitimate peripheral participation* in a community of practice. This concept is loosely based on a traditional master/apprentice relationship, but the CoP approach suggests that the target knowledge and practices that have to be learned do not reside in one person, but rather reside within, and are acquired from, a whole CoP. Learning, therefore, takes place through participation within a community and involves the appropriation of its practices. Thus, it is within the wider community that the totality of its knowledge and practices reside, and it is engagement and participation within the community by novice members that provide the means by which such knowledge and practices are acquired.

In his 1998 book, Wenger developed and extended the concept in his ethnographic study of insurance claims processors. The construct of CoP has since been used in various fields, including education, sociolinguistics, material anthropology and second language acquisition. An example of the application of the CoP concept to academic contexts involved consideration of the practices of North American graduate schools in the reporting of a range of *ex post facto* reflective case studies by doctoral students (Pearson-Casanave & Li, 2008). In these autobiographical case studies, the contributors reflect on their acculturation into North American academic practices through their interactions with academics and peers during their doctoral studies, invoking the CoP notion that knowledge resides within the community and that participation within the community leads to the acquisition of its knowledge. However, in relating the community of practice concept to academic contexts, there are a number of issues that need to be considered, such as the issue of common goals of academic communities, the nature of connectedness and relationships within academic communities, and the types of knowledge that may be derived from community relationships.

First, while Lave and Wenger's (1991) notion of communities of practice working towards common goals may relate closely to their original examples of occupational groups, such as midwives, West African tailors, quartermasters and butchers, the notion may be less easily applied to the academic world. For example, in relation to the organization and operation of academic communities, it may be that Wenger's (1998) CoP-defining attributes of 'mutual engagement' and 'joint enterprise' towards the achievement of a common goal may not accord with the differentiated nature of goals (and their related activities) of academic staff and students. For example, in a university context, the particular goals of academic staff may be the advancement of their particular research in a specialist area of their disciplinary domain (leading to the achievement of publications and bibliometric targets), whereas the academic goals of their undergraduate students will relate to mastery of the knowledge and concepts of the particular subject. Likewise, the primary research undertaken by postgraduate students, e.g. for a Masters dissertation or doctoral thesis may have quite a different type of outcome and purpose when compared with the research in the same field that is carried out by the thesis supervisor/advisor.

Second, the notion that the acquisition of knowledge derives from engagement with and participation within a particular community (situated learning) also requires scrutiny when it is related to academic contexts. In the context of academic communities, it may be necessary to delimit the types of knowledge that may be derived from this source as well as the nature of the relationship of the newcomer to the community. For example, in the reflective case studies reported in Pearson-Casanave and Li (2008), doctoral students' knowledge advanced through receiving feedback on their projects by means of critique by supervisors (advisors), such as the identification of design flaws and shortcomings in their research plans. This type of critical feedback, while potentially valuable to the novice, reflects the contested nature of the development of knowledge and bidding for membership of academic communities, and is evidence of what may be seen as the 'gate-keeping' roles of senior members, such as advisors, examiners and reviewers. In relation to participation in their academic communities, the same doctoral students self-report personal struggles in acquiring the necessary meta-knowledge, such as knowledge of the communities' patterns of organization, their relationships, hierarchies and techniques for gaining a voice – for example, in meetings with doctoral supervisors (advisors), research group meetings and conferences. As Lea (2005) points out, the application of the CoP model to academic contexts fails to account for the contested nature of membership of an academic community. She says:

> the focus has been on the benign nature of communities of practice, where there is a simple and smooth transition from peripheral participation as a novice to full membership at the core of the community's endeavour. This perspective does not take account of the more contested nature of participation in communities of practice, that is when participants are excluded from full participation in the practices of the community; for example, where students struggle to engage in the unfamiliar discourses or literacy practices of the academy, always feeling excluded and on the margins. (Lea, 2005: 183–4)

Third, the CoP model when applied to academic communities provides little theoretical basis for accounting for the role of language. Although Lave and Wenger (1991) acknowledge the role of *discourse*, it is not theorized or developed to any extent in the CoP approach when compared with the theorizing and researching of academic genres that has proliferated within the discourse communities approach.

2.4 Academic communities: summary

The brief review of these three approaches to theorizing community shows the different conceptual frameworks that may potentially be employed when examining the functioning of an academic community. However, when conceptualizing community for the purpose of investigating an academic context, it is important that whatever notion of community is adopted is suitable for the research purpose. This requires consideration of the object knowledge, ideologies and rationale behind any framework for community that is applied to a particular context. These aspects, then, have to relate to the aims or research questions that motivate the investigation.

For example, the *speech communities* approach particularly focuses on the sociologics of a particular community in terms of the types of social relationship that operate and influence the use of language. This may be entirely appropriate where the aim of an investigation relates to developing a detailed account of the use of language in interrelationships and interactions within an academic community that is located in one place, and whose activities and processes involve regular face-to-face interactions among its members. On the other hand, the *discourse community* approach focuses more closely on written genres as the mechanisms for communication within an academic community whose members are located in many different places. Such a widely dispersed discourse community may meet only infrequently at conferences, and its members communicate mainly through refereed research articles published in academic journals – a genre-based study may therefore be an appropriate approach to researching its activities. Yet, for a different type of context, it may be appropriate to employ the communities of practice approach in order to investigate the mechanisms by which situated learning takes place in terms of social relationships and participation within a community working towards identifiable common goals.

In EAP research, therefore, whatever theoretical approach is employed to examine academic communities, important factors to consider are whether or not the approach:

- accounts for academic communities that are located in one place or for those whose members are scattered in different cities or countries
- provides the means of accurately reflecting the relationships and processes that operate within the community
- acknowledges the role of the genres (categories of texts) used to communicate within an academic community and provides the means for deconstructing genre knowledge.

3.   Understanding the nature of knowledge within different disciplines

While the previous section focused on frameworks for describing and analysing the organization and practices of particular academic communities, this section considers differences in the orientations of different disciplines toward their particular areas of specialist knowledge. For example, when beginning to investigate the values that shape a particular academic community, such as the discourse community of a particular subject area, two fundamental aspects of the constitution of knowledge in the subject area need to be considered. These are the subject's position in relation to:

- *ontology* – the nature of being, existence; and,
- *epistemology* – the nature of knowledge and especially how it is validated or proven.

Issues relating to ontology often centre on is what is known as the *nominalist-realist* debate. A realist view of the world is that objects of thought have a real existence, independent of the human mind that perceives them. For example, in chemistry, the object of study, chemical compounds, are entities that exist in the real world and have an independent, objective, empirically provable existence. On the other hand, a nominalist view is that objects of thought are created by the human mind that perceives them. For example, in cognitive science, entities or objects of study tend to be seen as existing in terms how they are perceived by human beings.

The ontological view that characterizes a subject discipline influences its approach to carrying out research and creating new knowledge. For example, if a disciplinary subject emphasizes the nominalist position, research is likely to be carried out in ways that are rather different from its implementation in a subject that emphasizes the realist position. This is because a tendency to nominalism is likely to lead to caution about generalizations, such as generalizations about human behaviour. In other words, taking the nominalist approach, knowledge about things or abstractions exists only in people's minds. Because people are all individuals, they will have differing ways of construing and representing things. On the other hand, a realist ontological view will be concerned with establishing generalizable phenomena, aspects and trends supported by empirical or observable data that are often quantitative.

Issues relating to epistemology centre on how the people working in different subject areas view knowledge, such as how they create, validate (prove) and use knowledge within their particular field. Because those who tend to realism see knowledge as being more certain and more generalizable, they tend to employ positivist (scientific) approaches to investigating and validating new knowledge, where the emphasis tends to be on empirical data that are often quantifiable. On the other hand, because those who tend to nominalism see knowledge as being more personal and more subjective, they tend to employ an interpretative (naturalistic) approach to research.

A number of researchers and theorists, such as those in the *academic literacies movement* for example, see these fundamental ontological and epistemological perspectives and assumptions as exerting a strong influence on the ways in which knowledge is communicated through academic texts. This viewpoint suggests that these fundamental values need to be considered when approaching a new text and its contextual setting:

> what makes a piece of student writing 'appropriate' has more to do with issues of epistemology than with the surface features of form to which staff often have recourse when describing their students' writing . . . underlying disciplinary assumptions about the nature of knowledge affected the meaning given to the terms 'structure' and 'argument' (Lea & Street, 1998: 162).

For example, the reporting of knowledge that reflects a realist view will tend to value objectivity, empiricism and generalizability, whereas the values of a nominalist approach may tend to include contextual specificity, fine-grained detail and the acknowledgement of multiple viewpoints. In reflecting these underlying characteristics of subject knowledge, writers (including student writers), therefore, must adopt an identity and stance in their writing that reflects these fundamental (although often unexplicated) positions in relation to their target subject knowledge.

Thus the ontological and epistemological aspects of subject knowledge relate closely to characteristics of the written and spoken genres that are used to disseminate knowledge within a particular discipline. They also relate to the requirements of the written and spoken assignment genres that students, as novice members of the same discourse community, are expected to understand and master. The importance of this area of academic knowledge suggests that EAP courses should examine not only the modes and genres used to communicate within certain disciplines, but also these fundamental underlying assumptions in relation to disciplinary knowledge and its particular characteristics. When examining subject-specific texts, it is important to pose questions that uncover the subject-related views of reality and knowledge that form the background or contextual assumptions of the text and influence the types of language employed. Examples of such questions could be:

1. What is the topic/content of the text?
2. What view of reality relates to this type of knowledge?
3. How is this information uncovered? What research methods are used?
4. Can the findings be applied to a wider population or do they relate to a particular sample of people? (How is the connection between the research outcomes and other contexts communicated?)

5. Does the information aim to reflect one view or multiple viewpoints? (How is the particular viewpoint of the text communicated?)

4.   The meta-knowledge of academic settings: course organization, communication, assessment and ethical practices

In addition to developing awareness of the nature of the content knowledge of particular subject areas, EAP courses need to assist students to understand the operational norms and conventions of universities such as course organization, teaching methods, staff–student communication and assessment. Many of these are identified in the *Competency Framework for Teachers of English for Academic Purposes* (BALEAP, 2008). For example, in acculturating to a university and its practices, the range of organizational documents and communicative practices that new students need to understand and respond to may include:

- written communications outlining degree requirements and course summaries in university calendars and handbooks, including information about majors, supporting subjects and pre-requisite and co-requisite requirements
- written communications outlining the requirements for specific courses, as in course regulations, course outlines, lecture outlines, and guidelines relating to assignments and examinations
- the oral communications of course convenors regarding the online management and administration of courses, including their modes of communication with students
- key instructions in relation to task rubrics and assessment requirements.

Thus, when preparing EAP students for future study in particular subject courses, part of the target situation analysis involves deconstructing documents related to course organization and internal course communication. For the EAP course designer or teacher to access this area of knowledge requires them to analyse processes, materials and tasks from different subject areas.

In addition, EAP courses need to focus overtly on the ethical practices and demands of the academy as well as to build adherence to these practices within the assignment requirements and conventions, which can begin in the EAP course itself. Issues relating to intellectual property, what it is and the laws and conventions that relate to intellectual property in an academic setting, need to receive an overt focus in EAP courses, for example by:

- teaching knowledge of ethical practices, including the development of respect for intellectual property and its protection
- incorporating ethical training in the task/learning cycle
- requiring the use of citation and referencing in learning activities and prepared assessed tasks.

Also the assessment of EAP student assignments can include evaluation of conformity to citational and referencing requirements as part of the ongoing training of students in the rules of copyright, referencing and bibliographic skills.

5.   Three methods for researching academic knowledge and practices in specific disciplines: ethnographic, genre and corpus research

While the previous sections considered approaches to conceptualizing the types of academic community that an EAP student may aspire to join, including such a community's approaches to knowledge and organizational issues related to subject courses, this section moves to consider the types of data collection and analysis that may be employed when researching a particular academic community. As a basis for teaching the literacy practices of different disciplines within EAP courses, research has been carried out on the written and spoken texts and practices of a range of different disciplines. This research tends to be carried out using one or some combination of the following three research styles: ethnographic studies, genre-based studies and corpus research.

   This section of the chapter is not intended to be a substitute for a course in research methods; rather, what follows are brief summaries of how academic subject areas may be researched to inform EAP course design and delivery. When referring to research design, the terms used here – *research approach, research style, data-collection method* – are used in the way outlined by Cohen, Manion and Morrison (2007).

5.1   Ethnographic approaches to investigating disciplinary knowledge

Ethnography is a research style, originating from anthropology and sociology, which is based on the examination of human behaviour and language in naturally occurring settings. It is usually *interpretative* – in that it doesn't start with a hypothesis or theory that is being tested, rather the theory emerges from the data, and *qualitative* – in that it is less concerned with number information than with detailed descriptions of what people actually do with language in certain contexts.

Characteristics of a study that uses an ethnographic approach are:

- it provides participants' or insiders' descriptions of individuals' cultural practices
- it yields fine-grained detail in descriptions of target EAP contexts
- it combines several data-collection methods to gain a detailed picture of a specific context, e.g. observation, unstructured interview and personal accounts.

An example of an ethnographic study is Duff's (2002) study of classroom discourse in a mainstream high school class in one particular study area. Her particular research interest related to classroom interactions and the construction of identity and voice by ESL students within the speech community of a particular class. The methods of data collection that Duff employed included observation of the action of the class setting (as well as the wider school setting in which the class was located). She also performed discourse analysis, which in this study involved audio-recording, transcribing and analysing the classroom conversational exchanges between the teacher and students and among students. In particular, she examined the use of language in interactions and turn-taking in the class by a range of different types of learner. This study is illustrative of the ethnographic approach that focuses on contextualized use of language (ethnography of communication). In the findings, Duff developed a detailed qualitative description of the social setting. Through data-gathering using multiple methods and the analysis of the language used in this context, she uncovered a wide range of social, linguistic and educational behaviours and issues.

The principal problem in implementing ethnographic research is that there is always potential for researcher bias both in how situations are described (involving selection of data) and in how they are interpreted (involving the researcher's subjective judgement). However, there are various ways that this can be minimized in planning the research. A second issue that faces teacher-researchers is that it is time-consuming to gather, manage and organize such a large amount of data using several data-collection methods. Yet, the value of this research style is that it provides a close-up and detailed description of a particular academic context.

5.2   Genre-based approaches to investigating disciplinary knowledge

In the EAP context, a *genre* (category of texts) refers to a way that writers, within a type of recurring situation or context, typically create texts that achieve the same type of communicative purpose. This reflects the idea that the members of a particular discourse community expect that a type of text fulfilling a particular type of purpose (e.g. reporting research) will employ conventionalized forms that are recognizable to members of the same academic community. Because written texts are central to participation in academic communities, students need to understand, interpret and eventually master the particular genres of the community that they aspire to join. Therefore, investigations of genres have been used to investigate research texts in a variety of contexts to inform EAP. There are three main approaches to genre, each of which conceptualizes genre in a different way. The rest of this section will provide very brief outlines of the three approaches to genre that are used as a way of investigating disciplinary writing and speaking. (Further detailed discussion of the concept of genre and its application to EAP courses follows in Chapters 5 and 8.)

5.2.1   The approach to genre influenced by systemic functional linguistics (SFL)

The construct of genre identified by linguists working within the context of the systemic functional approach began to be applied to the teaching of writing in schools in the 1980s in Australia (see, for example, Macken *et al.*, 1989; Martin, 1989; Derewianka, 1990; Christie, 1990; Knapp & Watkins, 1994; Butt *et al.*, 2000 and Martin, 2000). This approach to genre typically describes texts in terms of *schematic structure*, described by Eggins (1994: 36) as the 'staged, step-by-step organization of the genre', and *linguistic* (lexico-grammatical) features such as syntax, lexis, types of cohesion and reference (which relate to the elements of the schematic structure).

Within the context of this approach, although some theorists focus on genres that are used to achieve a socially recognized, functional purpose, such as, for example, service encounters (Hasan, 1978, 1989; Ventola, 1984), attempts to identify genres for pedagogic purposes have tended to classify texts in terms of more general rhetorical categories, such as *recount, instruction, exposition/argument, narrative, report, explanation* (Derewianka, 1990) or *instructing, arguing, narrating, explaining, describing* (Knapp & Watkins, 1994).

An example of pedagogical implementation of the approach to genre influenced by systemic functional linguistics (SFL, but sometimes termed the *Sydney School*) is reported in a case study by Macken-

Horarik (2002) where a teacher in a 'disadvantaged schools programme' incorporated the teaching of the 'explanation' genre into the scientific writing requirements of a ten-week high school science unit that focused on human reproduction and its associated technologies. Specifically, the outcome task that the students had to write was a text that explained the in vitro fertilization process, and explicitly outlined how the 'material of inheritance' may be changed by this process. The case study reports how that the teaching learning cycle of *modelling, joint negotiation of text and independent construction of text* (Macken et al.,1989) was employed in the development of science writing in this particular teaching and learning unit.

5.2.2   The English for Specific Purposes (Swales) approach to genre

In another approach to genre, linguists working in the field of *English for Specific Purposes* have largely examined English texts used in academic and professional contexts, such as introductions to research articles (Swales, 1981, 1990), introductions and discussion sections of dissertations (Dudley-Evans 1986, 1989) as well as types of medical, legal and business documents. The motivation for this type of genre analysis is to identify the elements of specialized types of writing in order to teach them to second language writers who need to become familiar with the organizational patterns and characteristics of academic or professional texts. Analysis of genre in this tradition tends to involve examining the organization of the conventionally recognized stages of a text in terms of:

- *moves* and *steps*; this knowledge is then used as a basis for teaching the language and rhetorical patterns of the genres identified
- linguistic features associated with moves and steps.

An example of a genre study from the ESP tradition is Yakhontova's (2002) study of applied linguistics conference abstracts in which she examines the rhetorical and linguistic features of three samples of abstracts: one sample in English, one sample in Ukrainian and Russian and a third group written in English, but by Ukrainian or Russian writers. Although the publication in which Yakhontova's study appears locates it in a section labelled 'contrastive rhetoric', Yakhontova uses a fairly typical ESP approach to genre for her analysis of the abstracts and as a basis for considering their contrasting organization, linguistic and socio-cultural features. First, she identifies a set of five common moves that may occur in conference abstracts, and then examines each sample of texts for the frequency of occurrences of the moves. Through this analysis, she discusses cultural and historical differences for the variations that she finds among her three samples. She then examines linguistic differences among the three samples of texts in terms of their use of pronouns and evaluative language. The examination of linguistic features is framed somewhat by their occurrences within, and significance to, the move structure. Using this genre approach, Yakhontova is able to highlight the similarities and differences in the cultural and functional values that have influenced the development of the three different types of abstract.

5.2.3 The New Rhetoric/Rhetorical Genre Studies approach to genre

New Rhetoric or *Rhetorical Genre Studies* (see Artemeva, 2008) is a North American approach to genre, where genre is not defined in terms of the organizational or linguistic characteristics of categories of texts, but rather in terms of social actions that surround the regular creation of such texts. Genre research in this tradition focuses on the contexts in which genres occur. Researchers tend to investigate how users creatively exploit genres, and how genres change and evolve. This approach emphasizes the changing nature of genres, and eschews any view of genres as fixed templates that are regularly reproduced. A term that is frequently applied to this approach is that genres are 'stabilized-for-now' sites of social and ideological action (Schryer, 1993: 200). An example of this approach to genre is Schryer's (1993) study of a certain type of veterinary medical record as a genre, and specifically the development of novice veterinarians in the use of this genre when carrying out animal diagnosis. She carried out this study using an ethnographic research style, gathering data through interviews, observation and document analysis.

5.3 Genre-based research as an approach to data collection and analysis

The strengths of genre-based approaches to researching academic texts are that they allow researchers to examine knowledge about texts (and their related discourses) from multiple areas in a holistic way. This integration can include linguistic knowledge, procedural or organizational knowledge, and contextual knowledge.

However, the central problem in performing genre research to inform EAP course design is selecting from the multiplicity of approaches to genre for a particular research purpose. While this section has briefly presented the three main theoretical approaches to genre, there are also other approaches and terminologies used for analysing and classifying texts. This is not to deny that genre is a useful and productive basis for researching knowledge about academic texts and discourses and informing the design of EAP courses. Rather, the problem is identifying the most appropriate approach to genre for examining a certain type of written or spoken text. In Chapters 5 and 8, an approach to genre is proposed that attempts to address some of these difficulties of multiplicities of approach and terminology.

5.4 Corpus-based approaches to investigating disciplinary knowledge

Again, given the centrality of texts, corpus-based research has often been used as another way of investigating academic texts to inform the design and teaching of EAP courses. A corpus is a collection of naturally occurring texts used for linguistic study. Computer-mediated searches of a corpus can reveal insights about how language is actually used in texts. By using software programs, it is possible to selectively examine a body of quite a large number of texts and discover distributions of linguistic features. The following are key concepts in corpus research:

- A corpus is a collection of texts, sometimes (but not always) from one domain, for example, abstracts to articles that report chemistry experiments.
- Texts are typically converted into plain text files and then a group of texts of the same type are loaded into a corpus computer software program.
- The idea of frequency is central to most corpus studies. Frequency counts are a way of determining features that are underused or overused. Thus, often the first step in examining a corpus is to establish a *word list*. This is a list of all of the words arranged from most to least frequent. Most corpus programs also provide statistical information about the frequency occurrence of each word.
- In addition to exploring the frequency of the occurrence of words within a corpus, researchers also create *concordances* of words that they are interested in examining. A concordance is a type of list which shows each occurrence of a word with the parts of the sentence that occur before and after each occurrence of the word – sometimes termed *key word in context* (KWIC). Concordances can reveal information about common collocations that occur with certain words. They can also show the types of structures in which they commonly occur. (This makes it possible to see regularities of use that might otherwise be missed.)

Research in corpus linguistics that has examined language in academic contexts has included studies of vocabulary (see for example, Coxhead, 2000; Hirsh & Nation, 1992), grammatical features in different registers (for example, Biber, Conrad & Reppen, 1998; Flowerdew, 2002), features of language that signal writers' stance (Biber & Finegan, 1989; Charles, 2003) and language relating to addressivity and audience (Hyland, 2001, 2002a). An example of a corpus study that has examined academic language is a study by Lindemann and Mauranen (2001) that examined the use of the word *just* in the *Michigan Corpus of Spoken Academic English* (MICASE), where they found, through concordance and contextual analysis, that *just* is used as a 'minimizer' in academic speech (p. 172). As an example of a pedagogical application of a corpus finding, they suggest that in teaching students in an EAP context, it is important for them to learn that it has this mitigating function and that it is the unstressed rather than the stressed form that conveys this meaning in a polite way.

However, it is important to note what some see as the limitations of corpus linguistic research, articulated by Widdowson (2000: 6–7) in the following way:

> the computer can only cope with the material products of what people do when they use language. It can only analyse the textual traces of the process whereby meaning is achieved; it cannot account for the complex interplay between linguistic and contextual factors whereby discourse is enacted. It cannot produce ethnographic descriptions of language use.

What Widdowson is suggesting is that corpus findings involve decontextualized language, and for this reason such findings need to be recontextualized to actual contexts and situations of language use if they are to inform language teaching and learning. In other words, corpus findings are linguistic fragments of texts, and texts themselves are 'the overt linguistic trace of a discourse process' (Widdowson, 2004: 169). The discourses that give rise to the texts involve a range of socially driven operations involving both subject content and abstract organizational knowledge. Therefore, it may be problematic to account for the characteristics of a type of disciplinary writing by focusing merely on the linguistic elements of texts identified in corpus studies, since such an approach may have limitations in terms of construct validity. Rather, it may be that such research needs to begin by studying the discourse that gives rise to a category of text, including its functional role and purpose. The findings of this enquiry could then provide a rationale for the choice of texts included in a corpus and, thereby, address some of the objections to corpus-based research. Within such an approach, the micro-level focus of corpus studies further adds to the previous higher-level investigations. In this vein, two studies that link corpus investigations with genre theory (Flowerdew, 2005; Tribble, 2002) represent attempts to address some of these concerns about construct validity in corpus research.

6. Conclusion

In order to prepare students to participate in undergraduate and post-graduate courses in specific disciplines, EAP course design needs to be grounded in knowledge of the more general assumptions, values and practices of universities as well as understandings of the more specific differences that can occur among different subject areas. These foundational aspects of academic and institutional knowledge are integral to the organization, delivery and expectations of subject-specific courses, and are reflected in the types of textual and human interactions (staff–student and student–student) that are found in such courses. This chapter has examined some of the conceptual frameworks and research tools that provide a basis for theorizing and investigating academic subjects in ways that can inform EAP courses. However, it must be stated that such research, of itself, does not constitute a theory of EAP course design, but, as was pointed out at the beginning of the chapter, this type of research (that examines academic contexts and texts) can help to inform the second stage of a needs analysis – the *target situation analysis*, which will be addressed in more detail in the next chapter. Thus, the activities of theorizing and researching academic contexts are described in this chapter, and the subsequent process of carrying out needs analyses for particular groups of EAP students will be described in Chapter 3. Yet, while the activities described in these two chapters may inform EAP courses, of themselves they do not constitute a principled approach to EAP syllabus design; this is an issue that is taken up in the chapters of Part II.

3
Students' Needs and EAP Course Design

1. Introduction

While Chapter 1 introduced and defined EAP, and Chapter 2 considered approaches to performing research on the academy, its knowledge and practices, Chapter 3 focuses on the area of the needs of EAP students, beginning with the process of performing *needs analysis* as a basis for the design of EAP courses. Needs analysis involves gathering information about both students and their target learning situations, information that is then applied to the design of courses that prepare students to participate within the academy.

A number of stakeholders are interested in the progress of a student taking an EAP course. These stakeholders may include:

- the student him/herself seeking to enter or succeed in a certain university course for the purpose of achieving academic and career goals
- the student's parents who have paid course fees and expect that the EAP course will facilitate his/her entry into and success in a university degree course
- some kind of external funding agency (such as an employer or scholarship-awarding organization), which requires the students to reach a level of academic and language proficiency in order to enter particular courses
- receiving institutions wishing to accept students who are suitably prepared linguistically and academically to undertake undergraduate (or postgraduate) study.

Thus, EAP courses tend to be a high-stakes, needs-driven and expectation-driven educational activity. Within a relatively small time frame, such courses are expected, sometimes unrealistically, to facilitate rapid development of students' academic knowledge and language skills so that they are equipped to enter and succeed in university courses. Performing needs analysis and using the findings to inform the design of EAP courses is seen as a way of ensuring that students acquire the appropriate knowledge and skills. However, in this chapter I propose that needs analysis findings, when being incorporated into the design of EAP courses, should be related to theories of language (and specifically theories of discourse) and theories of teaching and learning.

To summarize this proposal, Figure 3.1 outlines a framework for EAP course design that links the processes of needs analysis and course development with theories of discourse, teaching and learning. This figure outlines three broad stages of a needs-driven design process for EAP courses. The first stage involves performing needs analysis to develop understandings of learners as well as the requirements and expectations of subject disciplines. The second stage involves framing course aims and objectives in ways that not only take account of information gained from the needs analysis, but also are informed by theories of discourse that account for its linguistic, cognitive/organizational and social elements. The third stage is the selection and staging of course content, which is informed by theories of teaching and learning. This chapter deals with the first two stages of the process outlined in Figure 3.1 – those of needs analysis and developing aims and objectives on the basis of the needs analyses. The following three chapters of Part II continue to develop the second stage of framing aims and objectives, and also address the third stage, which is the detailed planning associated with the selection and staging of course content.

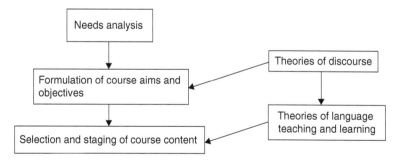

Figure 3.1　Needs analysis and EAP course design

2.   Performing needs analysis

As we saw in the definitions of ESP and EAP in Chapter 1, learner need is central to defining these areas of language teaching and learning. However, deconstructing learner need in relation to academic skills and competencies is complex and multi-faceted. As mentioned in Chapters 1 and 2, EAP practitioners have to consider two types of situation when performing a needs analysis: what knowledge and skills learners bring with them to the EAP course – *the present situation*; and where the learners need to get to – *the target situation*.

Consideration of factors that relate to both of these areas of knowledge and experience will then guide the planning and development of a course syllabus as well as the thinking about both the content and processes of the course. Table 3.1 presents questions that form a basis for performing present and target situation analyses. These questions are taken from Hutchinson and Waters' (1987) larger frameworks proposed for performing needs analysis to develop ESP courses.

2.1   Present situation analysis

Chapter 2 focused on approaches to fundamental research that informs EAP as an educational activity by providing background information that helps to inform the target situation analysis. However, as well as reviewing research and carrying out their own studies of target learning situations, EAP teachers and course designers also need to consider the specific groups that they are teaching and the particular needs of those groups – the 'present situation'. In relation to considering the EAP learners and what they bring into the course through *present situation analysis*, Hyland (2006: 78) suggests that gathering information may be carried out by using:

- questionnaires
- analyses of authentic spoken and written texts
- structured observations
- holistic observations
- informal consultations with faculty, learners and other EAP teachers
- assessment results.

The following summary tables and comments take some of the key questions posed by Hutchinson and Waters (1987) and use them as the basis for discussing the needs of various EAP learner groups. In relation to performing a 'present situation analysis', Table 3.2 relates some of

Table 3.1 Needs analysis

Present situation analysis	Target situation analysis
Who are the learners? • age, sex, nationality • What do they know already about English? • What subject knowledge do they have? • What are their interests? • What is their socio-cultural background?	Why is the language needed? • for study • for work • for training • for a combination of these • for some other purpose
Why are the learners taking the course? • Is it compulsory or optional? • Is there an apparent need or not? • Are status, money, promotion involved? • What do the learners think they will achieve? • What is their attitude towards the ESP course? Do they want to improve their English or do they resent the time they have to spend on it?	How will the language be used? • medium: speaking, writing, reading • channel: e.g. telephone, face-to-face • types of text or discourse: e.g. academic texts, lectures, informal conversations, technical manuals, catalogues
How do the learners learn? • What is their learning background? • What is their concept of teaching and learning? • What methodology will appeal to them? • What sort of techniques are likely to bore/alienate them?	What will the content areas be? • subjects: e.g. medicine, biology, architecture, shipping, commerce, engineering • level: e.g. technician, craftsman, postgraduate, secondary school
	Who will the learner use the language with? • native speakers or non-native • level of knowledge or receiver: e.g. expert, layman, student • relationship: e.g. colleague, teacher, customer, superior, subordinate.
	Where will the language be used? • physical setting: e.g. office, lecture theatre, hotel, workshop, library • human context: e.g. alone, meetings, demonstrations, on telephone • linguistic context: e.g. in own country, abroad
Questions selected from Hutchinson & Waters (1987: 62–3)	Hutchinson & Waters (1987: 59)

Table 3.2 Present situation analysis

Hutchinson & Waters' (1987) questions	Possible areas for investigation	Possible methods of data collection
Who are the learners?	• age, linguistic and cultural backgrounds • social position of learners vs. teachers in the prior learning situations • newly arrived or resident SL learners	• interview • questionnaire
Why are learners taking the course?	• pre-sessional students – seeking support to gain entry to tertiary education • in-sessional students – seeking support to gain a first degree • postgraduate students – seeking support to gain a professional or research degree	
What do the learners know?	• current language proficiency • prior language learning • previous educational experiences • prior cognitive training • students' understanding of teacher/learner roles • students' views regarding teacher-dependence vs. student autonomy • students' prior experiences in processing and creating text	• language testing • structured observations (e.g. of students' performance of orientation activities, tasks) • less structured observations (e.g. through teachers' reflective journals)
How do learners learn?	• preferred learning styles (related to prior cognitive training and previous educational experiences)	

Hutchinson and Waters' questions to the possible types of knowledge that need to be gathered from 'present situation' investigations and also suggests the types of data collection method that may be employed.

Thus, present situation analysis involves developing a multi-dimensional profile of the students taking an EAP course. From this part of the needs analysis process, teachers may gain an understanding of students in terms of their L1 educational and cultural background, which will include understanding their prior cognitive training and prior educational socialization. Embedded within these areas of learner knowledge and skills will be students' educational expectations of the EAP course that they are entering, which will inevitably be based on their previously developed beliefs about teachers' and learners' roles (and learning styles). It is probably fair to say that in most cases what students bring into courses in terms of these areas of prior knowledge and training (and expectations) will vary considerably from the teacher/learner roles, orientations and tasks of an EAP course, including the need to develop learner autonomy. The students' L2 proficiency and prior language skills development also has to be considered in relation to the EAP course that they are entering.

One important aspect of proficiency is the previous development of students' discourse competence in English in relation to processing and creating extended spoken and written texts. If, for example, students' prior learning has mainly been directed toward the testing of discrete-point items of grammar and vocabulary knowledge and there has been little requirement to process and produce texts, it is likely that the EAP course will need to focus strongly on developing this area of students' communicative competence. All of these elements of learners' knowledge and skills can, therefore, form part of a profile that provides an important source of information, which can inform the framing of objectives, selection of content and teaching methodologies of an EAP course. Also, while many of the elements of learner profiles will be gathered prior to or at the commencement of a course, other aspects of learner need will emerge through the interactions and activities of the course as it proceeds. These elements also need to be added to student profiles and taken into account, requiring the EAP teacher to be both reflective and adaptive during the delivery of a course. This may involve teachers performing ongoing observations and keeping reflective journals, especially during the early stages of students' acculturation into EAP courses.

2.2   Target situation analysis

As the previous two chapters have indicated, deconstructing learner need in relation the target study situation and related academic skills and competencies is complex and multi-faceted. Chapter 2 provided frameworks for approaching this activity. In effect, two sources of information may be drawn upon in relation to target situation analysis:

- the existing literature of EAP research; and,
- course-related, context-specific local investigations (such as employing the types of frameworks and methods proposed in Chapter 2).

Target situation analysis firstly requires consideration of the stage or level of academic education at which the EAP course is located. In Chapter 1, it was established that EAP is taught at different levels: pre-tertiary (often called pre-sessional), undergraduate level and increasingly at postgraduate level (in-sessional). At each level, because of the different types of learner need, the target situation focus of the course will be different. Using Hutchinson and Waters' (1987) questions, Tables 3.3, 3.4 and 3.5 suggest some of the key areas of target knowledge and skills required by students at each of these three levels of an EAP course.

Table 3.3   Target situation analysis: pre-sessional EAP courses

Questions based on Hutchinson & Waters (1987)	Possible target knowledge and skills
Why do the learners need the language?	The types of target-language academic and cognitive skills that students need in order to participate in tertiary (usually university) education in order to perform certain types of roles and tasks.
What will the content areas be?	A multiple-content, multiple-textual focus. Students at this level need to be gaining generic, procedural knowledge rather than topic-connected, discipline-specific knowledge – they need to be developing what Widdowson (1983) refers to as *capacity* as well as *competence*.
What genres will be used? (What is the typical structure of these genres?)	Pre-sessional EAP courses, such as senior secondary school and foundation studies courses, cannot meet student needs in terms of a single discipline-specific focus. For example, they cannot just focus on the genres

and practices of business, or of humanities or of science – unless of course it is known that all of the students within the group will be studying in only one of those areas. Students at this level need to focus on more general text types previously referred to by the author as *cognitive genres* (Bruce, 2008a).

Who will the learner use the language with? Where will the learner use the language?	Pre-sessional course situations and academic and proficiency examinations.

Table 3.4 Target situation analysis: in-sessional EAP courses

Hutchinson & Waters (1987) questions	Possible target knowledge and skills
Why do the learners need the language? What genres will be used? What is the typical structure of these genres? What will the content areas be?	These students need to develop the means to interrogate and respond to the requirements of undergraduate assignment genres. This involves understanding and employing the types of identity, orientation and discoursal resources that the assignments of particular disciplines require. This issue is intensified in the case of undergraduates who are taking broad-based degrees and facing courses and assignments in a variety of subject areas.
Who will the learner use the language with? Where will the learner use the language?	Undergraduate students tend to use language to participate in courses and to display knowledge in oral and written assignments primarily to teaching staff and sometimes to peers. Normally, this type of information display is in the social relationship of novice to expert although in some constructivist courses, peer discussion (sometimes online) is also part of the display process.

The next level is that of in-sessional EAP courses, such as first- or second-year undergraduate courses (see Table 3.4, above). Here the aim is usually to further address the language needs (and most urgently, the writing needs) of students at this level. In many countries, these students will usually have gained entry to undergraduate education on the basis of relatively low English proficiency requirements, such as IELTS (Academic Module) 6.0, TOEFL 550 or iBT 79–80. However, it is important to realize the limitations of these proficiency levels. For example, the *IELTS Handbook* recommends that an overall average IELTS score of 6.0 is probably suitable as an entry level to 'linguistically less demanding vocational training courses, such as in the areas of animal husbandry, catering and fire services' (IELTS *Handbook*, 2006: 5). Therefore, students entering undergraduate university courses with this English proficiency level will still face a range of language problems.

The third level of EAP is that of postgraduate courses (see Table 3.5). In some ways this area of EAP is the one that is informed by the most extensive body of research.

Table 3.5   Target situation analysis: postgraduate EAP courses

Hutchinson & Waters (1987) questions	Possible target knowledge and skills
Why do the learners need the language? What genres will be used? What is the typical structure of these genres?	The written and spoken genres used to report research.
What will the content areas be?	At this level, the EAP courses may be interdisciplinary – that is, taken by students from different subject areas. Therefore, there is still a need to provide opportunities to examine disciplinary differences in the research-reporting genres
Who will the learner use the language with?	Students at this level are beginning to create expert to expert communications within their disciplinary field. They are bidding to communicate new research knowledge as an equal expert in their particular field. To do this, they need to know intimately the literature and the forms of communication of the subject discourse community that they are bidding to join.
Where will the learner use the language?	At this level, students need to communicate through the written genres used to report research, but also the spoken genres of the oral seminar presentation, research group meetings and conference presentations.

The information gathered from needs analysis may provide a rich level of contextual information about the types of process and outcome that EAP course students need to master in order to study in disciplinary courses. However, needs analysis, of itself, does not provide a theoretical basis for the actual design of the EAP course, such as for the articulation of aims and objectives or the selection and staging of content that together support an appropriate teaching methodology. In Figure 3.1 needs analysis is identified as the first step in the process of course design leading to the second step, which is framing course aims and objectives.

3. Relating student need to aims and objectives for EAP courses

Following the progression of Figure 3.1, the findings of needs analysis are then related to the formulation of the aims and objectives of EAP courses and, as the figure suggests, this stage is informed by theories of discourse. This section, therefore, first provides a general discussion of the nature of EAP course aims and objectives that take account of learner need. The formulation of objectives is then related to discourse theory, and two principles are proposed that can guide their development. Chapter 4 will further relate these principles to more specific examples of EAP syllabus and course objectives.

The underlying language constructs that Widdowson (1983) terms 'capacity' and 'competence' provide a starting point when considering the framing of needs-focused syllabus objectives for an EAP course. Widdowson defines competence as 'the speaker's knowledge of the language system . . . [and] his [/her] knowledge also of social rules which determine the appropriate use of linguistic forms' (1983: 7). Capacity, on the other hand, is defined as 'the ability to create meanings by exploiting the potential inherent in the language for continual modification in response to change' (1983: 8). Capacity, therefore, relates to the ability to apply the different elements (or aspects) of competence to tasks that require complex language outcomes, such as may be encountered in academic or professional communities.

In relation to competence and capacity, Chapter 1 reviewed Widdowson's (1983) proposal that syllabus objectives will vary considerably between what he terms 'wide angle' and 'narrow angle' courses (p. 89). For example, if a course is narrow angle, it will be concerned mainly with developing competence. In this case, the course objectives will relate to the linguistic system, as well as to the social rules for its appropriate use. (In Chapter 1, the example of a narrow angle, competence-based course of teaching English to air traffic controllers was offered. The objectives of such a course can be established in terms of the known, occupational end uses of the language.) On the other hand, wide angle courses, such as most EAP courses, will be more concerned with objectives that aim at developing capacity.

It is suggested here that capacity development is central to EAP course design for two reasons. The first is that students in academic settings are faced with constantly changing contexts, such as different subject courses at undergraduate level or interdisciplinary postgraduate programmes. Participation in each disciplinary context involves different types of communicative or rhetorical purpose and language use in which students have to apply their competence knowledge. The second reason is that the language outputs that students are required to produce in academic contexts usually involve the preparation and presentation of extended texts – spoken or written. Thus, it is proposed here that framing objectives and designing EAP courses that promote *capacity development* require two essential elements embedded within and underpinning the curriculum. The first element is that EAP course objectives employ a principled approach to processing and creating the types of text (spoken and written) that occur in academic contexts, and the second element is that the framing of EAP course objectives will require exploration of the diversity of disciplinary contexts and their communicative differences.

3.1   Aims related to texts

Course aims and objectives that focus on text processing and text creation in EAP courses are important for two reasons. The first is the need to promote the development of what communicative competence models refer to as a *discourse competence*. Discourse competence refers to the ability to communicate through extended spoken or written texts that are characterized by an appropriate, integrated arrangement of content information and language. Most of the models proposed for the concept of communicative competence in a language include discourse competence (Canale, 1983; Canale & Swain, 1980; Celce-Murcia, Dörnyei & Thurrell, 1995; Council of Europe, 2001). Bachman (1990) uses the term *textual competence,* and Bhatia (2004) calls it *discursive competence.*

The second reason for textual objectives is to improve levels of linguistic accuracy by examining language features as they operate integratively within texts as functional wholes rather than trying to teach this type of knowledge in an atomistic way.

In order to develop syllabus aims that provide a basis for systematically presenting and deconstructing the types of texts identified in the needs analyses (and to make decisions about which types of texts to include within the curriculum and how to deal with them), EAP course designers need to look at existing research (including local target needs analyses) that examines actual assignment tasks in learning situations along with faculty expectations, and at theoretical approaches to deconstructing texts in ways useful for pedagogy.

Existing research that has examined the texts that university students have to write has been carried out through surveys of:

- undergraduates and the types of assignment tasks that they have experienced (Kroll, 1979)
- faculty, asking the types of tasks that they assign and their expectations of student responses (Braine, 1989; Bush, 1994; Eblen, 1993; Pearson–Casanave & Hubbard, 1992)
- university assignment tasks, for example, gathering and analysing a sample of assignments from a range of departments and faculties (Braine, 1989, 1995; Canseco & Byrd, 1989; Hale *et al.*, 1996; Horowitz, 1986; Moore & Morton, 1999, 2005)
- the assignment tasks and requirements of the target disciplines of students by EAP teachers' own target situation analyses.

Taking insights from this research about writing requirements and incorporating them into the curriculum in terms of aims related to creating texts requires the course designer also to consider approaches to classifying and analysing discourse – such as the various approaches to genre. However, relating genre theory to curriculum design is problematic, as the field of genre studies is an area of multiple (often overlapping) approaches, competing terminologies and different levels of constructs (see, for example, Hyon, 1996; Johns, 2002). A number of genre theorists propose that part of the confusion of constructs may be resolved by a dual approach to genre knowledge (Biber, 1989; Bruce, 2008a; Paltridge, 2002; Pilegaard & Frandsen, 1996). At one level is what is termed here *social genre* knowledge, which relates to the functional categories of whole texts (or their conventionalized sections). For example, essays, editorials, research articles and novels are examples of social genres. The second level of knowledge relates to *cognitive genres* – smaller, embedded stretches of text that realize a single, more general, rhetorical purpose, described in terms such as Recount, Explanation, Report or Argument. (The social genre/cognitive genre approach will be presented in more detail in Chapter 5.)

In relating these levels of text classification to syllabus development, it is proposed here that the textual aims of a particular EAP course should relate to the educational level and needs of the learner (be they pre-sessional, in-sessional or postgraduate). For example, because of the interdisciplinary nature of the student body in many foundation studies courses, the whole-text focus of a curriculum cannot begin with the social genres of particular disciplines. Rather, the focus should begin with the more general discourse-organizing structures, termed here *cognitive genres* (referred to by some writers as *text types*). Knowledge of these then becomes a basis for deconstructing the larger textual wholes of social genres at a later stage. On the other hand, the whole-text focus of discipline-specific courses, such as EAP courses for engineering or a specific science subject, needs to incorporate both levels of genre knowledge – the more general patterns of discourse organization (cognitive genres) as well as the larger social genres of their field.

3.2   Aims that include a focus on awareness of disciplinary diversity

By 'disciplinary diversity', I mean how subjects differ in the ways in which they create, use and report knowledge. In an interdisciplinary EAP course, such as a foundation studies pre-sessional course, members of the student body will be aiming to take a variety of different subjects at a university or polytechnic. However, even in this type of EAP course, it is important to include consciousness-raising activities so that students realize that academic expectations, conventions and orientations will vary greatly between disciplines and their particular genres. Examples of ways in which teachers can incorporate disciplinary diversity into their curriculum include:

- having a multi-context and a multi-textual focus when implementing different types of task, for example, when examining the language and features of critique, an extension activity could involve examining and comparing critique texts from a number of disciplines
- focusing on disciplinary differences in the areas of writer identity and positioning in relation to audience, such as examining the author's use of metadiscourse to address their audiences in a number of texts using the model referred to by Hyland (2005)
- examining the use of citation practices and the persuasive uses of citation in the texts of different disciplines (Hyland, 1999).

Thus, in meeting the needs of EAP students, the aims of EAP courses in their design have to take account of the needs of the learners, be framed in terms of textual outcomes, and be realized through diverse texts and contexts

Chapter 4 will focus in more detail on the specifics of the design of a syllabus for an EAP course. In that chapter, these general principles are related to the formulation of course objectives. However, course objectives also presume theories of language learning and teaching and in the case of EAP courses, these theories also need to support the needs-driven character of this type of course.

4. Conclusion

This chapter has proposed that, in addressing student need in the design and implementation of EAP courses, the concept of accounting for needs has three closely interrelated stages. This first involves performing present situation and target situation analyses of needs. Through gathering this type of information, EAP teachers and course designers can gather a considerable amount of information about the present knowledge and skills of students as well as information about the types of outcome that they will be expected to achieve in future courses. Needs analyses, therefore, identify the gap between students' present and target situations that EAP courses are expected to bridge. However, planning courses that equip students with the types of knowledge, strategies and skills that bridge the gap and achieve identified target outcomes means that the previously identified needs will then inform the development of course aims and objectives, the second stage of the process. It is proposed that these need to be centred around the processing and creation of texts (spoken and written), and that aims and objectives need to be formulated in ways that have the capacity to (a) acknowledge disciplinary differences, and (b) encourage the development of 'capacity' – more general procedural knowledge that enables students to adapt and apply their knowledge of language in a variety of contexts. Achieving this requirement involves drawing upon appropriate theories of discourse that provide a systematic, theoretical basis for the deconstruction and reconstruction of academic texts and the discourses in which they are embedded. The third stage of addressing needs relates to the selection and staging of course content, drawing upon theories of teaching and learning that support the needs-driven aims and objectives of EAP courses. Both the second and third stages of Figure 3.1 will be further developed in the chapters of Part II that examine syllabus development and the selection and specification of language for EAP courses.

Part II
The Design of EAP Courses

4
Developing an EAP Syllabus: Approaches and Models

1. Introduction

The chapters of Part I proposed a theoretical basis for EAP. Chapter 1 introduced EAP courses as a needs-driven educational activity, and presented a discussion of fundamental issues that need to be considered in the design of such courses. Chapter 2 considered approaches to researching different subject or disciplinary areas in order to inform EAP courses. Chapter 3 then considered the analysis of student needs as a basis for formulating aims and objectives for EAP courses. Against the background of the knowledge and issues presented in the previous chapters, the three chapters of Part II now turn to the design of EAP courses, beginning with Chapter 4 which considers the process of designing a syllabus for an EAP course.

In the conclusion of Part I, it was proposed that the aims and objectives of EAP courses should take account of the present and future needs of learners, be framed in terms of textual outcomes, and be realized through a variety of texts and contexts. These principles established in the previous chapters provide a basis for designing EAP syllabuses as frameworks around which courses can be developed. Hyland (2006) defines a syllabus as 'a plan of what is to be achieved through teaching and learning, identifying what will be worked on in reaching the overall course aims and [providing] a basis for evaluating students' progress' (p. 83). In considering the process of syllabus development, Chapter 4 is organized in two sections: identifying EAP syllabus knowledge and the stages of developing the syllabus.

The next section of the chapter, therefore, will examine types of EAP syllabus knowledge, and the third will look at the process of putting a syllabus together, taking account of the principles proposed in the chapters of Part I.

2.   Identifying and organizing EAP syllabus knowledge

While research that investigates academic disciplines and student needs analysis helps to identify the knowledge and skills that need to be taught in an EAP course, the next stage in the design of such a course is to develop a syllabus, a plan outlining what will be achieved through the teaching and learning. Developing a syllabus requires systematic, principled approaches to the organization of the content knowledge that is to be included in the future course. To address this issue, this section will consider the following classifications of knowledge and knowledge processing, which are expressed in contrasting pairs of terms:

- declarative vs. procedural knowledge
- atomistic vs. holistic objectives
- top-down vs. bottom-up processing
- synthetic vs. analytic syllabus types.

The contrastive discussion of each pair of classifications relates these areas of knowledge and knowledge processing to the types of purpose and function of EAP courses established in previous chapters. The discussion also has the aim of developing principles that should guide EAP syllabus design. To provide examples of the implementation of these principles, syllabus specifications for a unit of a general EAP writing course will be referred to. (These are summarized in Table 4.5 at the end of this chapter).

2.1   Declarative vs. procedural knowledge

Declarative knowledge is conscious knowledge of the systems of the language, such as vocabulary, grammar and syntax. *Procedural knowledge*, on the other hand, is knowledge about how to use declarative knowledge correctly, which relates to Widdowson's (1983) notion of *capacity*, introduced earlier in this chapter. For example, how one should use certain language appropriately in social situations is an area of sociocultural knowledge that should go hand in hand with the teaching of linguistic knowledge. Another type of procedural knowledge that is more abstract is knowledge about how to structure and organize texts in ways that achieve specific communicative purposes, such as how to arrange the content of an undergraduate essay in a way that presents a coherent argument or case. Clearly both types of knowledge are important, but in order to develop the area of capacity in EAP students, procedural, organizational (sometimes termed *strategic*) knowledge needs to be embedded within the syllabus so that it receives a central and ongoing focus in any course that is based on the syllabus. As a principle, therefore, declarative knowledge is not dealt with in isolation from procedural knowledge. However, to ensure that procedural knowledge is embedded within a syllabus requires objectives to be framed in such a way that its use is required when carrying out the objective. Therefore, a principle of *holism* is proposed here, which suggests that the aim or overall objective of a syllabus unit should be expressed in a way that will require a focus on procedural as well as declarative knowledge. This principle is reiterated in the discussion of the next pair of terms, atomistic vs. holistic objectives.

2.2   Atomistic vs. holistic objectives

Chapter 1 (Section 2) referred to Widdowson's (1983) proposal that syllabus objectives for wide angle courses, such as EAP courses, will require objectives that facilitate the development of the procedural knowledge necessary to exploit effectively the competence elements of language (and its use) in a range of contexts:

> With wide angle course design, the need to account for the procedural aspect of learning and use is more self evident. Here, the intention is obviously not to get students to internalize the topical realizations, but to use them for learning. It is the process of *relating these particular realizations to more general schematic structure* [emphasis added] which is the central concern and the process must . . . involve procedural activity. (Widdowson, 1983: 90)

Thus, in order to maintain an ongoing focus on procedural knowledge, it seems that objectives for an EAP syllabus should be holistic, possibly text- or genre-based. This type of objective will usually require the performance of a larger task that involves the integration of a number of different types of knowledge. For example, an aim (taken from Table 4.4) for a unit of a more general EAP writing course, such as a pre-sessional, foundation studies course, could be:

> *Students will be able to write a 200-word data report describing non-chronological data from a bar graph, pie chart or table.* (Chapter 6,

Table 6.1 contains a sample task and a text to exemplify this syllabus objective.)

To ensure that there is a focus on procedural knowledge in the realization of this objective, the unit has subsidiary objectives. One relates to schematic knowledge (applied to the organization of ideas) and two others to the textual structure (the organization of the written text). The objective relating to schematic knowledge is:

Students will use a WHOLE-PART schematic structure for whole reports and an UP-DOWN schema for the body section of information reports.

This subsidiary objective draws on the theory of cognitive genre (text type) that I have proposed previously (Bruce, 2005, 2007, 2008a). This type of procedural knowledge relates to the planning of ideas and draws on the idea that gestalts (shapes that relate to the physical world) are used metaphorically to organize abstract knowledge and ideas. Thus a simple information report of this type will contain a WHOLE (overall summary) and PART (description of the component parts of the WHOLE). The content of the PART section will be structured by an UP-DOWN (large to small/ more significant to less significant) organizational pattern. These elements of the schematic objective relate to prewriting planning in terms of the organization of ideas (this schematic organization of content relates to data that is non-chronological). The schematic objective then leads to two textual objectives for the actual writing that mirror the ideas organization of the schematic aim, which is organized in terms of a *Preview-Detail* discourse pattern (Hoey, 1983: 138–43). This pattern involves presenting an overview of the content of a text followed by a systematic presentation of the component details.

1. *Students will incorporate a Preview-Detail discourse pattern in writing an information report.*
2. *Students will have practice in writing topic sentences and developing paragraphs appropriate to this text type and the type of content data involved.*

Thus in a syllabus unit that has a larger textual aim that requires the integration of different types of knowledge, the requirement to integrate procedural knowledge into the course unit is in-built. However, if the aim of a syllabus unit focuses on linguistic features, such as different types of relative clause (an essential feature in writing that reports non-sequential data), there is less certainty that the higher-level, organizational elements of this type of writing will be included. Chapters 5 and 6 will further develop this idea by considering the types of textual units that can be used as a basis for identifying and developing a syllabus, particularly in relation to the writing skill. This issue will be taken up again in Chapter 8, which focuses on the teaching of writing within an EAP context.

2.3   Top-down vs. bottom-up processing of knowledge

In relation to human processing of knowledge, cognitive psychologists (e. g. Barsalou, 1992: 43) propose that the cognitive system has a hierarchical organization, with fundamental perceptual systems situated at lower levels of the hierarchy and more complex cognitive systems (e.g. memory and procedures for solving problems) situated at the top of the hierarchy. When processing knowledge, information can flow both from the bottom to the top and from the top to the bottom of the cognitive system. When information flows from the top to the bottom of the system, this is called 'top-down' processing – looking at the whole to make sense of the parts. For example, when reading, top-down processing occurs when reading for the gist or overall meaning of a text. When information flows from the bottom to the top of the system – focusing on specific details in order to understand something – this is called 'bottom-up' processing. Again, in the case of reading, bottom-up processing occurs during intensive reading for detail, such as at the level of noting individual words and their meanings. These types of information flow and their directions (top-down or bottom-up) can be influenced by what the individual already knows. For example, low-level language users process mainly using bottom-up processing, whereas proficient users tend to place more reliance on top-down processing, using bottom-up processing as a supportive strategy, for example to check the meaning of a word. According to Widdowson (1990: 136), syllabus design should be based on 'a reconciliation of the opposing principles of synthesis and analysis' – that is, it should involve both bottom-up and top-down processing.

   In the example syllabus unit in the following section (see Table 4.3), some objectives relate to the higher-level organization of knowledge – the schematic and the textual objectives – and some relate to lower-level, more specific knowledge – the linguistic devices that are used to achieve cohesion in this type of text (relative clauses, object noun clauses and various ways of showing contrast), along with vocabulary (related to data presentation). Following Widdowson's approach, the organization of the sample syllabus unit is principally top-down, but it also provides a framework within which salient elements of grammar and vocabulary can be presented and practised. Ideas relating to how these higher- and lower-level areas of knowledge connect and are related are further articulated in the next section, that considers syllabus types – synthetic syllabus vs. analytic syllabus.

2.4   Synthetic syllabus vs. analytic syllabus

Wilkins (1976) defined syllabuses as being mainly *synthetic* or *analytic*. A typical example of a synthetic syllabus is one that is organized around grammatical items, as Nunan says, 'based on the premise that learners acquire one grammatical item at a time and that they should demonstrate their mastery of one thing before moving on to the next' (Nunan, 1998: 101). With this type of syllabus, language learning is considered to be a process like laying bricks one upon another to build a wall. In teaching and learning from a synthetic syllabus, Wilkins says, 'the different parts of the language are taught separately and step-by-step so that acquisition is a process of gradual accumulation of the parts until the whole structure of the language has been built up' (1976: 2). The synthetic syllabus would appear to assume that language learning is a systematic and cumulative process. However, as Nunan also points out (1998: 102):

> [learners] do not learn one thing perfectly, one item at a time, . . . the rate of growth is determined by a complex interplay of factors related to speech processing constraints (Pienemann and Johnston, 1987), pedagogical interventions (Pica 1985), acquisitional processes (Johnston, 1987) and the influence of the discoursal environment in which the items occur.

A further problem with the synthetic syllabus approach is its capacity to integrate complex systems of the language, interrelated systems that are simultaneously engaged in any situation of authentic language use. These systems may include elements that are described in terms of pragmatics, semantics, phonology or orthography, morphology and syntax. As a solution to the problems of the atomistic nature and artificiality of the *synthetic syllabus*, Widdowson (1990) points to Wilkins' (1976: 2) proposal for another type of syllabus, termed an *analytic syllabus*, which Widdowson says (1990: 134),'presents language as synthesised units to be analysed in the process of learning'. Thus:

> [a]n analytic syllabus, on the other hand, would not be bottom-up but top-down. That is to say, it would present language in the form

of larger textual units and set tasks of different kinds which would direct the learners' attention to specific features, formal or functional, of the language they were exposed to. Analysis would then be induced by means of controlled procedural work. (1990: 136)

Thus, as an alternative to a linear, synthetic approach to language course design, Widdowson proposes that syllabus and course designers 'look for ways of defining the aims of our students in communicative terms *by devising a means of analysis which preserves the essential discourse* features of language use' (Widdowson, 1983: 85; emphasis added), this being essential to the development of syllabus and course materials that aim to develop the discourse competence of students, for example in relation to processing and creating texts in an EAP course. Hyland (2006: 83–6) suggests that *task-based, process* and *text-based* syllabuses are examples of analytic syllabuses that are used in EAP. Most EAP syllabuses are hybrids of these three approaches. Generally, EAP syllabuses (a) have outcomes-focused aims and objectives concerned with developing students' genre skills; (b) use tasks of various kinds; and (c) involve the integration of a variety of different types of knowledge and different skills. In particular, the text-based syllabus focuses on genres (categories of texts with similar characteristics) that students need to use. Furthermore, Hyland (2006) states that a text-based syllabus provides the basis for a scaffolded pedagogy to guide learners towards control of key genres.

2.5 Summary

To summarize, it seems that the design principles that should generally constrain the development of an EAP syllabus include:

- a focus on procedural as well as declarative knowledge
- a holistic rather than an atomistic approach to the framing of objectives
- a focus on top-down processing (as a balance to the bottom-up approaches of most second language learning)
- an analytic syllabus organized around larger units of language that are deconstructed and reconstructed in systematic ways.

3. Developing the syllabus

Hyland (2006: 282) says: 'course development starts with needs and rights analyses and uses the information to state the broad goals and the more specific outcomes on which a course is based. These, in turn, form the basis of a systematic plan of what needs to be learnt.' Thus the process of developing an EAP syllabus is a top-down one of formulating first general, then specific, details about the syllabus.

Step 1: Formulating course goals and overall objectives

The first step involves formulating a general course goal from the needs analysis. This is a global target statement that describes the overall expected outcomes of a course. In order to make this discussion more practical, a hypothetical target EAP class that has certain needs will be identified. Example goals for two language courses for the target group (in Table 4.1) will then provide the basis for the discussion.

The hypothetical group is a class of EAP students taking a pre-sessional, foundation studies course. Present situation analyses have identified that the group shares a number of characteristics. For most members of the class, their previous language learning has focused almost exclusively on discrete-point, decontextualized items of grammar and vocabulary – a backwash effect of the reliance on the multi-choice language tests favoured in certain countries. The learning experiences of members of the class have been teacher-centred, with little or no experience of any type of autonomous learning or requirement to work collaboratively or to complete larger tasks. As a result, the prior cognitive training of the students has mainly involved passive memorization and pattern recognition. The target situation analysis suggests, therefore, that the students have two overriding needs: first, the development of *discourse competence* and, second, preliminary acculturation into the day-to-day expectations and learning practices common to a range of faculties in a Western university. As part of the English component of the foundation studies programme, the students are taking two EAP courses, one that focuses on the development of reading and writing skills and the other concerned with developing listening and speaking skills. The overall goal for each course is presented in Table 4.1.

Table 4.1   Goals for two courses

Course 1
Students in this course will develop the reading and writing skills needed to undertake first-year undergraduate study in a range of disciplines.

Course 2
Students will develop effective listening and speaking skills in order to process input and meet the oral participatory requirements of first-year undergraduate courses in a range of disciplines.

In relation to these goals, the following questions need to be considered:

- What types of knowledge might be taught in the course? (What theory of language would you draw upon to identify and organize this knowledge?)
- How could this knowledge be broken down into course units or sections?

In the chapters of Part I, it was suggested that the aims of EAP courses should be realized through a range of texts and contexts. Thus, in implementing the syllabus of each course, texts (spoken and written) and related tasks need to be selected in relation to a variety of topic and subject areas, since the class members aim to study in a variety of undergraduate disciplines. Topic selection for units of the course could be based around the vocabulary needs of the learners (see Chapter 6, Section 4), and text selection needs to draw upon discourse theory, such as a pedagogic theory of genre, in order to have a principled approach to deconstructing and reconstructing whole texts.

As an organizational principle to ensure the development of the two skills in each course, tasks could be linked. For example, in Course 1, a focus on reading texts about a certain topic could lead into a writing task that recycles the same content and vocabulary. Because the class contains students who aim to study in a variety of disciplines, the writing outcomes cannot be discipline-specific genres, but rather, writing outcomes related to types of more general rhetorical purpose that are relevant to a range of subject courses. In relation to the development of reading skills, vocabulary development needs to be a strong feature of this course and can be included in the reading and recycled in the writing tasks.

Similarly, in Course 2, listening texts related to a certain topic could lead to speaking practice tasks and an oral presentation task on the same topic. In relation to the listening and speaking course, students need to develop the capacity to listen to and process extended listening texts, such as lectures, and to develop speaking (and listening) skills in order to meet the participatory requirements that now form an assessed part of many academic courses, along with more formal academic oral presentation skills. As with the reading and writing course, it would be desirable to integrate the two skills of listening and speaking. As an example, a topic that is developed through work on several extended listening texts could lead to a productive textual outcome, such as an individual or group oral presentation. In this way the principles discussed in the introduction to this chapter are implemented.

Table 4.2 takes the overall goal of the reading and writing course and presents some overall course aims that outline principles relating to the types of knowledge that are the object of each of the two courses.

Table 4.3 takes the overall goal of the listening and speaking course and adds the overall course aims that outline principles relating to the types of knowledge that are the object of the course.

Table 4.2   Course goal and overall objectives of the reading and writing course

Course goal
Students in this course will develop the reading and writing skills needed to undertake first-year undergraduate study in a range of disciplines.

Overall objectives
1. Reading: Students will be able to use a range of reading strategies to extract content meaning and identify discoursal, semantic and linguistic features from texts that relate to the topic areas of the course units.

2. Writing: In relation to the topic areas of the course units, students will be able to write extended responses to tasks that use four text types (termed here 'cognitive genres') that commonly occur in academic English prose: Recount, Report, Explanation, Discussion.

Table 4.3   Course goal and overall objectives of the listening and speaking course

Course goal
Students will develop effective listening and speaking skills in order to process spoken input and meet the oral participatory requirements of first-year undergraduate courses in a range of disciplines.

Overall objectives
1. Listening: Students will be able to listen to and process academic lectures and tutorial/seminar discussions for the purpose of extracting and organizing relevant information.

2. Speaking: Students will also be able to produce extended spoken discourse in oral presentations, including summaries and extended seminars drawing on multiple sources of information. Students will be able to engage in related follow-up interactions relating to presentations.

Step 2: Decide on the sequencing of units of the course

A number of factors can influence the staging of course units and their content. As pointed out in Step 1, the content of units may be related to vocabulary development, which is central to the needs of EAP students (see Cobb & Horst, 2001). However, the selection of texts (within which target vocabulary and language features are embedded) should draw upon theories of discourse in order to guide decisions about what language entities will form the basis for an individual course unit and how the different course unit entities relate to each other in the sequencing and progression of units within a course. For example, in a genre- or text-based approach to EAP course design, the logic of the ordering of units will relate to an appropriate staging of genre knowledge. (Also the old educational adage of 'proceed from known to unknown' is relevant here.) Given students' prior experience of narrative texts in literature, it may be appropriate to begin with factual recount texts that draw upon some familiar aspects of prior textual knowledge. For example, in the case of a 10-unit, pre-sessional EAP writing course that I have proposed elsewhere (see Chapter 8, Table 8.1), the course units are arranged around the four 'cognitive genres' (text types related to a single communicative purpose) beginning with factual Recounts.

Step 3: Formulating objectives for course units
Objectives describe behaviours that learners will be able to achieve by the end of a course unit. Therefore, they provide a framework for the planning and implementation of teaching and learning activities as well as a basis for assessment. The nature of the objective will also provide some direction concerning the types of tasks that are appropriate for teaching and learning activities. Objectives, therefore, are closely related to methodology. Individual course units will be described in terms of an overall objective for a unit and may also include subsidiary objectives that combine to help realize the overall aim. Thus, the nature of the overall and subsidiary objectives will be closely influenced by the theoretical basis of the syllabus. When framing objectives for a unit of an EAP course, it is important to think about the principles discussed in the first part of this chapter – that they:

- are framed in terms of textual outcomes supporting a holistic rather than an atomistic approach to knowledge
- include a focus on top-down processing as a balance to the bottom-up approaches of most second language learning
- include a focus on procedural as well as declarative knowledge.

To support these principles, objectives are expressed as performatives, something that the student will be able to do. Table 4.4 contains the overall objective for the writing component of a unit from the hypothetical foundation studies EAP reading and writing course discussed earlier in the chapter.

Expressing an objective in this way in relation to creating a whole language outcome requires the student to use a range of types of knowledge, both declarative knowledge in terms of the different systems of the language that will be used (vocabulary, grammar, syntax) as well as procedural knowledge in terms of the arrangement of language and content, to produce a text that is an appropriate outcome to achieve the objective of the course unit. The key elements that are essential to achieving the objective can be expressed in terms of subsidiary objectives and all of this needs to be related to an appropriate organization of these constituent elements of the unit.

Table 4.4 Sample general EAP writing syllabus unit objective

Overall objective

Students will be able to write a 200-word data report describing non-chronological data from a bar graph, pie chart or table (adapted from Bruce, 2005: 250; see also this volume, Chapter 6, Table 6.1 for a sample text).

(adapted from Bruce, 2005: 250)

Step 4: Decide on the internal staging of skills and knowledge within the course units

As mentioned in the first part of this chapter, the organization of knowledge should be informed by a coherent theory of discourse and text and should integrate the different aspects of language systems, e.g. vocabulary, grammar, syntax, rhetorical organization, meaning (semantics) and context (pragmatics). Previous discussion also proposed that the processing of knowledge (when realized in a course) should be a reconciliation of top-down and bottom-up processing (Widdowson, 1990: 136) and should enable cycles of learning that involve both analysis and synthesis (Skehan, 1996). Table 4.5 shows both the more general and more specific objectives for the previously discussed unit.

It is not the intention here to provide a detailed description of the theoretical approach to genre that that this illustrative unit draws upon; that is dealt with elsewhere (see Bruce, 2005, 2007, 2008a). However, if such a theoretical approach to a text-based or genre-based syllabus unit is employed, the principles proposed earlier are not violated. The organization of the syllabus unit is principally top-down. There is a focus on schematic, organizational knowledge – including both the organization of ideas and the organization of a text that represents the ideas. Salient elements of syntax, grammar and lexis may be examined so that the

Table 4.5 Sample general EAP writing syllabus unit

Objectives	
Overall	Students will be able to write a 200-word data report describing non-chronológical data from a bar graph, pie chart or table.
Schematic	The students will use a WHOLE-PART schematic structure for whole reports and an UP-DOWN schema for the body section of information reports.
Textual	Students will incorporate a *Preview-Detail* discourse pattern in writing an information report. Students will write topic sentences and develop paragraphs appropriate to this text type and the type of content data involved.
Cohesive	Students will have practice in using: restrictive (reduced) relative clauses (adjectival) syntactic and lexical markers of contrast.
Lexical	Students will review vocabulary related to statistics and data commentary.

language unit that is the object of learning of the unit is presented as a functional whole. This approach means that 'to identify something as a component is to recognize the operational complex as a whole in which it functions as a part' (Widdowson, 1983: 84).

4. Conclusion

The design of an EAP syllabus involves making connections between the present situation and target needs of learners and, on the basis of this knowledge, formulating the goals and objectives for the course. The identified goals and objectives then lead to the selection, sequencing and arrangement of knowledge within syllabus units in principled ways that are informed by theory and research. Thus, the development of a syllabus needs to occur in a systematic and principled way, as first outlined at the beginning of the previous chapter in Table 3.1, beginning with needs analysis, leading to the formulation of course goals and aims, which are then developed into units for teaching and learning. This developmental process should be informed by theories of discourse, language acquisition and pedagogy. Chapter 5 will continue the discussion of syllabus and course development by considering how (and when) knowledge from the subject disciplines can be incorporated into EAP courses.

5
EAP Courses and Subject Discipline Knowledge

1. Introduction

Chapter 4 considered issues relating to the design of syllabuses for EAP courses, including the types of knowledge to be included and how such knowledge may be organized. The ideas and principles that were proposed were exemplified in the design of an EAP syllabus unit at pre-sessional level. In continuing the idea of how EAP syllabuses and courses can be developed, Chapter 5 considers issues related to identifying and integrating academic subject knowledge into EAP courses. The chapter begins by considering the nature of subject knowledge as it relates to the different levels of EAP course (pre-sessional, in-sessional and postgraduate). It then discusses models of engagement between EAP teachers and staff in academic disciplines, along with theoretical issues involved in gathering and analysing discipline-specific knowledge for the EAP curriculum. The final section of the chapter considers a genre-based approach to classifying and deconstructing disciplinary texts as a basis for developing the holistic types of syllabus objectives discussed in the previous chapter.

2. EAP course design and delivery: a balancing act

EAP course designers, materials writers and teachers in effect have to balance a number of considerations. First they have to provide opportunities for the systematic and comprehensive development of academic language skills, and in particular the development of discourse competence, which was defined in Chapter 1. Secondly, they have to facilitate the development of other areas of academic meta-knowledge, skills and practices in order to equip students to participate in present or future courses. Such participation requires students to be acculturated into the interdisciplinary aspects of academic practices as well as aspects of subject-specific learning cultures. This second area of development involves understanding and adopting appropriate student roles, learner autonomy, independently accessing, using and citing knowledge. It is often the case that this second area of development must be addressed gradually and incrementally at first because of the nature of EAP students' prior educational experiences and their levels of language proficiency.

Both of these two areas of knowledge and skill need to be developed in tandem and in systematic ways that are informed by theory and research. In terms of their relative importance, it is proposed here that the first area (the ongoing development of academic language competence, and particularly discourse competence) is the core concern of an EAP syllabus, along with the courses and materials that are created to realize the syllabus. The second area (of academic meta-knowledge, skills and practices) relates to the implementation of a syllabus. This includes the teaching methodologies employed, approaches to skills development, tasks and assessments that together constitute the detailed aspects of the course realizations of a syllabus. Thus, the second area can be developed in terms of the types of learning culture and practices that EAP teachers adopt and establish in the classroom. (Aspects of academic meta-knowledge can also be incorporated into unit topics that incorporate academic vocabulary development.) However, implementing these two areas of learner development through the content and delivery of courses is predicated on the assumption that EAP course developers and teachers are themselves able to access and interpret the academic learning cultures of different disciplines, and that they can somehow introduce relevant elements of these disciplinary cultures into the EAP classroom in ways that students can understand and appropriate. (Chapter 7 reviews the types of teacher competencies that are necessary to implement the type of *pedagogic transfer* that needs to take place in an EAP course, that is, introducing students to the knowledge and practices of the academic world by means of an EAP course.)

Developing these two aspects of EAP learning in the classroom is, therefore, contingent upon the knowledge and professional practices of the teacher. In the EAP context, it may be that the approaches and methodologies of general English language teaching (ELT) need to be modified in order to reflect aspects of the learning culture of the university along with the types of disciplinary difference that operate within that culture and influence language choices. Adapting more general language pedagogy and professional practice to meet the needs of the academy goes to the heart of the challenge faced by many competent ELT practitioners who are asked by employers to develop and teach EAP courses in order to meet the increasing demand for this type of course. In effect, such teachers are being required to create and deliver courses in a specialized area of English language teaching (an area that differs considerably from more general ELT courses) without the requisite specialist training and support. They are being asked to introduce students to academic discourses and practices in systematic and theorized ways although they themselves may only be able to draw upon their own personal, eclectic experiences and intuitions about the academic world that is the object of their pedagogy.

Thus, in considering these issues, the following sections of this chapter address two central questions about the issue of connecting EAP teachers with the academic learning cultures of the university.

- How can EAP teachers access knowledge about subject disciplines in order to inform their courses?
- What are some of the theoretical and analytical issues that need to be considered when analysing disciplinary knowledge in order to incorporate it into EAP courses?

3.   Levels of EAP and knowledge from academic subjects

To provide a background for considering approaches to gathering subject-disciplinary knowledge and its incorporation into EAP courses, this section will review ideas about the different levels of disciplinary engagement in relation to different types of EAP courses.

One of the two areas of needs analysis examined in Chapter 3 is the future language and academic needs of students as they enter particular disciplines – the target situation analysis. Understanding this aspect of learner need is central to identifying the areas of language teaching and learning of an EAP course. However, deconstructing learner need in relation to academic skills and competencies is complex and multi-faceted, and the degree to which an EAP course will focus on situated language use within specific subject disciplines will vary considerably in the case of pre-sessional and in-sessional undergraduate and postgraduate courses. At each of these levels, because of the different types of learner need (present needs and target situation needs), the focus of the EAP course will be different. Thus, whether one needs to focus on the texts and practices of specific disciplines or to provide a more contrastive overview in relation to disciplinary practices depends on the needs of students at each of these levels.

Pre-sessional EAP courses, at lower levels, such as senior secondary school and foundation studies courses, often cannot meet student needs in terms of a single discipline-specific focus, because the students in such courses will be intending to study in a wide range of disciplines. Therefore, at this level academic knowledge and related topics may be introduced by following a more contrastive, cross-disciplinary approach. The overall goal of such courses tends to be to provide the maximum possible benefit to all of the participant students by focusing on language and content that will be relevant to future study in a wide range of disciplines. This suggests a need for the selection of themes and topics that have an academic focus and provide a vehicle for ongoing language development, such as the vocabulary identified in Coxhead's (2000) *academic word list* (AWL). On the other hand, pre-sessional courses that have the aim of preparing students for a single discipline, such as engineering or business management, may be formulated in terms of a more specific EAP focus. Such specialized, pre-sessional EAP courses may be offered at various levels, such as prior to undergraduate, postgraduate or doctoral study. The academic language and practices of the target subject need to be researched and analysed so that they can be incorporated into the EAP teaching and learning programme.

The second type of EAP is that of *in-sessional EAP* support. Here the aim is usually to address further the language needs (and most urgently, the writing needs) of students already engaged in undergraduate and postgraduate study. In Chapter 3, it was pointed out that these students will usually have gained entry to undergraduate courses on the basis of an overall average IELTS score of 6.0 (TOEFL 550) or to postgraduate courses with the slightly higher grade of 6.5 (TOEFL 600). Therefore, students entering university courses with these English proficiency levels will still face language difficulties, the most pressing of which usually relates to academic writing tasks.

In relation to language proficiency development in academic writing, students need to develop the means to negotiate and respond to the requirements of assignment genres, often in several disciplines. Typically, undergraduate students, especially in their first year, take a variety of courses in different subject or disciplinary areas. Students at this level, therefore, need to be provided with frameworks to explore disciplinarity in order to understand the types of identity, orientation and discoursal resources that the assignments of each discipline require. This issue is multiplied in the case of undergraduates who are taking broad-based degrees and facing courses and assignments in a variety of subject areas. The same issue is faced by students at postgraduate level taking interdisciplinary degrees in applied sciences, such as health sciences, social work or urban planning. EAP support to such students will, therefore, need to be tailored to provide a principled and systematic approach to the written and spoken assignment genres that they are confronted with.

The third area of EAP courses identified in earlier chapters are those courses that focus more specifically on the written and spoken genres used to report research. Developing this type of course requires a developed and systematic approach to deconstructing research-reporting texts and the discourses that give rise to such texts. This will involve evaluating and drawing upon a suitable, genre-based approach to course design. Such an approach needs to be sufficiently robust to provide a basis for exploring disciplinary differences in the research-reporting genres, such as abstracts, journal articles or dissertations.

4.   Models of engagement between EAP teachers and disciplines

The idea of relating the content, processes and skills focus of EAP courses to potential future situations of use has led to a considerable variety of approaches to engagement between language teachers (such as EAP teachers) and the teaching staff of subject disciplines. In relation to ESP courses, Dudley-Evans and St John (1998: 42–8) propose three types of engagement between language teachers and teachers of subject disciplines: co-operation, collaboration and team-teaching.

4.1   Co-operation

Dudley-Evans and St John suggest that co-operation is the first level of engagement with the disciplines, and involves the language teacher investigating the academic and language requirements of the subject disciplines that their students are preparing to enter. This could, for example, involve visiting relevant departments, gathering course outlines (curricula) and examples of assignment tasks and, where possible, using academic staff as subject informants. It may even involve the EAP teacher reading some of the literature and attending lectures, seminars and tutorials in the subject area to develop a sense of the writing and speaking needs of the discipline. (The activities of co-operation, in effect, refer to the target situation analysis aspect of performing a needs analysis.)

Dudley-Evans and St. John (1998) suggest that co-operation 'means finding out about the conceptual and discoursal frameworks of the subjects students are studying and occasionally introducing material [into the EAP course] that provides a slightly different perspective on that content' (p. 43). Thus, the activities that relate to co-operation can present a considerable challenge for EAP teachers and course developers in that they are required to analyse and interpret appropriately the teaching and learning practices and the textual and discoursal resources central to a particular subject discipline. Therefore, for an EAP course developer or teacher to be able to analyse and exploit the texts, discourses and practices discovered by co-operation, they need to have at their disposal knowledge and skills as discourse analysts in order to be able to analyse and make a pedagogic transfer into their teaching of the types of subject discipline knowledge that they uncover. Approaches to investigating this type of knowledge and expertise are discussed in Section 5 of this chapter.

4.2 Collaboration

While co-operation involves the EAP teacher/course developer unilaterally gathering information about specific subjects to inform the design and delivery of EAP courses, *collaboration* is a more direct working together by the language and subject instructors. Dudley-Evans and St John (1998: 44) suggest that this may take place in three ways:

1. The planning of a series of classes where the language class prepares the students for a subsequent subject class taught in English.
2. The running of a class on a specific skill or related to a specific task where the subject department has a specific input to the materials or the language teacher uses materials produced by the department.
3. The North American 'adjunct' model, in which the adjunct acts as a back-up class to the subject, helping students who have difficulties with the subject class.

Again, as with co-operation, in the collaboration model the knowledge and skills of the EAP teacher as a discourse analyst are essential so that they can deconstruct subject texts and their related discourses in useful ways to inform the EAP course. The principal difference in this model of engagement is that the teaching of the EAP teacher is more closely integrated with subject-course teaching.

4.3   Team-teaching

The most integrated model of engagement between EAP/ESP teachers and subject disciplines is that of team-teaching, which involves subject specialists and language teachers working together to teach the content and content-specific language of a particular discipline. This approach was successfully implemented at Birmingham University in the 1980s (Dudley Evans & Johns, 1981). Although various models of team-teaching have been developed in different contexts, the core element appears to be classes and tutorials designed in collaboration with the content teacher and which focus on the language requirements of the teaching and assignment tasks of a course.

More recent models that are a combination of collaboration and team-teaching have been developed and reported in the literature. For example, Sloan and Porter (2009) report on an ongoing study and the implementation of its findings in a team-teaching situation that involves the embedding of specific EAP instruction within graduate courses in the Newcastle Business school (University of Northumbria, Newcastle Upon Tyne). They propose a model (the CEM model) that involves three aspects: *contextualization, embedding* and *mapping*. 'Contextualization' involves analysis of the language and practices of the actual business courses. 'Embedding' means the EAP tutor is integrated within a team that teaches an academic programme, and has responsibility for teaching subject-specific language and study skills as part of the subject programme. 'Mapping' ensures that the focus on academic language is carefully timed to relate to the academic tasks and assignment needs of students.

In relation to collaboration with the disciplines, Dudley-Evans and St. John (1998: 47) suggest that teachers begin with co-operation, and perform investigations of subject texts and their discoursal interpretations. As part of this process, they suggest that it is important to engage with content-teaching staff from the disciplines as informants about the ways language is used in disciplinary spoken and written texts. When these types of engagement are established and successful, they suggest that the EAP and subject teachers seek institutional support for collaboration and team-teaching that builds on the relationships established through co-operation.

5. Analysing academic subject texts and related discourse knowledge

This section considers the activity of analysing subject discipline knowledge so that it can be incorporated into an EAP course. The section begins by discussing some of the issues that arise when EAP course designers and teachers engage with subject disciplines, and then proposes an approach to analysing this type of knowledge. While engagement between an EAP teacher and a subject discipline can potentially be a useful source of information for course development, it is proposed here that:

- EAP teachers first need to possess and understand theoretical frameworks in order to analyse and understand disciplinary knowledge and practices so that this knowledge can then be introduced into EAP courses in principled and systematic ways.
- Second, learners need to participate in tasks and activities that ensure an active rather than a passive engagement with the types of disciplinary knowledge uncovered; that is, it is not just the EAP teachers, but also their students who need to become trained and engaged in the processing and understanding of disciplinarity.

5.1 Understanding and approaching disciplinary knowledge: a need for frameworks

As well as drawing upon the findings of published ESP and EAP research on disciplinary practices, teachers also need to gather their own primary information about the disciplinary genres (spoken and written), values and practices needed by their own students in local, subject-discipline contexts. However, in order to be able to analyse and then teach the types of knowledge that they gather, teachers need to employ appropriate analytical frameworks, such as the ways of conceptualizing academic communities that were discussed in Chapter 2, and genre-based approaches to analysing texts and their related discourses, which are described later in this section. In relation to this process, there are a number of important issues that need to be considered by a course developer when gathering data about different disciplines to inform the design of EAP courses. These include:

- the limitations of subject informants' knowledge
- the beliefs and values of subject informants
- the wording of assignment tasks.

In engaging with the disciplines, an issue that it is important to acknowledge is the limitations of subject informants when attempting to relate their descriptions of disciplinary knowledge to EAP courses. For example, subject informants can describe the texts and processes of their discipline from the point of view of an insider. Such informants will have discipline-specific ideals and expectations of student assignments and communications. However, the same informants are not applied linguists; they do not usually have the linguistic knowledge or meta-language needed to describe the textual and discoursal requirements of assignments in consistent and transparent ways that provide a basis for an EAP course that then seeks to teach such knowledge to current or future students of the same discipline. For example, Lea and Street (1999) suggest that subject specialists are not necessarily able to help their students acquire disciplinary skills and they often view academic writing conventions as self-evident. In addition, Elton (2008) suggests that subject lecturers tend to lack the declarative knowledge necessary to make explicit the discoursal principles that underlie assessment criteria. Therefore, in order to relate knowledge gathered from subject informants to course design, EAP teachers need their own frameworks for the analysis of discipline-specific tasks, texts and the surrounding discourses.

In engagement with the disciplines, it is important to consider the beliefs and values of subject informants about what knowledge in their particular field is, how it is created and reported – beliefs that relate to the ontology and epistemology of their field. A crucial element of the epistemology of a field relates to its research methods – how knowledge is created and validated within a field. Also, an EAP teacher's own epistemological views cannot be mapped onto other subject disciplines. Barron (2003) exemplifies this point in reporting a case where collaborating EAP teachers' and science teachers' core values concerning knowledge and its reporting differed when considering what constituted assessable knowledge in a science poster presentation project. The project involved groups investigating and reporting community knowledge of a scientific issue. While science teachers were concerned with content that constituted scientific facts, EAP teachers focused on the language employed in the communication of the study, such as its methodology and findings.

An additional issue of EAP/subject discipline engagement relates to interpreting and responding to the prompts of assignment tasks in ways that meet the expectations and conventions of a particular subject discipline. Although the wording of assignment tasks may not always be consistent (often in terms of the instructional verbs used), academic staff will still have clear, subject-driven expectations about the form that the response to the task should take. Therefore, unpacking assignment prompts in terms of the types of discoursal and textual resources that they require needs to draw upon a developed theory of text and discourse that can be applied in principled and systematic ways.

5.2 Approaches to analysing subject texts and discourses

Much of the disciplinary knowledge that EAP course developers and teachers will need to pass on to their students relates to conventionalized spoken and written forms of communication that occur within every discipline, such as the genres of written assignments and oral presentations. In discussing the elements of these forms of communication, I will use the terms *text* and *discourse*. In defining these terms, Widdowson says that:

> text is the overt linguistic trace of a discourse process. As such, it is available for analysis. But interpretation is a matter of deriving a discourse from the text, and this inevitably brings context and pretext into play. (2004: 169)

Text, therefore, is the written record on the page (such as a written document or the written transcription of a spoken event), while discourse includes the written record as well as the social and cognitive operations that surround it in both its creation and processing. EAP course developers and teachers need to have systematic and transparent frameworks for analysing both the texts and also the related discourses of particular disciplines. In effect, teachers themselves need to be discourse analysts, but they also need to be training EAP students as discourse analysts in more fundamental ways so that they themselves can acquire the tools and knowledge to deconstruct the subject-specific discourses of their own subject areas.

To frame the investigations of different aspects of subject discourses and their texts, three data-collection methods were briefly considered in Chapter 2: ethnographic, genre-based and corpus linguistic approaches. It seems that some combination of these methods may be needed to fulfil Bhatia's (2004) proposal that the investigation of professional and academic genres needs to include both textual and ethnographic dimensions. Corpus linguistic studies can provide objective, linguistic information from a large sample of texts, e.g. about frequencies of use and collocations of words. Specific corpora (in terms of subject and genre) may be useful to uncover knowledge about linguistic features as they occur within a particular genre (category of texts) of a subject discipline. Ethnographic investigations of specific subject contexts using multiple data-collection methods, such as observation, interview and document analysis, are important for understanding disciplines in terms both of their specific contextual information and their practices. However, for close examination of both subject discourses and texts, genre-based approaches are also important tools, as they make it possible to integrate knowledge from multiple areas. This integration can include contextual knowledge relating to subjects and their subject-specific disciplinary practices, procedural or organizational knowledge, and linguistic knowledge.

However, as I have mentioned previously (Bruce, 2005, 2008a), the central problem in accessing genre theory to perform this type of task is the multiplicity of approaches to genre that may be employed to deconstruct disciplinary discourses and their associated textual patterns. For some, genre classification is largely a social phenomenon whereby theorists see genre as being reflected in the socially recognized functions and conventionalized structures of written or spoken texts that occur in specific contexts. These events may be shaped by contextual elements, participant relationships and communicative and transactional purposes. This type of genre analysis has been applied to legal cases, research articles and dissertations (see, for example, Bhatia, 1993, 2004; Swales, 2004). For other theorists, genre as a classifier of language entities is a more rhetorically motivated, cognitive phenomenon, often described in terms of general, rhetorical categories such as argument, explanation, recount and description. Following this approach, gaining genre knowledge involves the study of texts including their internal organizational and linguistic characteristics (see, for example, Knapp & Watkins, 1994; Macken-Horarik, 2002). Within the two broad approaches, it is possible to group a wide range of classifiers, as evidenced by the list presented in Table 5.1.

Any review of theory or research related to classifying texts in terms of such categories as genre and text type needs to address the fact that terminology (as is evident in Table 5.1) is used in very different ways by different writers. This is not simply a problem of naming or designation. It is a problem that arises out of fundamental disagreement about the very nature of the object of enquiry – what it is that is being investigated and classified. Thus, when it comes to defining genres, there is a multiplicity of overlapping theories along with a range of competing terminologies (see Hyon, 1996; Johns, 2002).

Table 5.1 Approaches to text classification

Proposer	Social focus	Rhetorical focus
Hasan (1989)	genre	
Swales (1990)	genre	
Bhatia (1993)	genre	
Martin (1994, 1995, 1997)	macro-genre	
Schryer (1993)	genre	
Knapp & Watkins (1997, 2005)	text type	genre
Werlich (1976)	text genre	text type
Biber (1989)	genre	text type
Virtanen (1992)	discourse type	text type
Paltridge (2002)	genre	text type
Van Dijk (1980)		macro-structure
Derewianka (1990)		genre
Lackstrom, Selinker & Trimble (1973)		rhetorical mode
Silva (1990)		rhetorical mode
Jordan (1997)		rhetorical mode
Hoey (1979, 1983)		discourse pattern
Adam (1985, 1992)		séquence
Bhatia (2002, 2004)		generic value
Council of Europe (2001)		macro-function
Grabe (2002)		macro-genre

In providing a framework for my own research and syllabus development, I have proposed that the different approaches to classifying extended discourse (both spoken and written) fall within two broad categories – *social genre* and *cognitive genre*.

> Social genre refers to socially recognized constructs according to which whole texts (or conventionally recognized sections of texts, such as Methods sections in research articles) are classified in terms of their overall social purpose and function. Thus, for example, personal letters, editorials, novels and academic articles are examples of different social genres, which are created to fulfill different types of socially recognized and understood purpose. Purpose here is taken to mean the intention to consciously communicate a body of knowledge related to a certain context to a certain target audience . . . .

The term cognitive genre is used here to refer to the overall cognitive orientation and internal organization of a segment of writing that realizes a single, more general rhetorical purpose to represent one type of information within discourse. Examples of types of general rhetorical purpose relating to cognitive genres are: to recount sequenced events, to explain a process, to argue a point of view, each of which will employ a different cognitive genre. (Bruce, 2008b: 39)

Social genres and cognitive genres are not mutually exclusive categories, but, in effect, two sides of the same coin, or two complementary approaches to examining a category of texts. The social and cognitive genre model proposed involves detailed frameworks for performing both ethnographic and also textual analysis. They involve analysing texts at different levels and acknowledging that each level employs different types of knowledge, all of which are integrated, and which include:

- context
- epistemology
- stance
- content schemata
- cognitive genres.

I propose that when examining academic written and spoken texts (and their surrounding discourses) in a particular subject discipline, it is important to consider the different dimensions of knowledge of the social/cognitive genre model as a basis for making a pedagogic transfer of such knowledge into the EAP course in ways that are accessible to students. In the remainder of this section, each of these areas of genre knowledge are unpacked a little further and discussed in terms of how they may inform an EAP course.

5.3   Context

Widdowson (2004) proposes that the relationship between texts and their contexts is indivisible. He says that 'there is no "understanding" of texts as a semantic process, separate from, and prior to a pragmatic "evaluation", which brings context into play' and that context involves both 'intralinguistic and extralinguistic factors' (p. 35). I suggest that, in relation to academic or professional genres, extralinguistic factors are the types of specialist, technical knowledge of the field to which the text belongs and intralinguistic factors include the particular forms of communication and technical vocabulary used in the particular field. Thus, the process of unpacking the genres of a particular discipline should first consider the contextual factors that give specialist meanings to a subject-specific genre or category of texts. This includes considering:

- the context-specific communicative purposes of a text
- the types of specialist subject knowledge that are needed to understand the text
- the related subject-specific vocabulary necessary to understand the text.

5.4 Epistemology

As already mentioned in Chapter 2, Section 3, another important aspect of contextual knowledge that influences a particular genre is epistemology – how experts working in a particular field view and use knowledge. However, it must be acknowledged that developing a full understanding of the epistemology of a particular field or subject cannot be achieved solely by deconstructing texts in an EAP reading and writing class. Rather, understanding the theory of knowledge that academics or professionals working in a particular subject area subscribe to involves understanding how they create knowledge. In any particular discipline, the knowledge-creating paradigms that are used shape its knowledge-communicating forms, such as its written and spoken genres. The written texts of the discipline and their related discourses are a consequence of its approaches to knowledge creation.

As I have suggested elsewhere (Bruce, 2008a: 134), it seems that the problem faced by novice academic writers is that information about knowledge-creating within their particular field, such as the research methods of a discipline, tends to be withheld until the students reach postgraduate level. As a result, undergraduate novice writers (native speakers and non-native speakers) have only a partial understanding of the writing of their discipline and the influences that shape it until they develop an understanding of the subject's research methodology later in their studies. Therefore, tasks that relate to uncovering the influences of epistemology on the writing of a particular field need to examine knowledge-creating (such as the research methods that are used in the subject) and how the subject's knowledge-creating influences the knowledge-reporting in particular texts.

5.5   Writer stance

The overall context and the epistemological values of a subject area, in turn, both influence the *stance* or *standpoint* of a writer in relation to his/ her audience. Bakhtin proposes that writing, like speaking, is *dialogic* – a dialogue between the writer and the reader – and, as a consequence, writing is constructed with the expectations and knowledge of the reader in mind. Like Bakhtin, Hyland (2005) emphasizes the dialogic nature of writing because, he says, '[writing] presupposes and responds to an active audience, and because it makes links to other texts' (p. 88). Hyland (2005: 49) proposes a set of language devices that are used to connect writer with reader, which he groups together under the term *metadiscourse*. (The different language features of metadiscourse are described in Chapter 6, Section 3, Table 6.9, along with examples of metadiscourse in different types of text.) Examples of metadiscourse are *hedges* and *boosters*. Hedges are expressions that withhold commitment and open dialogue, such as 'might', 'perhaps'. Boosters are expressions that emphasize certainty and close dialogue, such as 'definitely, it is clear that'. To date, Hyland's model appears to be the most comprehensive approach to categorizing the types of language used for this purpose and metadiscourse features from Hyland's model can be used as a basis for novice writers to analyse texts and develop a sense of the types of language used by writers to address their audiences.

5.6   Staging of content

In the main pedagogic approaches to (social) genre, a cornerstone of how they define genres has always been regularities (or regular patterns) in forms of communication used to achieve a particular purpose. For example, in the approach to genre influenced by systemic functional linguistics, the content organization of a genre is described in terms of *schematic structure* (Eggins, 1996), and in the approach of the English for specific purposes (ESP) movement, patterns of content organization have been described in terms of *moves and steps* (Swales, 1981). In relation to academic texts, genre analyses have tended to follow the ESP approach. Introductions and 'Discussion' sections of academic articles that report research have been quite intensively analysed in this way. Other academic or professional genres that have been analysed include dissertations, popularized medical texts, job applications, sales promotion letters, legal case studies and grant proposal applications.

The question is: how does one, therefore, apply this type of genre knowledge (such as a move and step structure) to a teaching and learning situation? (That is, if it is possible to identify such a structure.) The idea is that presenting such a structure to novice writers means that it can be used as an heuristic to analyse further texts (of the same genre) within a discipline. However, the pattern that is offered should be sufficiently general to apply to the range of intertextual differences that may occur among the texts of a single genre. After some guided analysis of one or more sample texts, in terms of the genre move and step structure, learner-writers can then be encouraged to use it critically to examine other texts (of the same genre).

5.7   Cognitive genres

A cognitive genre, as stated previously, is a stretch of text that realizes a single rhetorical purpose, such as explanation, report (of non-sequential data), recount or discursive argument (see Bruce, 2005, 2007, 2008a: 95–9). Cognitive genres are sometimes described as text types or rhetorical functions, depending on the research tradition that is drawn upon. Cognitive genres tend to manifest as small stretches of text embedded within a larger social genre, a whole text. Therefore, when teaching the writing of larger, more complex texts, such as research reports or dissertations, it can be helpful for novice writers to examine parts of texts or conventionalized sections intensively in terms of their regular use of one or more cognitive genres. For example, in a research-writing EAP course, students can examine Methods sections in research articles in their field in terms of their use of cognitive genres. In a previous study (Bruce, 2008b), I proposed that Methods sections in research-reporting journal articles in the physical sciences mainly draw on the *Explanation* cognitive genre and Methods sections in the social sciences draw on *Report* and *Recount* cognitive genres. This type of focus can provide a basis for examining the textual resources employed, aspects of cohesion and coherence, and key linguistic features of textual patterns that are often recursive. Chapter 6, Section 2 provides examples of a pedagogic analysis of two cognitive genres in terms of these areas of knowledge.

6.   Conclusion

In order for EAP courses to be helpful for students, they need to be relevant and prepare students effectively for their future study; they need, in effect, to be connected to target subject disciplines. This chapter has considered the nature of this type of engagement and also the ways in which subject disciplinary knowledge may be investigated in order to inform EAP courses.

In relation to the nature of teacher relationships between an EAP course and a subject discipline course, the chapter has considered the three approaches of Dudley-Evans and St John (1998) of co-operation, collaboration and team-teaching, although it is acknowledged that there will be variations on, and combinations of, aspects of each of these approaches. Whatever approach to engagement with subject disciplines is used will involve an EAP course developer or teacher making contact with and gathering information from subject disciplines. Such information-gathering may be achieved by ethnographic observations of the use of language in context, interviews with subject staff and collecting and analysing documents, such as the course outline (syllabus), tasks and texts of a disciplinary course. However, as has been mentioned in the chapter, although subject informants may be able to provide insider disciplinary knowledge to the EAP practitioner, they will not have at their disposal the tools to analyse and deconstruct the disciplinary knowledge in ways that can pedagogically inform the EAP course. For such a pedagogic transfer (of disciplinary knowledge) into an EAP course to be achieved effectively, the EAP course developer or teacher has to have at their disposal the means to deconstruct the discourses and texts of particular subject disciplines in ways that are systematic and principled. Carrying out this activity requires the skills of discourse analysis. The dual approach to genre of *social* and *cognitive* genres is proposed as a possible framework for identifying and analysing complex areas of knowledge, for formulating syllabus objectives in EAP courses and also for training EAP students as discourse analysts. This does not mean that it is necessary for students to access complex theories of text or discourse; but the types of understandings that the course developer or teacher has uncovered can then be used in pedagogic ways to promote inductive analyses of target texts and their related discourses in ways that are meaningful for students.

6
EAP Courses and Language Knowledge

1. Introduction

In Chapters 4 and 5, which discussed syllabus design and approaches to identifying and analysing discipline-specific knowledge, it was proposed that any learning focus on language used in academic contexts should examine linguistic elements as they are integrated within texts and their discoursal settings. This integrative principle supports an important overall goal of EAP courses, which is development of students' *discourse competence*. A preliminary definition of discourse competence is the ability to achieve 'the appropriate arrangement of both content information and language in order to create extended spoken or written discourse' (Bruce, 2008a: 4). (The concept of discourse competence and various definitions that have been proposed for it are further discussed in Chapter 8, Section 2.) Thus, when designing a syllabus and developing related pedagogic materials for EAP courses, linguistic knowledge is presented as part of an integration with other types of knowledge. This accords with the principle of holism advocated by Widdowson, who says:

> [t]o identify something as a component is to recognize the operational complex as a whole in which it functions as a part. If analysis isolates elements from this complex, then it must deny them the functional features which alone can give them their component status. (1983: 84)

In accord with this principle of holism, it was proposed in Chapter 5 that a genre-based approach to the organization of the curriculum content of EAP courses enables three areas of knowledge to be integrated:

- contextual knowledge (including subject content)
- organizational knowledge (sometimes termed rhetorical or procedural or strategic knowledge)
- linguistic knowledge (such as syntax, grammar and vocabulary).

In Chapter 5, Section 5, the social genre/cognitive genre approach to analysing the texts and related discourses of particular subjects was proposed as a systematic and principled way to examine contextual, organizational and linguistic knowledge. This chapter continues this discussion by focusing on the third part of this integration, linguistic knowledge, which is divided into three areas: textual grammar, metadiscourse and vocabulary

However, as these three areas of linguistic knowledge are examined, the underlying idea is that they cannot be usefully presented and explored in isolation, but rather they must be part of larger operational wholes, in accordance with Widdowson's principle. Therefore, in the three sections that follow, the approach taken is to consider linguistic features (of textual grammar, metadiscourse and vocabulary) in terms of their functional roles in relation to the texts within which they occur as well as the discourses that are derived from interpretations of the texts.

2.   EAP curriculum and textual grammar

Textual grammar in this section refers to the use of items of grammar and syntax as integrated features of a text. This approach contrasts with much language teaching, where grammar and syntax tend to be taught as abstract rules and exemplified in sentence-level examples, an approach that ignores the role of a target item within a larger piece of text and the related discourse that can be derived from interpretations of the text. This latter atomistic approach to grammar and syntax can lead to two problems. First, learners' understanding of the actual meanings and uses of syntactical and grammatical items can be limited as a result of teachers explaining and practising an item in a decontextualized way without a pedagogic focus on the salient contextual and co-textual elements. That is, an atomistic approach does not assist students to understand that the meaning and use of a grammatical or syntactic item may depend entirely on the textual setting and the larger context in which it is located. As examples, the meaning relationships between the clauses in the following sentences, when analysed in terms of

Crombie's (1985) binary interpropositional relations, are quite different, but each sentence uses the co-ordinating conjunction *and*:

> *He went to his mother's house and showed her the document.* (Chronological Sequence)
> *Do that again and I will call the police!* (Condition Consequence)
> *He spent beyond the limit on his credit card and the bank called him to say that it had cancelled his card.* (Reason Result)

The second problem with a decontextualized approach to the teaching of linguistic knowledge is that the actual selection of features of grammar and syntax included in study skills or academic writing textbooks may not actually focus on the linguistic elements that the learner needs to know to write a certain text type or genre. As a positive illustration of this point, Table 6.1 presents a brief data commentary text (exemplifying the syllabus objectives proposed in Chapter 4, Tables 4.4 and 4.5), followed by an analysis of the elements of textual grammar

Table 6.1 Data commentary text (Report cognitive genre)

Road deaths in New Zealand – 12 months to September 2002				
Age group	Drivers	Passengers	Motorcyclists	Pedestrians
Under–15	0	15	1	8
15–24	53	45	8	8
25–34	39	12	10	9
35–44	32	12	7	5
45–54	32	8	2	6
55–64	19	8	3	1
65–74	16	5	0	4
75+	23	12	0	9
Unknown	1	1	0	0
Total	215	118	31	50

The information in this table shows an analysis of road deaths that occurred in New Zealand during the twelve month period from September 2001 to September 2002. The road deaths are separated into eight age groups and five types of road user including: drivers, passengers, motorcyclists, pedestrians and cyclists.

The road user group which has the largest number of deaths is drivers, with 215 deaths. Among drivers, the largest number of deaths occurs in the 15–24 year age group, with 53 deaths. This is followed by the 25–34 year age group, with 39 deaths.

The next largest number of deaths occurs among passengers, with 118 deaths in total. The age group with the largest number of deaths among passengers is also 15 to 24 years, with 45 deaths. This is followed by passengers aged under 15, with 15 deaths.

The total numbers of deaths for motorcyclists and pedestrians are considerably lower than for the other two road user groups, with 31 and 50 respectively.

From this table it can be seen that the most at-risk group of road users are drivers and passengers, especially those in the 15 to 24 years age group.

Table 6.2 Analysis of the data commentary text

Social genre	Metadiscourse	Cognitive genre	Discourse pattern	Cohesion/ Coherence (Reference)	Vocabulary	Morphology
Data commentary (possibly relates to the Result section of a research-reporting academic article.)	*From the table*, it can be seen that . . . (endophoric reference)	Report (presentation of data that is non-sequential)	General–Particular Preview–Detail (organization of the actual written text)	Prepositional adjective phrases Restricted relative clauses Reference – use of the definite article (the) to show specificity This is followed . . . (Why not 'it' . . ?)	(transportation-related) road death driver passenger motor cyclist pedestrian cyclist	shows road deaths occurred aged at-risk

that are salient to this type of writing and that would be the object of a pedagogic focus.

Table 6.2 presents a top-down analysis of the data commentary text presented in Table 6.1. The analysis is adapted from the social genre/cognitive genre model. While aspects of the model involve more technical analysis, especially at the cognitive genre level (gestalt structure, discourse patterns, interpropositional relations), the findings are presented here in terms of more conventional language categories.

The analysis of the text in Table 6.2 shows a variety of linguistic items that could potentially be included in any text-based lesson using the model provided. In relation to textual grammar (syntax, reference, grammar), one particularly salient point (and one that is not often found in writing instruction textbooks) relates to the referential uses of the definite article (*the*) in this type of writing. Analysis of the text shows that there are 15 occurrences of the definite article *the*, and among these occurrences, five different uses are identified. The five 'defining' or 'specifying' uses of *the* are outlined in Table 6.3. The rules relating to each use are provided in the superscript number beside each occurrence, as shown in Table 6.4.

Table 6.3   Five uses of *the* for defining or specifying nouns

The definite article *the* defines nouns – makes the meaning of nouns more specific. This is done in a number of ways, including:

1. Previous mention
   An analysis of road deaths that occurred
   The road deaths are separated into . . .
2. Uniqueness, only one of its kind
   the largest number of deaths
3. Defined by another noun or noun phrase
   before the noun e. g. the *15–24 year* age group
   after the noun, joined by *of*, e.g. *the age group of 15–24 years*
4. Defined by a prepositional phrase
   The information *in this table . . .*
   the twelve-month period *from September 2001 to September 2002*
5. Defined by a relative clause
   the road user group *that has the largest number of deaths*

It is proposed here that any piece of text that involves the presentation of quantitative data that is non-sequential (such as proposed in the Report cognitive genre) will make heavy use of the definite article as a referential device, and the five rules outlined here (along with the related structures) are particularly salient to this type of writing. In relation to

Table 6.4   Use of *the* in the data commentary text

The[4] information in this table shows an analysis of road deaths that occurred in New Zealand during ***the[3]*** twelve month period from September 2001 to September 2002. ***The[1]*** road deaths are separated into eight age groups and five types of road user, including: drivers, passengers, motorcyclists, pedestrians and cyclists.

The[5] road user group which has ***the[2]*** largest number of deaths is drivers, with 215 deaths. Among drivers, ***the[2]*** largest number of deaths occurs in ***the[3]*** 15–24 year age group, with 53 deaths. This is followed by ***the[3]*** 25–34 year age group, with 39 deaths.

The[2] next largest number of deaths occurs among passengers, with 118 deaths in total. ***The[4]*** age group with ***the[2]*** largest number of deaths among passengers is also 15–24 years, with 45 deaths. This is followed by passengers aged under 15, with 15 deaths.

The[3] total numbers of deaths for motorcyclists and pedestrians are considerably lower than for ***the[1]*** other two road user groups, with 31 and 50 deaths respectively.

From this table it can be seen that ***the[2]*** most at-risk group of road users are drivers and passengers, especially those in ***the[3]*** 15–24 year age group.

---

the other cognitive genres outlined in the model, different relational structures realized by different linguistic features will provide salient elements of textual grammar that could be focused on.

As a further illustration of this point in relation to textual grammar, a brief contrastive argument text (Discussion cognitive genre) is presented in Table 6.5.

Table 6.5   Contrastive argument text (Discussion cognitive genre)

Compare and contrast evidence, opinions and implications.

It has always been the case that considerable numbers of people from poorer countries emigrate to richer, developed countries in search of work and improved educational opportunities.

TASK
Compare and contrast the arguments for and against migration to developed countries.

MODEL RESPONSE
Many people in developing countries are faced with the problems of poverty and lack of opportunities for education and employment. As a solution, some choose to migrate to a more developed country in order to achieve a higher standard of living and better employment and educational opportunities. This essay will consider the arguments both for and against migration as a solution for lack of opportunities.

For many people, migration to another country offers them a chance to improve their lives. Through hard work migrants are often able to re-establish themselves in better circumstances and with more freedom than they had enjoyed in their countries of origin. For such migrants, this means being able to own a business or pursue a career, which would not have been possible in their home countries.

Conversely, migration may not necessarily offer all of the advantages that some people imagine. An immigrant is always an outsider, in terms of background, language, accent and culture or colour. This can mean that many jobs or business opportunities are simply not available to him or her in the same way they are available to someone who was born and grew up in the country. In the worst cases, immigrants encounter prejudice and discrimination and even violence.

Migration can offer advantages and disadvantages for people who relocate to another country. It is never an easy solution for someone who is seeking to improve his or her life, and the difficulties should not be understated. However, it can provide opportunities and bring advantages, and there are many people who have benefited from the decision to become migrants.

Table 6.6 (on p. 90) again presents a top-down analysis of the contrastive argument text presented in Table 6.5. Based on the social genre/cognitive genre model, the categories used are the same as for the analysis of the data commentary text.

The analysis of the text in Table 6.6 which is marked on the text in Table 6.7 (on p. 91) shows that a variety of items could potentially be included in any lesson based on the model text. A salient element is the use of the 'discourse pattern' *Problem-Solution* in a text that presents arguments for and against a proposition. Essay tasks that require a contrastive argument response tend to embed the 'problem' and 'solution' (situation and response) within the title of the essay task itself, which is revisited in the introduction, while the body of the essay presents contrasting evaluations of the solution.

In relation to textual grammar, the analysis suggests that salient markers that could be extracted and practised in relation to this type of writing are those that signal *purpose* and *means*. The example of purpose marking 'in order to' is embedded in the text. This could provide the vehicle for a focus on markers of purpose. Table 6.8 (on pp. 92–3) shows the range of linguistic features that could be employed in any such focus on markers of purpose.

Similarly, a textual grammar focus in relation to a contrastive argument text could focus on markers of *means* or *contrast*. The examples in this section are only intended to be illustrative of the importance of presenting and practising items of grammar and syntax in an EAP course as

Table 6.6 Analysis of the contrastive argument text

Social genre	Metadiscourse	Cognitive genre	Discourse pattern	Cohesion/ Coherence	Vocabulary	Morphology
Evaluative argument (such as part of a discussion section of research report)	Endophoric reference e.g. *This essay will consider . . .* hedging, e.g. use of modal verbs to hedge claims (*can, may, are often able*)	Discussion – focus on the organization of data in relation to (possible) outcomes/ conclusions/ choices	Problem – Solution – Evaluation – signallers of problem/ solution	Signallers of: purpose, e.g. *in order to* means, e.g. *through* contrast, e.g. *conversely, however*	(Migration-related) poverty standard of living migration employment opportunity re-establish outsider	re-establish

parts of operational wholes in order to support the wider development of the discourse competence of students. However, such an approach assumes that linguistic selection will be systematic and principled, informed by theories of text and discourse.

Table 6.7 Mark-up of the contrastive argument text

Discourse pattern	Discourse signalling
Problem *Solution*	Many people in developing countries are faced with the <u>problems</u> of poverty and lack of opportunities for education and employment. <u>As a solution</u>, some choose to migrate to a more developed country <u>in order to</u> achieve a higher standard of living and better employment and educational opportunities. <u>This essay will consider</u> the arguments both for and against migration <u>as a solution</u> for lack of opportunities.
Evaluation 1	For many people, migration to another country offers them a chance to improve their lives. <u>Through</u> hard work, migrants <u>are often able to re-establish</u> themselves in better circumstances and with <u>more freedom than</u> they had enjoyed in their countries of origin. For such migrants, <u>this means</u> being able to own a business or pursue a career, which would not have been possible in their home countries.
Evaluation 2	<u>Conversely</u>, migration <u>may not necessarily offer</u> all of the advantages that some people imagine. An immigrant is always an outsider, in terms of background, language, accent and culture or colour. <u>This can mean</u> that many jobs or business opportunities are simply not available to him or her in the same way they are available to someone who was born and grew up in the country. In the worst cases, immigrants encounter prejudice and discrimination and even violence.
Conclusion	Migration <u>can offer</u> advantages and disadvantages for people who relocate to another country. It is never an easy solution for someone who is seeking to improve his or her life, and the difficulties <u>should not be understated</u>. <u>However</u>, it <u>can provide</u> opportunities and bring advantages and there are many people who have benefited from the decision to become migrants.

Table 6.8 Markers of purpose

A with verbs (the base form of a verb):

    1. For positive purpose use: *to/so as to /in order to* plus verb

    EXAMPLE

                              to
    I have come to New Zealand *so as to*   have a better life.
                                in order to

    2. For negative purpose use: *so as not to/in order not to* plus verb

    EXAMPLE

    I shut the door *so as not to*   disturb the class.
                    in order not to

    1. To show alternatives use: . . . . *not to.* plus verb . . . , *but to*. . . . plus verb

    EXAMPLE

    I came to New Zealand *not to* study business *but to* learn English.

B with present participles (the -ing form of a verb):

    Use: *for the purpose of/with a view to* . . . plus the -*ing* form to express positive purpose

    EXAMPLE

    He applied to enter the best university *with a view to*   pleasing his father
                                             for the purpose of

    NB *for plus verb/-ing* can only be used:
    1. *for actions that relate to things, not people*
    2. *after a passive voice verb*
    ✓ This brush is used for *cleaning* the machine.
    ✗ He came to New Zealand *for studying*. (wrong)
    ✓ [He came to New Zealand to study.] (correct)

C with nouns

    1. Use *for* plus noun to express positive or negative purpose

    EXAMPLE

    I am (not) going to Australia *for a holiday*.

    2. To show contrast or alternatives use *(not) for* plus noun,
    but for plus noun

    EXAMPLE

    I'm *not* going to Australia *for* a holiday *but for* business.

D with clauses

1. Use *so (that) in order that/with the intention (that)* with clauses to express positive or negative purpose.

2. Note that the modals *could* and *would* used in the purpose clause e.g.

   could – make it possible for something to happen

   would – make certain that something will happen (or not happen) – stronger meaning

EXAMPLES

I gave her my telephone number *so that* he *could call* me. (possibility)
I went home early from work so that I *could rest*. (possiblity)
I hurried *so that* I *would not be* late. (stronger personal intention)
He studied diligently *in order that* he *would pass* the examination.
(strong personal intention)

3. EAP curriculum and metadiscourse

Chapter 5, Section 5, discussed language devices that specifically relate to the writer connecting with the reader as an element of social genre knowledge, language devices termed *metadiscourse*. As was pointed out, this aspect of the social genre model draws on Bakhtin's proposal that writing, like speaking, is *dialogic* – a dialogue between the writer and the reader, and that writing is constructed with the expectations and knowledge of the reader in mind. Hyland (2005) defines metadiscourse as 'the means by which propositional content is made coherent, intelligible and persuasive to a particular audience' (p. 39), and proposes a model for interpersonal metadiscourse features involving interactive and interactional resources; see Table 6.9 .

In the outline of the social genre/cognitive genre model presented in Chapter 5, 'metadiscourse' is located within the part of the model that deals with writer stance (see also Bruce, 2008a: 137). In continuing the principle of holism discussed at the beginning of this chapter, a pedagogic focus on metadiscourse devices could involve directing students to examine texts for:

- the parts of the text that specifically guide or speak directly to the reader
- the features of language that show the writer's attitude towards the content
- language features that are trying to influence or persuade the reader in some way
- language features are regularly used to connect ideas.

Table 6.9 Hyland's interpersonal model of metadiscourse

Category	Function	Examples
Interactive	Help guide the reader through the text	Resources
Transitions	express relations between main clauses	in addition; but; thus, and
Frame markers	refer to discourse acts, sequences or stages	finally; to conclude; my purpose is
Endophoric markers	refer to information in other parts of the text	noted above; see Fig; in Section 2
Evidentials	refer to information from other texts	according to X; Z states . . .
Code glosses	elaborate propositional meanings	namely; e.g.; such as; in other words
Interactional	Involve the reader in the text	Resources
Hedges	withhold commitment and open dialogue	might; perhaps; possible; about
Boosters	emphasize certainty or close dialogue	in fact; definitely; it is clear that
Attitude markers	express writer's attitude to proposition	unfortunately; I agree; surprisingly
Self mentions	explicit reference to author(s)	I; we; my; me; our
Engagement markers	explicitly build relationship with reader	Consider; note; you can see

(Hyland, 2005: 49) reproduced by kind permission of Continuum International Publishing Group.

Table 6.10 Metadiscourse features in the contrastive argument text

---

Many people in developing countries are faced with the problems of poverty and lack of opportunities for education and employment. As a solution, some choose to migrate to a more developed country in order to achieve a higher standard of living and better employment and educational opportunities. *This essay will consider[1]* the arguments both for and against migration as a solution for lack of opportunities.

For many people, migration to another country offers them a chance to improve their lives. Through hard work, migrants *are often able to re-establish[2]* themselves in better circumstances and with more freedom than they had enjoyed in their countries of origin. For many migrants, this means being able to own a business or pursue a career, which would not have been possible in their home countries.

Conversely, migration *may not necessarily offer[3]* all of the advantages that some people imagine. An immigrant is always an outsider, in terms of background, language, accent and culture or colour. This *can mean[4]* that many jobs or business opportunities are simply not available to him or her in the same way they are available to someone who was born and grew up in the country. In the worst cases, immigrants encounter prejudice and discrimination and even violence.

Migration *can offer[5]* advantages and disadvantages for people who relocate to another country. It is never an easy solution for someone who is seeking to improve his or her life, and the difficulties should not be understated. However, it *can provide[6]* opportunities and bring advantages and there are many people who have benefited from the decision to become migrants.

---

[1] *endophoric reference* – guiding the reader through the text
[2/3/4/5/6] *hedging*, examples of cautious language using modal verbs to soften claims or statements

In relation to a certain category of texts, it may be salient to focus on only one or two commonly recurring metadiscourse features. In relation to writing that presents an argument or a case, for example, it may be appropriate to focus on *hedges* and *boosters*, particularly if they are in evidence in a sample of texts. This will require textual analysis and awareness by the teacher of such specific features before undertaking a pedagogic focus on the features with students. For example, in the contrastive argument text first presented in Table 6.5, *hedging* appears to be the principal metadiscoursal device employed particularly in relation to the writer's claims in paragraph topic sentences (see Table 6.10). Therefore, it may be appropriate to focus on this metadiscoursal device when teaching this type of writing.

Again, as in the case of textual grammar, the selection of particular metadiscoursal items to be taught in a particular lesson or course unit will need to be in relation to the 'functional whole' of certain types of texts that relate to certain contexts and communicative and rhetorical purposes.

4.   Vocabulary knowledge

The third area of linguistic knowledge is that of vocabulary knowledge. As Jordan (1997) points out, vocabulary development is often neglected in EAP courses, and if there is a focus on it, this tends to relate to the reading skill. This is usually the pre-teaching of key vocabulary items needed to process a reading text. He says that 'the result of this neglect is that it [vocabulary development] may be left to the students' indirect learning, which may be inefficient' (Jordan, 1997: 149). Supporting this idea, several research studies indicate that vocabulary knowledge is an essential element of the EAP learner's development and that vocabulary deficit can be one of the biggest problems that students can face when undertaking academic study (see, for example, Cobb & Horst, 2001). The findings from these studies, therefore, suggest that vocabulary needs to be taught more actively and intensively in EAP courses in order to enable students to cope with the requirements of academic study. In order to consider this area of learner need, this section will first consider the types of vocabulary knowledge that relate to EAP courses and second, will discuss some approaches to the teaching of vocabulary knowledge.

Corpus linguists, such as Coxhead and Nation (2001), divide the vocabulary used in academic English into four groups:

- *high-frequency words*: They suggest that these involve about 2,000 word families. They include most of the 176 *function* words in English and they will typically provide about 80% of the running words in an academic text. These are most of the words that occur in Michael West's *general service list of English words* (GSL). This list was updated in the 1990s to 2,300 words by Bauman and Culligan (1995).
- *academic vocabulary*: This consists of about 570 'word families' identified in Coxhead's (2000) *academic word list* (AWL). These words are reasonably common in different types of academic texts. Coxhead and Nation (2001) suggest that the AWL accounts for 8.5–10% of the running words in an academic text. They state that knowing the AWL (in addition to the GSL) 'makes the difference between 80% coverage (one unknown word in every five running words) and 90% coverage (one unknown word in every ten running words' (p. 252).

- *technical vocabulary*: Coxhead and Nation (2001) suggest that technical vocabulary differs from subject to subject, but for any one subject, it consists of up to 1,000 words and provides coverage of up to 5% of the running words in a text.
- *low-frequency words*: these consist of words that have a low frequency of occurrence and specialized meanings.

Coxhead and Nation suggest that when learners have mastered the approximately 2,000 high-frequency words, vocabulary learning should then focus on more specialized areas that will be useful for the learners. They propose that for EAP learners, there is considerable value in focusing on the second level of vocabulary identified in Xue and Nation's (1984) *university word list* or Coxhead's (2000) *academic word list* (AWL), which these corpus researchers propose is a set of vocabulary that is shared by a variety of disciplines. However, the cross-disciplinary usefulness of such lists of academic vocabulary has recently been challenged by Hyland and Tse's (2007) study. In particular the research of Hyland and Tse examined the AWL in relation to its actual occurrence in three disciplinary corpora (engineering, sciences and social sciences). First, they found that if you combined the three corpora, the AWL accounted for approximately 10.6% of the overall word use, which is close to Coxhead's original claims. However, the AWL words were not evenly distributed across the three corpora. The GSL and the AWL failed to account for 22% of the words in the science corpus, which meant that the learner would stumble on one word in five, making a text incomprehensible. They found that of the 570 items:

- 283 occurred in the engineering sub-corpus
- 244 occurred in the sciences sub-corpus
- 128 occurred in the social sciences sub-corpus.

The conclusion of Hyland and Tse (2007) was that the AWL was relevant in a general sense to academic texts if you take a unitary approach to academic writing (that is, by combining all of the texts of the disciplines that they examined), but that the vocabulary in discipline-specific texts will be more specialized, and may not reflect the proposed percentage occurrences of words from the GSL and AWL lists. The issue then really is the level at which one is teaching EAP (be it pre-sessional or in-sessional), and whether or not it is a more general or specific EAP course. However, as a general principle it seems that a focus on vocabulary should probably include both the researched lists (the GSL and

AWL) and the more specialized vocabulary of the subject discipline areas, in order that students receive adequate coverage of vocabulary related to their future needs.

Thus, while it is important to acknowledge the limitations of such researched lists of vocabulary, they nevertheless provide a basis for considering the types of vocabulary that learners need to cope with the language that is used in academic contexts.

In approaching the teaching of academic vocabulary in EAP courses, there are two possible approaches. The first involves following the principle of elements of language being part of a functional whole, which is termed the *contextual analysis* of vocabulary. This may provide a basis for identifying vocabulary items that are relevant to academic writing. However, once certain categories of lexical item have been identified as important, such as reporting verbs in summary and paraphrase writing, this type of lexical item may be examined more intensively using analytical approaches, such as *concordancing, componential analysis grids* and *word networks*.

4.1   Contextual analysis

The preliminary tasks that introduce many EAP reading texts often have a strong focus on developing vocabulary knowledge, in order that students can process and understand target texts. However, contextual analysis can be employed with texts that are also used in the teaching of writing and listening skills. Using a contextual approach, vocabulary can be presented and practised in context, and then students can be required to carry out inductive learning tasks that involve inferencing based on contextual clues. Dunmore (1989) proposes four main types of vocabulary exercises that involve inferring the meaning of vocabulary items from contextual clues. Some of the more inductive activities are:

1. matching a given synonym with a word appearing in a text
2. filling a blank space in a text with a suitable word (cloze)
3. using contextual clues to identify the meaning of an underlined word in a text
4. inferring the meaning of a word by studying its occurrences in different parts of a text.

There appears to be a considerable amount of evidence that the effective learning of a vocabulary item involves a learner encountering the word several times (Nation, 1990; Stahl & Fairbanks, 1986). Therefore, it may be that a staged combination of activities that require the learner to use the item several times is needed.

4.2 Concordancing

The use of corpus software and concordancing has conventionally been used as part of a bottom-up approach to building vocabulary knowledge. Vocabulary items that have been identified as essential and high-frequency are presented and practised in ways that encourage learners to relate the target item back to a type of context. As an example, the students in Cobb's (1997) study had to match a meaning to a word that occurred in a set of concordance lines and then performed different types of gap fill tasks in an effort to re-contextualize what begins as a decontextualized vocabulary item.

In an EAP context, students can use an academic corpus to create concordances of items that have already been presented in a context and embedded in a text in order to review their meanings and uses more intensively, or concordance lines can be used as cloze activities in which to insert previously taught or presented items.

4.3 Componential analysis

This requires students to consider different components of the meaning of a word and is a way of providing an approach to the overlapping similarities as well as the differences of meanings of words within a wider 'semantic field'. Semantic componential analysis can use a scale or a cline to contrast differences of meaning of words from a similar field. Examples of componential analysis are found in Swales and Feak (2004) relating to the objectivity of reporting verbs (p. 165) and strength of evaluative adjectives (pp. 195–6). These examples suggest that ready-made grids should be used, but in fact they can be constructed by students working in pairs/groups advised by the teacher. In many ways, grids that are developed as part of students' developing language hypotheses may be the more effective way of using this approach to vocabulary learning.

4.4 Word networks

While componential analysis, for example by using grids, can be useful for understanding the shades of meaning of vocabulary items, a way of dealing with vocabulary items that relate to a topic is that of *word networks*, originally proposed by Ellis and Sinclair (1989). For example in relation to the topic of migration and the argument points in the

Table 6.11   Word networks

Push factors for emigration	Pull factors for immigration
overpopulation	living space
overcrowded cities	labour shortages
limited job market	educational opportunities
lack of educational opportunities	higher standard of living
unemployment	lower population
poverty	health services

essay first presented in Table 6.5, word networks could be proposed as in Table 6.11 .

Such word networks could be developed as part of a class 'brainstorming' activity as feedback from pair or group activities when planning the writing of such an essay task.

5.   Conclusion

Following the principle proposed by Widdowson (1983), this chapter has argued that the teaching of linguistic knowledge should, as much as possible, examine and present linguistic items as part of an integrated, functional whole rather than as atomized, decontextualized elements. The three areas of language knowledge: textual grammar, metadiscourse and vocabulary, are proposed as broad areas within which linguistic knowledge can be examined in relation to the texts and the related discourses within which they occur. In relation to each of these areas, illustrative examples are provided. Although the scope of the chapter does not present a comprehensive theory of text and discourse, it draws on a theory of genre that I have proposed elsewhere (Bruce, 2008a). As it stands, this chapter aims to provide EAP course designers and teachers with some approaches to deconstructing and practising the linguistic elements of texts in ways that support the ongoing development of students' discourse competence.

Part III

The Implementation of EAP Courses

7
EAP and Teacher Competencies

1. Introduction to Part III

While the chapters of Part I were concerned with establishing what EAP is, and those of Part II considered the design of EAP courses, the six chapters of Part III move on to consider aspects of the delivery of EAP courses. In this group of chapters, discussions of issues of course implementation are framed by (and refer back to) the definitions and theoretical principles established in Parts I and II. Chapter 7 begins this shift of focus by considering the skills and knowledge required by EAP teachers. The overview of teacher requirements is based on the *Competency Framework for Teachers of English for Academic Purposes* developed by the British Association of Lecturers in English for Academic Purposes (BALEAP, 2008). Following this focus on the EAP teacher, Chapters 8 to 11 examine the development of the four language skills as they relate to EAP teaching and learning, dealing with writing, reading, listening and speaking respectively. However, this particular chapter arrangement does not ignore the fact that many EAP tasks and activities will involve the use of more than one language skill. Therefore, across these four chapters there is also considerable emphasis on the integration of language skills in EAP tasks. Finally, Chapter 12 provides a brief overview of selected issues relating to assessment in an EAP context.

2. Introduction to the chapter

While the content and discussion of earlier chapters have focused centrally on the student, reflecting the fact that EAP is a needs-driven, learner-centred activity, Chapter 7 turns to consider issues relating to the expertise of the teacher. Specifically, this chapter presents an overview of the areas of knowledge and professional skills that are required by a teacher of EAP. The chapter draws on the *Competency Framework for Teachers of English for Academic Purposes* (hereafter referred to as CFTEAP). This document was developed by a specialized sub-group of members of the British Association of Lecturers in English for Academic Purposes as a comprehensive statement of the knowledge and skills required by teachers of EAP.

Following the organization of the CFTEAP document, this chapter aims to describe the areas of knowledge and skills that are essential to teach EAP. The CFTEAP begins with an overall EAP teacher competency statement followed by 11 specific teacher competencies grouped within four areas:

- competencies relating to academic practice
- competencies relating to EAP students
- competencies relating to curriculum development
- competencies relating to programme implementation.

Each of these four areas also begins with a competency statement followed by a more detailed description of what the competency area involves.

In the discussion of the CFTEAP document the key elements of each competency area will be quoted and discussed, but it is emphasized that readers will need to refer to the actual document for more specific detail about each competency area, including related activities and recommended outcomes. Therefore, what is provided here is an overview of key elements of the CFTEAP document with reference to landmark theoretical works and research studies as well as to the specific chapters and sections in this book that focus on each particular area of teacher knowledge and skill.

3. Overall CFTEAP teacher competency statement

An EAP teacher will be able to facilitate students' mastery of the language, skills and strategies required for studying in a further or higher education context and to support students' understandings of approaches to interpreting and responding to the requirements of academic tasks and their related processes. (CFTEAP, p. 3)

The overall teacher competency statement assumes that EAP teachers are familiar with the academic practices and processes of higher education contexts as well as possessing an understanding of the types of language used in these settings. Predicated on these assumptions, the statement emphasizes teachers' capacity to assist students' development of the types of language and related academic knowledge and skills that they need in order to study in higher education contexts.

Clearly the overall teacher competency statement assumes a wide range of knowledge and skills on the part of the teacher whose job it is to create and deliver EAP courses. However, a problem arises when teachers who have pre-service teacher training for general English language teaching are then required by employers to organize and teach EAP courses without any further training or preparation for this more specialized area of English teaching. In creating and delivering EAP courses, such teachers can only draw upon their own personal experiences of academic study and the academic world. However, this situation is now changing, and higher education institutions are beginning to acknowledge that EAP teaching requires areas of knowledge and skills that go well beyond those considered necessary for general language teaching. As a result, managers and recruiters increasingly are requiring staff with EAP-related skills and experience to teach this type of course. Therefore, specialized training courses and qualifications are being developed and offered to prepare and equip teachers of EAP. However, it is also important to state that general English language teacher training and experience do provide a strong background for anyone seeking to become an EAP teacher, although this needs to be supplemented by further specialized EAP teacher training.

In this chapter, the various areas of knowledge and skill necessary for teaching EAP are briefly outlined under the various competencies. However, it must be emphasized that such competency specifications are relatively open-ended, as EAP is a rapidly developing field. Therefore, practising teachers need to be developing, revising and adding to their knowledge of the academic world and its practices on an ongoing basis. They also need to access regularly the growing body of research that is being carried out in the field through the relevant journals (e.g. the *Journal of English for Academic Purposes, Journal of Second Language Writing, English for Specific Purposes, Text and Talk*) and through EAP-specific conferences and workshops.

4.   Competencies relating to academic practice

The first group of teacher competencies in the CFTEAP document focus on academic practice, and include four specific competencies relating to:

- academic contexts
- disciplinary differences
- academic discourse
- personal learning, development and autonomy.

4.1   Academic contexts

The competency statement that relates to academic contexts states: '[a]n EAP teacher will have a reasonable knowledge of the organizational, educational and communicative practices, values and conventions of universities' (CFTEAP, p. 4). In relation to this competency, the document states that teachers need to have knowledge and understanding of the

- norms and conventions of universities in relation to course structure, teaching and learning, staff/student communication and assessment
- modes of knowledge communication and publication, including: print media, electronic media and oral genres
- university policies relating to ethical practices, respect for intellectual property disciplinary procedures, student support. (CFTEAP, p. 4)

As part of their overall background knowledge, EAP teachers need to be familiar with the day-to-day educational assumptions, values and practices of universities, and need to be aware of how these ideas shape the organization and delivery of courses across the academy. These areas of knowledge also involve EAP teachers understanding the range of expected staff–student and student–student relationships that may operate in academic courses and underpin formal and informal communications.

Understanding the knowledge communication that takes place in various academic disciplines requires the teacher to draw on discourse analysis in deconstructing discipline-specific spoken and written texts for the purpose of pedagogy. In this book, Chapters 5 and 6 (dealing with syllabus development, content selection and language knowledge) propose tools for deconstructing these areas of knowledge using genre analysis. A genre-based approach can also provide the basis for cycles of teaching and learning in the EAP course that involve the presentation, analysis and synthesis of texts through tasks that help students to understand the requirements of target undergraduate courses and that provide training in meeting their communicative, textual and ethical requirements.

Uncovering and teaching the elements of knowledge listed in the document under 'academic contexts', therefore, requires the EAP teacher to engage with and investigate various aspects of subject courses. This issue of teacher engagement with subjects and subject specialists has been discussed previously in Chapter 3 (in relation to needs analysis, and specifically target situation analysis) and in Chapter 5, where approaches to gathering and analysing this type of knowledge are proposed (see Johns, 1997: 71–91). However, it has been emphasized in earlier chapters that effective engagement between EAP teachers and staff from other disciplines requires the EAP teacher to have a level of theoretical knowledge and skills to be able to identify, analyse and make use of the discipline-specific knowledge that can be gathered from this type of collaboration. The ability to interpret and analyse academic knowledge in these areas relates to aspects of academic discourse competence, which form the third group of competencies in this section of the CFTEAP document.

4.2 Disciplinary differences

The competency statement that relates to disciplinary difference states: 'An EAP teacher will be able to recognize and explore disciplinary differences and how they influence the way knowledge is expanded and communicated' (CFTEAP, p. 4). In relation to this competency statement, the document goes on to specify that this involves knowledge and understanding of:

- discourse communities and how membership and full participation is achieved
- audience within discourse communities
- the importance of evidence-based reasoning in knowledge creation.

Chapter 2 (Section 2) provided an extended discussion of approaches to conceptualizing and investigating academic communities and their particular practices and approaches to knowledge. In the conclusion of that section, it was proposed that the choice of a framework to examine an academic community may vary according to how its members engage with each other, such as whether communication is primarily through speaking or writing. Furthermore, understanding the nature of engagement and communication with an audience in a discourse community relates closely to two key elements of the texts and discourses of different academic subjects. These are epistemology (Lea & Street, 1998) and knowledge of how to engage in what Bakhtin (1986) terms *diologism* (writing as a dialogue between the reader and the writer).

It was emphasized in both Chapters 2 and 5 that acquiring the epistemological knowledge of a particular discipline is developed over an extended period of engagement with the discipline, and requires an understanding of its knowledge-creating processes, such as the assumptions and practices of its research methods. Although this is an area of knowledge that cannot be acquired solely through the tasks of EAP courses, students can be encouraged to consider the connections between the knowledge-creating paradigms of their disciplines and their influence on its knowledge-communicating forms.

The issue of addressing a disciplinary audience, what Adam and Artemeva (2002) term *addressivity and audience*, is also considered as one of the key elements of the approach to genre analysis discussed in Chapter 5, which draws specifically on Hyland's (2005: 42) metadiscourse model, outlining the types of language devices that writers use to connect with readers. Using Hyland's model (2005), learner-writers can be encouraged to examine the metadiscoursal features of the common genres of their particular discipline through some fairly objective textual analysis.

In relation to the issue of 'evidence-based reasoning', teachers need to be aware that one size does not fit all subjects, and that what constitutes the presentation of an argument or development of a case may vary considerably among subject disciplines (see Bruce, 2010). This is an area of EAP teacher competence that relates to understanding and use of discourse and genre analysis in order to identify the discoursal and textual resources that particular disciplines draw upon to achieve different types of communicative purpose, such as to explain the methodology, report or discuss the findings of a piece of research.

4.3   Academic discourse

The third of the general academic competencies relates to a teacher's ability to analyse academic texts and the discourses that are derived from interpretations of such texts. The statement says: '[a]n EAP teacher will have a high level of systemic language knowledge including knowledge of discourse analysis' (CFTEAP, p. 5). Under the overall competency statement, the document further specifies that this teacher competency involves:

> knowledge and understanding of discourse features and sub-technical vocabulary which would allow teachers to read and make sense of texts without being subject specialists:
>
> - grammar and syntax at the level of sentence or clause
> - language features at discourse level
> - approaches to cohesion and coherence
> - semantics, pragmatics
> - approaches to text classification, such as the various theoretical approaches to genre and text type.

Thus, an EAP teacher's language awareness has to be more than awareness of categories of discrete linguistic features. It has to involve knowledge of approaches to the analysis of both texts and the discoursal processes that give rise to and shape texts, and relate to their salient interpretation by readers or listeners. Thus, the teacher needs more than a passing acquaintance with textual grammar and discourse analysis and approaches to text classification as a basis for identifying units of discourse around which curriculum or syllabus units can be organized. In the present volume, this area of knowledge is developed in a number of chapters in Parts I and II, especially in Chapters 5 and 6. An EAP teacher's discourse knowledge also has to enable them to give knowledgeable and targeted feedback to learners about their outputs. This has to be done in ways that promote an ongoing development of the learner's accuracy and fluency in the processing and creation of extended spoken and written texts. These areas of systemic language knowledge are essential tools in the repertoire of the EAP teacher or lecturer who is seeking to address the language needs of higher-level EAP learners.

4.4   Personal learning: development and autonomy

The final competency relating to general academic practice is that of teachers' awareness of their academic field, its research literature, current issues and developing practices. The statement says: 'An EAP teacher will recognize the importance of applying to his or her own practice the standards expected of students and other academic staff.' The statement goes on to say that this involves knowledge and understanding of:

- the importance of continuing professional development
- appropriate professional terminology
- current issues in teaching and researching EAP
- the role of ambiguity in academic enquiry
- the importance of critical reflection on one's own practice. (CFTEAP, p. 5)

These statements emphasize the fact that EAP itself, because it is deeply concerned with preparing students for effective participation in academic life, has developed into an academic discipline in its own right with its own discourse community of teacher practitioners, theorists, researchers and teacher trainers as well as articulated threshold levels of practitioner knowledge and expertise (such as outlined in the CFTEAP document). A teacher's access to the areas of knowledge and understanding listed under this competency statement, therefore, derives from specialist training, ongoing reading of EAP-related research literature and involvement with the EAP community of practitioners. This competency statement and its subsidiary points, therefore, relate to a teacher's bid for membership of, and participation in, the EAP discourse community. At the present time, pathways into this community are not always clear.

5. Competencies relating to EAP students

The second group of teacher competencies in the CFTEAP document are those relating to EAP students, with competencies listed relating to three areas: EAP students' needs, critical thinking and its development and student autonomy (pp. 6–7).

5.1 EAP students' needs

In relation to teachers' understanding of students' needs, the CFTEAP document states (p. 6):

> An EAP teacher will understand the requirements of the target context that students wish to enter as well as the needs of students

in relation to their prior learning experiences and how these might influence their current educational expectations

The more detailed specifications under this statement say that this involves knowledge and understanding of:

- the prior learning, expectations and values that students are likely to bring from their original learning cultures
- the specific language knowledge and skills, educational values and roles necessary for participation in the target learning culture
- the different content and focus required at pre-sessional, undergraduate in-sessional and postgraduate in-sessional levels.

In relation to learner need, Chapter 1 (Section 5) discussed the role of the EAP course in terms of the 'bridge' metaphor, which is the idea that the EAP teacher and his/her course provide the link to facilitate students' progression from where they have come from to where they need to go in terms of the academic language, knowledge, values, roles and expectations they require to participate in English-medium higher education. In developing this idea, Chapter 3 provided an extended discussion of a number of aspects of students' present and future needs, drawing on Hutchinson and Waters' (1987) proposals for present situation analysis (what students bring to their study from their prior learning experiences) and target situation analysis (the language and skills that students need for their target learning situation). The chapter proposes frameworks for performing needs analyses for EAP students at different levels, including pre-sessional, in-sessional and postgraduate classes, and considers how the findings of needs analysis inform the development of aims and objectives for EAP courses.

5.2   Student critical thinking

The second of the student-related competencies relates to student critical thinking and its development.

An EAP teacher understands the need for critical approaches to knowledge-processing and knowledge creation in academic contexts and will employ tasks, processes and interactions that require students to exercise and display critical thinking skills.

The document goes on to say that this involves knowledge and understanding of:

- how critical thinking underpins academic practice
- the elements of critical thinking and critical approaches to knowledge (to achieve its advancement)
- student autonomy and the development of an individual voice in relation to knowledge. (CFTEAP, p. 5)

In relation to teacher competencies, the issue for the EAP teacher is to develop clear approaches to understanding what critical thinking involves, and to employ principled and systematic ways of assisting students to develop this skill. Critical thinking in relation to EAP in general, and particularly in relation to the writing skill, will be further discussed in Chapters 8 and 11. The discussions there challenge some of the conventional approaches to critical thinking, and aim to provide some discussion for an EAP teacher who is grappling with this area. The approach taken accords with the views of Ramanathan and Kaplan (1996a), who propose that the development of a 'critical' voice occurs within a particular disciplinary context, and that it involves the ability of students to make evaluations 'within their field's accepted standards of judgement' (Swales & Feak, 2004: 180). It is proposed here that understanding part of what constitutes the 'accepted standards of judgement' within a discipline arises partly from familiarity with both its knowledge-creating processes and knowledge-reporting forms (disciplinary genres). Therefore, modelling critical thinking and the modes of its expression, such as in writing that presents a reasoned case (argument), is a core activity of the EAP teacher. It is important, however, to recognize that critical thinking should not be restricted to the arrangement of propositions in certain argument writing tasks or in constructing oral debates – that would be a very simplistic view – but rather, it relates to the development of attitudes, values and norms that will pervade the whole range of processes and tasks of an EAP course.

5.3   Student autonomy

The third of the student-related competencies relates to student autonomy and its development. The teacher competency statement asserts: 'An EAP teacher will understand the importance of student autonomy in academic contexts and will employ tasks, processes and interactions that require students to work effectively in groups or independently as appropriate' (CFTEAP, p. 6). The document goes on to say that this involves knowledge and understanding of:

- the principles of student autonomy
- the use of new technologies to support autonomous learning
- how to support student autonomy through group activities and individual tutoring. (p. 7)

For most students entering EAP courses, comparison of the present situation and the target situation aspects of the needs analysis will reveal the students' need to develop autonomous learning practices in order to cope with the expectations and requirements of academic courses in higher education.

In terms of EAP teacher practice, it is proposed here that the competency in developing student autonomy relates to the types of methodology and staging of courses that teachers employ. Understanding the future requirements for student autonomy (in performing disciplinary processes and tasks) will derive from the teacher's investigation of the requirements and expectations of discipline-specific courses. The teacher then develops students' familiarity with these through the methodologies, tasks and materials of the EAP programme. Therefore, there will be a need to stage the processes and tasks of EAP courses in ways that promote and develop both co-operative and autonomous learning.

6.   Curriculum development competencies

The third area of EAP teacher competencies relates to curriculum development and is divided into syllabus and programme development and text processing and text creation.

6.1   Syllabus and programme development

In relation to syllabus and programme development, the CFTEAP competency states that '[a]n EAP teacher understands the main types of language syllabus and will be able to transform a syllabus into a programme that addresses students' needs in the academic context within which the EAP course is located' (p. 7). The competency goes on to specify that this involves knowledge and understanding of:

- a range of EAP syllabus types
- the need in a syllabus for progression and recycling and transfer of knowledge and skills to other learning contexts
- constraints and their impacts on syllabus design.

In this volume, Chapters 4, 5, 6, 8, 9, 10 and 11 relate to the planning of a syllabus and its implementation in an actual programme. Chapter 4 considered the types of knowledge and processes that are the focus of an EAP syllabus as well as organizational principles that should constrain the design of such a syllabus. These are:

- a focus on procedural as well as declarative knowledge
- a holistic rather than an atomistic approach to the framing of objectives
- a focus on top-down (as well as bottom-up) processing
- an analytic syllabus organized around larger units of language that are deconstructed and reconstructed in systematic ways.

From the syllabus, the teacher will develop a programme that realizes the syllabus aims and is appropriate for the target learner group in terms of the teaching methodology, tasks and activities employed. Chapter 5 focused on the incorporation of subject discipline knowledge within an EAP programme and Chapter 6 considered the incorporation of linguistic knowledge. Chapters 8 to 11 will consider tasks and their implementation in EAP courses in relation to the four skills. A strong influence on a programme that implements any syllabus is the *washback effect* of the assessments of learning that are employed. Teacher competency in relation to assessment, however, will be discussed separately.

6.2   Text processing and text creation

In relation to curriculum, the CFTEAP document also proposes a competency statement that relates to text, its creation and processing:

> An EAP teacher will understand approaches to text classification and discourse analysis and be able to organize courses, units and tasks around whole texts or text segments in ways that develop students' processing and production of spoken and written texts. (p. 8)

In relation to texts, the competency further states that this will involve knowledge and understanding of:

- approaches to text classification and analysis, such as those used in genre research, including the functional and rhetorical features of texts
- disciplinary differences evident in academic genres

- text processing skills and strategies
- text production skills and strategies. (p. 8)

Issues relating to analysing text and discourse are dealt with in Chapters 5 and 6, as well as in the following four chapters in Part III. The fundamental view presented in this book is that a text-focused, genre-based approach is necessary for facilitating the development of discourse competence by EAP students, and this thinking also underpinned the previous chapters that relate to syllabus and programme development.

Text processing involves knowledge of reading and listening strategies and sub-skills. The role of vocabulary knowledge as an important element of text processing is discussed in Chapter 6, Section 4, which addresses the issue of levels of vocabulary knowledge or thresholds that are necessary in order to process texts. Text creation relates to the development of academic writing skills (often the biggest challenge to EAP students) along with the development of oral presentation skills. As indicated previously, the teacher needs knowledge of discourse theory to deal with texts, but this also has to be combined with a discourse-based teaching methodology. That is, teachers need to know how to deconstruct and reconstruct whole texts in ways that promote student writing and speaking outputs.

7. Competences related to programme implementation

The CFTEAP document divides competences relating to programme implementation into those relating to teaching practices and assessment practices (pp. 8–9).

7.1 Teaching practices

EAP teachers should be familiar with the methods, practices and techniques of communicative language teaching and be able to locate these within an academic context and relate them to the exercise of language skills required by academic tasks and processes. (CFTEAP, p. 8)

The teaching practices competency statement goes on to say that it involves knowledge and understanding of:

- the key differences between the needs and processes required for an EAP class compared with a general ELT class
- a developed repertoire of teaching techniques and the rationale for their appropriate use.

While general ELT is concerned with a learner's development of overall language proficiency (communicative competence), EAP is the study of language in academic contexts along with the educational and research practices that influence and shape texts and their interpretations. As a result, EAP courses will often employ a text-focused, genre-based syllabus, such as is proposed in Chapter 5, underpinned by a genre-based teaching methodology. The methodological basis for such an approach can be found in the teaching and learning cycle of Burns and Joyce (as cited in Hammond *et al.*, 1992: 17). Important ideas here are that elements of language are presented and practised as part of a functioning whole (Widdowson, 1983: 84), along with the need for cycles of analysis and synthesis (Skehan, 1996). Thus, teacher knowledge of academic contexts and their influences on language use, along with more text-analytical approaches to language teaching, are among the characteristics of EAP that distinguish it from general ELT.

7.2 Assessment practices

This competency states '[a]n EAP teacher will be able to assess academic language and skill tasks using formative and summative assessment'. This includes knowledge and understanding of:

- different modes of EAP assessment
- the link between assessment and teaching and learning in EAP
- the purpose and structure of international proficiency tests e.g. IELTS and TOEFL. (CFTEAP, p. 9)

The EAP teacher, like teachers in other areas of ELT, should have a developed knowledge of approaches to assessing the four skills and, in particular, knowledge of assessing the productive skills in terms of *performance-based* assessment. Formative assessment of these skills should provide ongoing and cumulative feedback to EAP students. In relation to the writing skill, for example, my view is that this should include knowledge of *analytical* approaches to assessing the writing skill (see Hughes, 2003: 100–6) alongside the use of portfolio assessment. Chapter 12 will focus on approaches to the assessment of speaking and writing and the use of holistic, analytical approaches to the provision of feedback.

8. Conclusion

The work of the BALEAP working group in developing the CFTEAP document strongly supports the idea that the EAP teacher needs

knowledge and skills that build on, but also go beyond, the requirements for general English language teaching. This detailed specification
of knowledge and skills for EAP teachers raises two important issues.
The first is a need for appropriate pre-service training and ongoing professional development of teachers who work in the area of EAP. This
is an area that is currently under development in a number of teacher
training institutions. The second issue is the need for ongoing participation by EAP teachers in their own discourse community, which is
rapidly growing and internationally located. This discourse community
possesses its own literature that draws upon theories of language and
discourse, and is informed by research. Therefore, becoming an EAP
teacher involves both initial specialized training and knowledge and
ongoing professional development and engagement within the EAP
discourse community.

8
EAP and Teaching the Writing Skill

1. Introduction

Previous chapters have emphasized that the core characteristic of EAP courses is that they are needs-driven. Their prime purpose is to meet the needs of students (for whom English is an additional language) by preparing them to cope with the language requirements of academic courses in higher education. Central to the language needs of EAP students is competence in academic writing, because of the importance placed on written assessments in academic courses at all levels. Competence in academic writing also relates to the future needs of graduates to communicate within professional or academic communities through written publications. As Prior (1998: 27) points out: '[i]n disciplinarity, much of the work on alignment is centering around texts, around the literate activities of reading and writing'. Thus, an essential part of any student's bid to join an academic or professional discourse community is the development of their academic writing ability, since proficiency in this skill is essential, not only at the stage of their formative participation in higher education, but also later when bidding for full membership of a specialist discourse community.

In relation to the need of students to develop the writing skill, the overall aim of this chapter is to consider the teaching of writing in EAP courses. Writing is sometimes taught on its own as a separate skill, sometimes taught in conjunction with reading and sometimes as a part of an integrated skills approach, for example where a course unit may include activities involving the four skills of listening, speaking, reading and writing. The skills combination through which writing is taught will depend on the aims and projected outcomes of a particular course unit, task or activity.

In this chapter, the focus on teaching the writing skill for academic purposes is divided into three sections. The first section considers the underlying construct of discourse competence in relation to writing extended texts; the second section reviews the main pedagogical approaches to writing instruction in terms of their capacity to develop discourse competence in the writing skills of EAP students; and the third section considers the issue of an appropriate curriculum for the teaching of writing in EAP contexts.

2. EAP student need and discourse competence

In relation to writing for academic purposes, a key issue is that of students developing *discourse competence* as a basis for writing extended texts, as might be required for university assignments. This is an area of communicative competence that can be problematic for many students undertaking higher education through the medium of a second language. The problem often stems from the capacity to understand the differences between the ways in which extended texts (and their related discourses) are typically organized in their own languages and textual (and discoursal) patterns of the target language, in this case English. Thus, for EAP students, it is important to develop discourse competence in academic English writing.

In relation to this capacity to process and create extended spoken and written texts, a number of theorists have proposed definitions of the concept of discourse competence. For example, as part of a model proposed to describe the overall concept of *communicative competence* in a language, Canale (1983) includes discourse competence as an essential component, which he defines as 'mastery of how to combine and interpret meanings and forms to achieve unified text in different modes by using (a) cohesion devices to relate forms and (b) coherence rules to organize meanings' (p. 339). Similarly, in proposing a model of communicative competence relating to language assessment, Bachman (1990) includes what he refers to as *textual competence*:

> involving both *cohesion* and *rhetorical organization*. Cohesion comprises ways of explicitly marking semantic relationships, such as reference, substitution, ellipsis, conjunction and lexical cohesion, as well as conventions such as those governing the ordering of old and

new information in discourse. Rhetorical organization pertains to the overall conceptual structure of a text, and is related to the effect of the text on the language user. (p. 88)

Celce-Murcia, Dörnyei and Thurrell (1995), in developing another communicative competence model for pedagogical purposes, also include discourse competence as one of the five components of their model. Within the area of discourse competence, they include: '*cohesion, deixis, coherence, generic structure* and *conversational structure* inherent to the turn-taking system in conversation' (1995: 13).

As well as being included in these models, discourse competence is also included as part of a broader category of *pragmatic competence* in the Council of Europe's *Common European Framework of Reference for Languages*. This document states that 'discourse competence' is:

the ability of a user/learner to arrange sentences in sequence so as to produce coherent stretches of language. It includes knowledge of and ability to control the ordering of sentences in terms of:

- topic/focus
- given/new
- natural sequence e.g. temporal . . .
- cause/effect (invertible) . . .
- ability to structure and manage discourse in terms of: thematic organization; coherence and cohesion; logical ordering; style and register; 'rhetorical effectiveness' the *co-operative principle*' [Grice 1975].
(Council of Europe, 2001: 123)

Bhatia (2004) proposes that students wishing to participate in the discourses of a particular academic or professional community need to develop what he terms a *discursive competence*, which includes the three subsumed areas of *social competence, generic competence* and *textual competence*.

Social competence . . . an ability to use language . . . to participate effectively in a variety of social and institutional contexts
Generic competence means the ability to identify, interpret, construct and successfully exploit a specific repertoire of disciplinary genres to participate in the daily activities and to achieve the goals of a specific professional community . . .

Textual competence represents not only an ability to master the linguistic code, but also . . . to use textual, contextual and pragmatic knowledge to construct and interpret contextually appropriate texts . . . (Bhatia, 2004: 144–5)

While Bhatia's proposal for discursive competence includes many of the knowledge elements of earlier discourse competence models, it also addresses the issue of participation within a discourse community, acquiring elements of voice and identity that are appropriate to communication in a particular disciplinary community.

However, as an extension of the three component competences that form part of Bhatia's discursive competence, it is proposed here to add a further element, that of *critical competence*. Critical competence refers to a writer's ability to employ textual and rhetorical resources in analytical, evaluative writing that is appropriate within a particular discipline. This critical dimension in the use of textual and discoursal resources within a particular professional or academic community relates closely to elements of Bhatia's *generic* and *social competences*.

Thus, taken together, the elements of knowledge included within the descriptions of discourse competence (including discursive competence and critical competence) relate to high levels of writer and speaker proficiency within specific academic or professional communities. They refer to a consummate ability to process, respond to and create extended texts that are appropriate to the contexts, discourse conventions, values and identities of a particular community. As such, in relation to academic writing, these levels of competence represent the endpoint or goal for most EAP students.

The various proposals for discourse competence agree that it is a central component of communicative competence in a language, and that it involves a number of elements that relate to the processing and creation of extended texts. Thus, in the teaching of academic writing in EAP courses, the task is to help students to develop and use these competence elements integratively and autonomously as they undertake their writing tasks. Therefore, in assisting EAP students to develop these competences in academic writing, there appear to be two fundamental issues for syllabus designers, materials writers and teachers: to identify and use the most appropriate teaching methodology in order to develop the various elements of discourse competence of EAP student writers; and to employ the types of curriculum and materials that best support the development of discourse competence of EAP students. This chapter addresses these questions by first considering methodologies of writing instruction and then curriculum and course content.

3.   Teaching the writing skill in EAP contexts: towards an appropriate pedagogy

This section reviews pedagogical approaches to writing instruction in terms of their capacity to develop student writers' knowledge and skills in the context of the definitions of discursive competence and critical competence discussed in the previous section. In terms of their capacity to advance these areas of writer competence, four different theories of writing instruction are reviewed: the *process writing, post-process, genre-based* and *critical literacies* approaches. It is proposed here that a critical understanding of these theories and the ways in which they underpin currently available materials and teacher practice is essential if EAP teachers are to be able to provide a well-argued rationale for the assumptions, knowledge, skills and ideologies that underpin their teaching of writing.

Although there is an extensive literature dealing with the theories of writing instruction discussed here, this brief review considers the capacity of each to underpin frameworks (curricular and pedagogical) that assist students to progress from student to competent writer within the particular academic discourse community of which they are 'bidding for membership' (Widdowson, 1998: 10). To provide a basis for reviewing the four pedagogical approaches to the teaching of academic writing, it is proposed that there are three key stages in the development of academic writers, and that these stages are loosely sequential:

- developing knowledge frameworks in order to be able to deconstruct and reconstruct the discourses of the discipline that writers aim to enter (relating to the elements of 'discourse competence')
- developing an authorial 'voice' and an 'identity' within the target discourse community (relating to elements of 'discursive competence')
- developing a critical competence to innovate, challenge, resist and reshape the discourses of their academic discourse community.

These developmental stages are not the stages of an academic writing course; they are the stages of the successful launch of an academic or professional career. Indeed the EAP writing course, because it tends to be brief and transitory, will probably only relate substantially to the first developmental stage, but it should help to establish the basis for those following by assisting writers to acquire the tools and frameworks that they need to become discourse analysts (Johns, 1997) and writers in their chosen disciplines.

Before examining some of these approaches to writing instruction in relation to their potential to assist academic writers in their development, it is instructive to contextualize them within the research traditions from which they arise:

- *Process* (and *post-process*) approaches to the teaching of writing derive from the North American writing and rhetoric tradition (including *composition theory*). This is an academic community with a long history, a large membership and its own distinctive organs of communication, such as the *College Composition and Communication* journal and *College English*. This tradition tends to employ a humanities approach to scholarship and research, and employs a variety of genres for the communication of ideas, including the research essay.
- *Genre-based* approaches to the teaching of writing, for example in mainstream schooling and second language teaching, have emerged from the fields of systemic functional linguistics (SFL), discourse analysis and educational studies. Research in this tradition, therefore, tends to select from the range of approaches, styles and methods available to social science research, and is communicated through the genre of the research article. In its broadest sense, genre-based pedagogy involves examining and deconstructing examples of a target genre text in order to acquire the knowledge necessary for students to recreate their own examples of the same category of text.
- The *critical literacy* approach derives from theories of the relationship between the exercise of and response to power (Foucault, 1977, 1980) and the obstacles to learners posed by power structures in education (Freire, 1979, 1994). Drawing on the *critical theory* approach to research, critical literacies approaches to writing instruction have questioned both the *basis* of pedagogy, including the assumptions and practices of writing instructors, as well as the *object* of the pedagogy, such as the extent to which instructor-trained writers will perpetuate rather than resist and shape the writing practices of their future disciplines.

Thus, the various theoretical perspectives on writing instruction arise from different educational or theoretical traditions that employ differing approaches, styles and methods in research. However, in this chapter, rather than discuss these various theories of writing pedagogy in terms of oppositional binaries (e.g. process vs. genre-based approaches), they are considered in terms of their potential to develop the previously mentioned, three developmental stages of EAP student writers.

Stage 1: Development of the capacity to deconstruct and reconstruct disciplinary discourses
The previous section of this chapter introduced and discussed various proposals for the concept of discourse competence, referring to a language user's ability to process and create extended texts (spoken or written) that are the appropriate, competent and coherent 'linguistic trace[s] of discourse processes' (Widdowson, 2004: 169). Discourse competence is more than textual competence, as it involves socially constructed knowledge, general rhetorical knowledge and linguistic knowledge; also, to intermesh these knowledge areas within discourse, it requires more abstract procedural or organizational knowledge (Bruce, 2005, 2007, 2008a, 2008b, 2009, 2010).

In order for student writers to develop a discourse competence, the view taken here (like that of Johns, 1997) is that they need to be trained as discourse analysts. They need to develop heuristic processes and knowledge frameworks to analyse and deconstruct the texts (and related discourses) of their subject areas in order to be able to construct their own texts competently. Therefore, the first criterion for the review of theories of writing instruction applicable to tertiary contexts is their capacity to support a methodology that enables the student writer to develop their discourse competence within a discipline-specific setting.

Consideration of the use of language in specific domains (such as within an academic community) has not been integral to the various interpretations of the 'process approach' to writing instruction, an approach centrally concerned with uncovering and applying knowledge of the cognitive processes employed by writers in order to develop self-awareness and self-confidence in exercising the writing skill (Flower & Hayes, 1981; Elbow, 1981; Emig, 1971; Murray, 1982). In the process approach, the object of writing is a focus on issues of personal relevance and interest to the writer. Language-related knowledge and skills are addressed on a 'need-to-know' basis in relation to the writer's own self-expression, and in an inductive way through conferencing, often at the stage of editing a draft text.

Post-process theorists moved from a focus on the writer's cognitive self to consideration of the social situation and construction of writing and, in some cases, from the perspective of external ideological positioning, as for example, from a feminist position. The *social situatedness* of writing was reflected in the classroom with tasks and activities that reflected social constructivism (Lave & Wenger, 1991) and collaborative learning (Bruffee, 1995). Thus post-process theory, in moving from a focus simply on the writer, considered the *sociologics* of writing, including its interactive character. However, in post-process theories, the writer and the social activities that surrounded the writer were not linked in any systematic way to features of language in specific domains or contexts. In keeping with the post-process notion of the social situatedness of writing, North American (New Rhetoric/Rhetorical Genre Studies) genre theorists (Artemeva, 2008; Devitt, 2004; Freedman & Medway, 1994; Miller, 1984) consider genres (as categorizers of texts) by focusing more on the social actions that surround texts than their realizations *as* texts. These theorists tend to view linguistic analysis of genres as categories of texts, such as within specific disciplinary domains, as 'prescriptivism and [an] implicit static vision of genre' (Freedman & Medway, 1994: 9).

On the other hand, approaches to genres (as categories of text) that have attempted link the construction of meaning in a social context to the actual language of texts have been proposed by genre theorists influenced by systemic functional linguistics (Eggins, 1994; Hasan, 1989; Martin, 1986, 1992, 1997, 2000; Ventola, 1984) and those working in the field of *English for Specific Purposes* (hereafter ESP) (Dudley-Evans, 1986, 1989, 1994; Swales, 1981, 1990, 1998, 2002; Bhatia, 1993, 1998, 2004; Johns, 1997, 2001). Of the two, it is the latter ESP approach from which has arisen a considerable body of theory and research relating to the analysis and teaching of genres relating to specific academic disciplines. The aim of this stream of genre research has been to inform academic writing courses for students for whom English is an additional language. The theoretical basis for the ESP approach to genre analysis is pragmatic and developing, so that it now accounts for both ethnographic and textual knowledge (Bhatia, 2004; Swales, 1998) as well as propositional and metadiscoursal knowledge (Hyland, 2005). A developing body of work on genre pedagogy has also addressed the charge of prescriptivism in the implementation of genre-based courses (see Badger & White, 2000; Hyland, 2003).

Writers who are aspirant members of particular academic disciplines need to access the discourses and written texts of those disciplines. Within the limited time frames of EAP writing courses, it would seem that a well-theorized, genre-based approach may potentially provide access to this type of knowledge. However, an adequate theory of genre needs to be able to account for the socially constructed, general rhetorical and linguistic elements of texts (Bruce, 2008a). Furthermore, the incorporation of genre knowledge into pedagogy requires a learner-centred methodology that employs cycles of learning that involve both analysis and synthesis (Skehan, 1996), where students have opportunities to deconstruct (actively and critically) and reconstruct the particular genres of their discipline.

Stage 2: Development of writer voice and identity
Among the theories of writing pedagogy, the notion of writers developing a *voice* in order to be able to communicate their own ideas in individuated and innovative ways is generally seen as an essential element of competence. In relation to the idea of 'voice', the process approach introduced the notion of writer-centredness to language classrooms, moving away from authoritarian teaching roles and a sole focus on linguistic knowledge. Learner writers were encouraged to harness cognitive principles of thinking, generating and organizing ideas, and to use recursive strategies for encoding their ideas into written texts. However, as previously mentioned, the process approach places less emphasis on the external factors of contextual knowledge and context-related communicative purposes and forms, and how these elements ultimately shape the communication of interactions within specific contexts.

Communicating in one's own voice through writing (within the context of an academic community) would appear to relate closely to reading and processing the written texts of the same discipline. Therefore, many writing instructors see that the skill of writing cannot be taught in isolation, without reference to reading. Hirvela (2004) proposes *reader response theory* as a basis for connecting reading and writing in the context of instructing non-native speakers in writing. Reader response theory privileges a reader's individualized response to a text, which inevitably would be based on their personal frameworks of prior knowledge, life experience, cognitive training and previous experience of texts. While these types of personal knowledge may well provide a valid basis for processing and responding to everyday and literary texts, the approach would appear to be less suitable as a basis for processing and responding to discipline-specific, academic texts. Rather, the requirements for deriving appropriate discourses from academic texts would appear to admit less breadth of validity to a range of personal interpretations of the text, and require a greater understanding of the socially constructed knowledge and communicative values and practices of the discourse community within which the text is located, including what Widdowson (2004) refers to the *pretextual* values of specialist readers.

Our understanding of a text, its realization as discourse, depends on the degree to which we can ratify the linguistic and contextual knowledge that its author presumes we share. This has to do with how far we can engage with the text at all. But there is a second condition that also comes into play: this has to do with what we are processing the text for, what we want to get out of it, the pretextual purpose which controls the nature of the engagement, and which regulates our focus of attention. (Widdowson, 2004: 80)

Thus, in an academic context, it seems that the development of writer voice may not be merely an individualized voice based on a heightened self-awareness of personal thinking and information processing and organizing skills. It is an identity and a voice established and grounded within a particular disciplinary discourse community, and it communicates by drawing upon the identities, genres and communicative values of that community.

It is still feasible that the development of a disciplinary voice and identity in writing would be closely connected to reading; however, it will be reading that involves processing and analysing disciplinary genres (categories of texts). It is proposed here that this will involve a focus on two closely related areas of genre knowledge that concern the development of voice, which are epistemology (Lea & Street, 1998) and knowledge of how to engage in what Bakhtin (1986) terms *diologism* (writing as a dialogue between the reader and the writer). It was proposed in Chapter 3 that epistemological knowledge is developed over an extended period of engagement with a discipline, and particularly requires an understanding of its knowledge-creating processes, such as its research methods. Although this is an area of knowledge that cannot be acquired solely in the EAP writing classroom, students can be encouraged to consider the connections between the knowledge-creating paradigms of their disciplines and their influence on its knowledge-communicating forms. To help to understand this, activities can include analytical reading and ethnographic tasks used to engage with disciplinary experts (Bruce, 2008a: 135–40). In relation to the specific generic elements involved in addressing and audience, Hyland (2005: 42) proposes a model for the types of language devices that writers use to connect with readers, termed *metadiscourse*. Using Hyland's model (2005), learner writers can be encouraged to examine the metadiscoursal features of the common genres of their particular discipline through some fairly objective textual analysis.

Stage 3: Development of critical competence

Across all sections of the academy, students' capacity for *critical thinking* (hereafter CT) is generally considered to be a core and necessary academic skill. However, operationalizing CT and fostering its development through the tasks and activities of tertiary writing courses can be problematic since, like the concept of genre, there is a multiplicity of approaches and views as to what critical thinking is, and how it is developed.

Traditionally, writing and rhetoric courses have promoted the teaching of CT through writing as a set of cognitive skills that are not specifically bound to a context. It was thought that writers, once trained in the use of a set of generalizable CT skills, would be able to transfer them later into disciplinary contexts. This view has been challenged by a number of theorists and researchers reviewed by Ramanathan and Kaplan (1996a), who conclude that 'the transfer and general applicability of critical thinking/reasoning skills is at best a debatable one', but rather, the incorporation of CT into writing 'is situated and context/discipline-dependent' (p. 242). This is a view that resonates with the views of theorists in the academic literacies movement about the discipline-specificity of skills relating to academic writing.

Some also see a possible approach to the development of critical thinking by using *critical literacy* theory (Lankshear & McLaren, 1993) (hereafter CL) and the related theory of *critical pedagogy* (Kincheloe, 2008). Both theories have a socially transformative agenda in that they reject the notion that learning should focus on a body of 'canonical' knowledge, the teaching of which is seen as reifying present inequalities and power structures. In relation to pedagogy, CL supports a critical, rather than a rule-governed approach to enquiry, beginning (like the process approach to writing) with the cultural experiences and orientations of the learner as a basis for making sense of new cultural material. Texts are seen as social constructions and CL involves their deconstruction to examine power relations that can be derived from different 'readings' or approaches to their interpretation. However, even an early supporter of this approach, Bizzell (1993), like Ramanathan and Kaplan (1996a), has questioned the idea of the transferability of critical thinking skills across domains. Specifically, she questioned the notion of causal relations existing between teaching academic discourse and developing critical thinking that, in turn, has the wider potential to transform or democratize societies.

In the approach taken here (in accord with the views of Ramanathan and Kaplan, 1996a), it is proposed that the development of a 'critical' voice occurs within a particular disciplinary context, and involves the ability of students to make evaluations 'within their field's accepted standards of judgement' (Swales & Feak, 2004: 180). It is proposed here that understanding what constitutes the 'accepted standards of judgement' within a discipline arises partly from familiarity with both its knowledge-creating processes and knowledge-reporting forms – its disciplinary genres. Like Hyland (2003), it is also proposed here that 'learning about genres does not preclude a critical analysis but provides a necessary basis for critical engagement with cultural and textual practices' (p. 25).

Ultimately, employing a critical competence involves a writer exercising their own authorial voice (within their particular discourse community) in creative ways that potentially involve individuated and innovative use of the various aspects of discourse knowledge that are at their disposal. Or, as Canagarajah (2002: 599) puts it: '[t]o be really effective, I need to work from within the existing rules to transform the game'. This is the endpoint or goal for student academic writers. To reach this endpoint, however, requires a well-developed, analytical knowledge of the practices of a discipline and the disciplinary genres that a student writer aims to control and eventually exploit.

3.1 Theories of writing instruction: conclusion

The teaching of academic writing within EAP courses generally occupies a very small curricular space. Within a small time frame, teachers are expected to effect major improvements in the writing of students. In this section it was proposed that in developing the writing skill in an EAP course, pedagogy needs to:

- help the student writer to develop their discourse competence within a discipline-specific setting in order to be able to deconstruct and reconstruct its texts and their related discourses
- help the writer to develop an authorial voice and identity within a particular discourse community
- help the writer to develop the competence to communicate in writing that is analytical and critically evaluative in terms of their field's 'accepted standards of judgement'.

Given the need to develop these different elements of knowledge and skill, this review suggests that, in an EAP context, a genre-based approach to writing instruction would provide the methodological basis for a writing course that focuses on these types of textual outcomes in systematic ways. A genre-based pedagogy (see Hammond *et al.*, 1992) will involve examining, deconstructing and reconstructing (collaboratively and individually) the target genres of the discipline community in ways that provide a close focus on the development of the types of discourse knowledge that are essential to the novice, disciplinary writer.

4.   Developing the writing skill in EAP courses: curriculum and course content

Having considered approaches to the teaching of academic writing, this section turns to consideration of approaches to curriculum and course content that are salient to the teaching of writing within the context of an EAP course. For a theoretical basis for specifying the curriculum in relation to writing, this section refers back to key ideas and principles for the design of EAP courses presented in the chapters of Part II, and in particular in Chapter 4. Section 2, which presented the ideas of holism, an analytic, top-down syllabus, and cycles of synthesis and analysis.

Thus, in earlier chapters it was emphasized that it is important to retain language components as functioning features of a whole – a larger discoursal system, and to avoid atomistic approaches to language teaching. This principle of holism relates to the analytic syllabus also reviewed in Chapter 4, which Widdowson (1990) says, 'presents language as synthesized units to be analysed in the process of learning' (p. 134).

These ideas have long been part of the rationale for the various genre-based approaches to language course design and teaching. In previous chapters, there has already been considerable discussion of genre as a basis for researching and implementing EAP courses. Specifically, genre theory has been discussed:

- as a research tool to uncover subject knowledge to inform EAP courses (Chapter 2)
- as a way of providing textual categories to conform with the principle of holism in curriculum design (Chapter 4)
- as a basis for EAP syllabus objectives (Chapter 4)
- as providing a systematic approach for investigating disciplinary texts (Chapter 5)

In using a genre-based approach for the teaching of writing in an EAP context, the object of learning will be the types of text likely to be encountered in the future study contexts of EAP students. These categories of text provide a basis for course units and their written, textual outcomes. A genre-based approach to instruction involves sequencing teaching and learning activities around the deconstruction and reconstruction of categories of text. Using sample texts (as examples of a particular genre), learners engage with tasks that focus on the organizational and linguistic features of the text in order to identify and acquire the types of knowledge necessary for creating their own examples of the same genre. Often the outcome of the learning cycle will be tasks that require students to use knowledge of the target genre (which they have been analysing) to create new examples of the same genre. For the teaching of writing, it seems that genre-based courses have three major strengths:

- they make it possible to focus on units of language above sentence level
- they can provide a focus on the organizational or procedural elements of written discourse
- they make it possible to retain linguistic components as functioning features of a larger unit of discourse, thereby avoiding atomistic approaches to language teaching.

As Paltridge (2001: 6) observes:

> [a] genre-based approach to language program development aims to incorporate discourse and contextual aspects of language use that are often under-attended to in programs based only on the lower-level organizational units of language, such as structures, functions, or vocabulary.

The crucial issue, however, (and one that gives rise to much confusion) is the discourse entity that should provide the basic unit of a genre-based, analytic syllabus, such as one designed for an academic writing course. In beginning to respond to this issue, Chapters 4, 5 and 6 provide discussion about, and examples of, the use of genres in relation to implementing an EAP course. In Chapter 5, Section 5, it was emphasized that there are a number of approaches to conceptualizing genre and that section focuses on the social genre/cognitive genre approach (Bruce, 2005, 2007, 2008a). I have proposed this approach as a way of resolving some of the problems of the multiplicity of ways of conceptualizing genre by integrating a range of types of knowledge: contextual, organizational and linguistic. However, in developing the writing skill in an EAP course, it is important to identify the types of genre and text that are the object of teaching and learning. This issue will be considered in relation to two types of EAP course: pre-sessional courses for students preparing to take undergraduate courses, which may involve students preparing to study in a range of disciplines, and in-sessional courses or pre-postgraduate (pre-sessional courses), which will include students preparing to study in one particular discipline. In considering the selection of writing content in EAP courses at these two levels, the dual approach to genre (the social genre/cognitive genre model presented in Chapter 5, Section 5), will frame the discussion.

4.1 Genre and writing content in pre-university EAP courses

For the selection of the content for a pre-undergraduate, EAP bridging course that aims to develop the writing skill of students intending to study in a range of disciplines, the question remains whether the language entity that provides the basis for each syllabus unit should be a cognitive genre or social genre construct. Since EAP courses at this level are relatively wide-angle, and the core writing need of students is the development of a fundamental discourse competence (relating to Widdowson's notion of 'capacity'), I have proposed that cognitive genres (extended units of language sometimes referred to as 'text types' or 'rhetorical functions') should provide the basis for writing instruction in such course units. The cognitive genres proposed as prototypes in academic writing are: Recount, Report, Explanation and Discussion (Bruce, 2005, 2007, 2008a).

Cognitive genres are essential to a writer's discourse competence; they are cognitively organized, textual building blocks that are combined in socially driven ways to create whole texts, which I have termed *social genres*. For example, the body of an extended undergraduate sociology essay (a social genre) may be structured by using several cognitive genres, relating to the writer's shifting rhetorical purposes. In such an essay, the body may begin with a Recount to establish a context, followed by an Explanation, and conclude with a Discussion (see, for example, Bruce, 2010). However, in basing the writing instruction of an EAP syllabus unit on a cognitive genre (which is, in effect, a segment of a whole text), it is suggested that any model text and target language elements still need to be strongly contextualized in terms of topic, content and vocabulary. This background knowledge should be established before undertaking the activities of deconstructing the text, practising its elements and creating new examples of the same genre. Thus, establishing a clear context, clarifying content knowledge and pre-teaching essential vocabulary related to the topic of the syllabus unit are essential first stages of any such unit.

I have proposed elsewhere (Bruce, 2008a: 119) that the syllabus of a general EAP writing course may reasonably include more than one unit based around a particular cognitive genre. Where two or three syllabus units relate to one particular cognitive genre, each unit could recycle the higher-level, more general, organizational elements of the genre (gestalt structure and discourse patterns), but include a different, linguistic focus, based on one or more of the interpropositional relations that are salient to the particular cognitive genre. (Each unit could also have a different topic and vocabulary focus.) It would be unrealistic for example, to introduce too many different items of grammar and syntax within a single syllabus unit. Table 8.1 (taken from Bruce, 2008a: 119) outlines a possible ten-unit general EAP writing course based on the cognitive genre model, in which each cognitive genre provides the basis for two or three units within the course.

By sequencing the cognitive genres in the particular order of Table 8.1 (Recount, Report, Explanation, Discussion). It is intended that the development of linguistic knowledge will be cumulative. For example, a previous study (Bruce, 2008a: 99–100) shows that Discussion is the most linguistically complex cognitive genre, combining linguistic elements that occur in the other cognitive genres. Therefore, the order of Recount, Report, Explanation, Discussion is recommended as an appropriate sequence for any syllabus that aims to cover these four types of writing systematically. In using *genre-based instruction* (GBI) as a teaching methodology in conjunction with this syllabus, it is proposed to use the cognitive genre model as a basis for analysing texts and identifying the types of knowledge that can be extracted and practised in preparing joint and individual writing of texts (Bruce, 2005: 245, 2008b: 43).

Unit 3 of the syllabus outlined in Table 8.1 is exemplified in previous chapters. For example, Chapter 4, Table 4.5 proposes an outline of a possible syllabus for Unit 3. Chapter 6, Table 6.1 provides an example Report text and Table 6.2 shows the types of syllabus knowledge that may be derived from this particular text. It is proposed that analysis of the cognitive genre will examine the elements of gestalt structures, patterns and interpropositional relations.

The first step in deconstructing the input text involves identifying a schematic (gestalt) structure, which provides novice writers with a framework that can be used for structuring content ideas when confronted with the need to write similar kinds of text. The discourse pattern aim

Table 8.1 Proposal for a general EAP writing course syllabus (Bruce, 2008a: 119)

Cognitive genre: rhetorical purpose	Possible unit aims for a general EAP writing syllabus
Recount the presentation of data or information that is essentially sequential or chronological	Unit 1 Students will be able to write a 200-word chronological recount of events from a timeline and other source information.
	Unit 2 Students will be able to write a 200-word chronological recount of events from a line graph that displays sequential information.
Report the presentation of data or information that is essentially non-sequential	Unit 3 Students will be able to write a 250-word report describing non-sequential data from a data table.
	Unit 4 Students will be able to write a 250-word report describing non-sequential data from a bar graph.
	Unit 5 Students will be able to write a 250-word report describing non-sequential data from a pie chart or pictograph.
Explanation the presentation of information with the orientation on means	Unit 6 Students will be able to write a 250-word explanation of the stages of a simple manufacturing process.
	Unit 7 Students will be able to write a 250-word explanation of an abstract process from a flow chart.
Discussion a focus on the organization of data in relation to (possible) outcomes/conclusions/choices	Unit 8 Students will be able to write a 300-word contrastive evaluation of the solution to an environmental world problem.
	Unit 9 Students will be able to write a 300-word discussion of arguments for and against a response to a social problem.
	Unit 10 Students will be able to write a 300-word critical evaluation of a selected text.

then leads to examining organization of the paragraph structure of the input text exemplifying the particular cognitive genre. Specifically, this could involve a focus on the types of information in the introductory paragraph and its relationship with the content of the subsequent paragraphs. It may also involve examination of the signallers of larger sections within the discourse, such as words or phrases that introduce a contrasting viewpoint or a move to a summary of viewpoints that are represented in the text. When dealing with each of the linguistic features that signal the interpropositional relations, examples can be extracted from the model text of the syllabus unit and practised in tasks that have a discoursal focus. Tables 6.3 and 6.4 provide an example of textual grammar based on the Report text presented in Table 6.1.

Once the cognitive genre has been presented, deconstructed, reconstructed and practised, a possible extension activity could be to examine its use in other contexts. For example, larger texts from other contexts could be examined for their used of the particular cognitive genre, thereby supporting the notion of shifting rhetorical purposes within larger textual wholes and the different textual resources that such texts draw upon.

4.2   Genre and writing curriculum in more advanced EAP courses

This section now turns to considering the elements of a genre-based curriculum that relate to teaching the writing skill in higher-level EAP courses, such as in-sessional courses for students already participating in higher education or pre-sessional courses that aim to prepare students for postgraduate study. In such EAP courses, it is likely that writing instruction will focus on the types of whole texts (social genres) that students are required to write in order to meet specific study or research requirements in their particular disciplines. Therefore, in planning such a course, local needs analyses that examine the requirements and expectations of target disciplines along with any salient studies in the existing EAP/ESP research literature will provide information about the genres that the students will be required to write. Subsequently, the writing requirements of the course and their outcome texts may then become the object of the pedagogy, with writing instruction focusing on student analysis and mastery of these target genres.

As an illustrative example of a genre-based approach to identifying curriculum content at this level, this section considers the sub-genre of the *Results section*, which could be the section of a dissertation or an article for an academic journal reporting the results or findings of research. Teaching this sub-genre would occur in an EAP course for postgraduate students who have to undertake and report research. When identifying

Table 8.2   Studies of Results sections

Study	Field	Results texts	Content staging/moves
Brett (1994)	sociology	20	metatextual, presentation, comment (cyclical, recursive pattern)
Williams (1999)	medicine	9	metatextual, presentation, comment (linear pattern)
Yang & Allison (2003)	applied linguistics	20	preparatory information, reporting results, summarizing results, commenting on results, evaluating the study and deductions from the research
Kanoksilapathan (2005, 2007)	biochemistry	60	restating methodological issues, justifying methodological issues, announcing results, commenting on results

the types of curriculum knowledge for a course unit on Results writing, it is important to examine previous research studies of Results sections. Drawing mainly on the ESP approach to genre, previous studies of Results sections tend to focus on text-organizing structures, either in terms of more general communicative categories (Brett, 1994) or of move and step structures (Yang & Allison, 2003), organizational structures that are linked to particular linguistic features. While there are some similarities in the content-organizing patterns proposed (see the summary in Table 8.2), there also appears to be variation between disciplines, but 'presenting' and 'interpreting' findings appear to be obligatory stages in most disciplines.

In a relatively recent study (Bruce, 2009), I examined the Results sections from sociology and organic chemistry articles in terms of the social genre/cognitive genre model. Part of the social genre analysis of this study involved conducting semi-structured interviews with a sociologist and an organic chemist in order to elicit their views about Results reporting in their respective disciplines. Also, as part of the social genre focus, Results section texts were analysed – 20 from sociology and 20 from chemistry articles. (These were taken from the three academic journals in their respective fields to which the two interviewees most frequently refer.) The textual analysis focused two social genre elements: the use of metadiscourse features using Hyland's summary (2005: 49) and potential content organizing schemata, such as Swales' (1990) *move and step* structures.

The cognitive genre focus involved further analysis of the two samples of Results section texts. First, following a bottom-up approach, a copy of each text was marked-up with the model elements of interpropositional relations, discourse patterns and gestalt structures. Where a segment of a Results section text appeared to conform *mostly* to the features of a particular cognitive genre it was classified in terms of that category. Second, each sample of Results sections was examined using corpus software. This involved creating a word list for each sample and performing concordance searches of frequently occurring cohesive devices. This was to provide further linguistic data that could be compared with the rater analysis of cohesion and coherence in terms of Crombie's (1985) interpropositional relations. Table 8.3 summarizes the findings of the study.

Creating a genre-based curriculum unit that focuses on both the social genre and cognitive genre elements of a category of texts, therefore, involves drawing upon the contextual elements of genre that relate closely to the processes and values of the discipline in which it is located as well as the elements of textual organization. Thus, drawing upon the existing research that has investigated Results sections, it is proposed that a curriculum unit (following a top-down approach) involves:

- contextualization
- present knowledge/studies of the genre
- students' ethnographic investigation of their field
- textual analysis and writing outcomes.

Contextualization
In the case of Results sections, the function of Results sections within an *introduction, methods, results, discussion* (IMRD) structure (Swales & Feak, 2004: 222) and its relative role in relation to the other three parts of the structure need to be examined. This may involve joint analysis of sample research-reporting articles and students individually gathering a small sample of Results sections from their own discipline for future study and analysis. Issues about the approaches to reporting Results in particular disciplines can be considered at this stage.

Review findings of existing research on Results sections
The findings of any existing studies of the genre in other domains, such as other disciplines, then form the basis for comparison with

Table 8.3 Findings of Results section study: sociology and organic chemistry articles

Genre elements	Sociology Results sections	Organic chemistry Results sections
Context	The study of inter-human behaviour, in terms of interrelationships and interactions.	The study of carbon-containing compounds, most of which are involved with life processes.
Epistemology	Research approach may be positivist or interpretative, yielding quantitative and qualitative data about human behaviour. (Informant's approach interpretative, research style ethnomethodology, one data-collection method interview.)	Positivist or scientific research approach – on the basis of present knowledge of chemical compounds and their constituencies, new 'target' compounds are proposed and investigated following established techniques and procedures; the data tends to be quantitative.
Writer stance	Findings need to account for the multiplicity of intentions and views of the human subjects being examined. Metadiscourse features used: endophoric reference, evidentials, self-mention, hedging.	Key values – near absolute preciseness of detail and conciseness, no author presence. Metadiscourse features used: endophoric reference, evidentials.
Schematic structure	No conventionalized move structure.	No conventionalized move structure.
Cognitive genres	*Report* cognitive genre found to structure just over 80% of the texts of the sample, often recursively – several small adjacent reports.	*Explanation* cognitive genres found to structure just over 60% of the texts of the sample (usually recursive); the *Discussion* cognitive genre also occurred in eight of the texts.

the function and structure of the genre in a student's own subject area. Students can be asked to compare the findings that relate to other disciplines with their sample of Results sections from their own discipline.

Ethnographic focus
In order to make the genre focus relevant to their own disciplines, the students develop enquiry questions, such as those suggested in Bruce (2008a: 132–9), which are used to interview researchers and analyse texts of their own field.

Textual focus

Students can carry out guided analysis of common texts for the social genre elements of metadiscourse, schematic structure (for example moves relating to presenting data and commenting on data) and the types of cognitive genres that are employed as textual resources. They can then apply the same analytical procedures to their own sample of Results sections from their own particular discipline. This can then lead to tasks that require students to use data to create their own Results section texts.

5.   Teaching the writing skill: conclusion

In discussing the development of the writing skill in EAP courses, this chapter considered the areas of underlying knowledge and skill that EAP students need to master in order to write extended academic texts, and discussed approaches to writing pedagogy and the selection of curriculum. The chapter began by considering students' need to develop discourse competence in relation to writing extended written texts that are responses to academic tasks. Approaches to this underlying construct of discourse competence and its constituent components were reviewed. Student writers' needs then framed a brief review of pedagogical approaches to writing instruction, which concluded that EAP courses need a systematic and principled approach to teaching the writing of extended texts, and an approach that accounts for disciplinary contexts and disciplinary discourses. To meet these requirements, genre-based instruction is identified as an efficient and holistic approach to the teaching of EAP writing. Finally, the chapter considered the types of genre that can be used to provide a basis for the teaching of writing in EAP courses at two levels.

9
EAP and Teaching
the Reading Skill

1. Introduction

The overall aim of this chapter is to consider the issue of the teaching of reading in EAP courses. Reading is sometimes taught on its own as a separate skill, sometimes in conjunction with writing, and sometimes as a component of a study skills programme. Whether a single skill or an integrated approach is taken, the main focus of reading instruction often tends to be on the development of sub-skills related to extracting different types of information from texts, such as skimming for gist and scanning for specific details. However, pedagogy that focuses mainly on such sub-skills reflects a particular view of the reading skill that may not necessarily take account of all of the areas of knowledge that converge when processing and deriving discourses from academic texts. Therefore, this chapter, rather than immediately considering the teaching and learning of discrete sub-skills, first examines the physical and psychological processes of reading, along with the different areas of knowledge that are drawn upon when processing extended academic texts.

The chapter then has three sections. Section 2 begins by considering the nature of the reading skill with particular reference to EAP students and their needs. It examines a range of areas of knowledge and skill including:

- the psycho-linguistic process of reading with reference to academic contexts
- the role of contextual knowledge and pre-textual expectations in reading
- the notions of separate *study skills* and an overall *study competence* with particular reference to reading

- discourse competence and reading
- different purposes of, and strategies for reading in academic contexts, including sub-skills, such as skimming, scanning, intensive and extensive reading.

Section 2 considers these areas of knowledge and skill as a basis for reading instruction in an EAP context. Section 3 then considers how reading may be integrated within an EAP course; this is a brief section that proposes some general principles relating to (a) the position of reading within a programme that integrates the four language skills, and (b) where the reading skill may occur in the actual staging of teaching and learning. Section 4 then discusses two major challenges faced by students required to process extended texts in academic contexts, those of reading speed and vocabulary knowledge.

2. Elements of the reading skill with reference to academic contexts

This section aims to provide a brief overview of the types of knowledge and skill that converge in the reading of extended academic texts. The section begins with a brief review of theories of how the reading process takes place. Knowledge of this area is important for the reason that course designers' and teachers' understanding of the nature of the process of reading influences their professional practice, such as the design of syllabuses and materials and the implementation of pedagogy. Following this review of the reading process, the section focuses on the contextual knowledge that is necessary for the appropriate interpretation of a text, drawing on Widdowson's (2004) idea of *pre-textual knowledge*. This term refers to the expectations and presuppositions that readers bring to their interpretations of texts, such as those that specialist readers in a particular discipline apply to the interpretation of texts of their field. This section then turns to the areas of study competence, discourse competence and the sub-skills that relate to different types of reading purpose. Several of the categories of organizational knowledge discussed in relation to reading in this chapter are also included when considering the listening skill in Chapter 10. However, in terms of the exercise of the psycho-linguistic and physical processes of the two skills, there are considerable differences because of the actual language inputs, such as orthography and text in the case of reading, and phonology and (usually) paralinguistic information in the case of listening.

2.1   The process of reading

Approaches aiming to account for the psycho-linguistic processing that takes place when an individual is reading, have variously focused on *top-down* processing (Goodman, 1967) that stresses importance of topic and contextual information, or *bottom-up* processing (Gough, 1972) that emphasizes individual word by word inputs. An *interactive* processing model proposed by Rumelhart (1977: 588) suggests that the reading process occurs as a synthesis of top-down and bottom-up processing, that is, bringing together background and topic knowledge and the word by word inputs from a text. In a flow chart of the interactive model, Rumelhart proposes that *graphemic input* enters a *VIS* (visual information store) from which a *feature extraction device* identifies the critical features which provide input to a *pattern synthesizer* that may draw on syntactic, semantic, orthographic or lexical knowledge. However, Rumelhart cautions that:

> [t]he flow chart does little more than list the relevant variables. We need a representation for the operation of the pattern synthesizer itself. To represent that we must develop a means of representing the operation of a set of parallel interacting processes. (1977: 589)

However, while Rumelhart avoids representing the process of reading as sequential and emphasizes parallelism, subsequent research has tended to suggest a more bottom-up direction in the reading process which gives primacy to word recognition, such as readers matching new word inputs to what they already know about the text and their prior knowledge of the topic (the higher-level elements). Evidence for this has been drawn from studies that have examined eye movement during reading and considered the phenomenon of word *fixation*, which refers to the action of the eye pausing on separate words (Just & Carpenter, 1986; Rayner & Pollatsek, 1995). Summarizing descriptions of the physical process of reading, Nation (2009: 62) states that

> when people read, three types of action are involved – fixations on particular words, jumps (saccades) to the next item to focus on, and regressions (movements back to an item already looked at) . . . A skilled reader reading at around 250 to 300 words per minute makes 90 fixations per 100 words.

Thus, for fluent readers these steps of recognizing, matching and integrating processes are more rapid and automatic than is the case for less proficient readers. Studies of eye fixations also suggest that readers tend to focus more on content words than function words (see, for example, Just & Carpenter, 1980). If, therefore, the predominant direction of the physical and cognitive processes of reading is bottom-up, the directionality of the process suggests the importance of lexical knowledge, particularly in relation to the processing of complex academic texts. However, a bottom-up directionality of the reading process does not necessarily diminish the importance of knowledge of contextual frameworks, discourse, syntax and areas of meta-knowledge and skills, since all word inputs still have to be processed in relation to these different areas of knowledge.

2.2   Contextual knowledge and pre-textual expectations

Because the common element of all EAP courses is that they are needs-driven, one of the first issues to consider in developing any course is the projected future needs of its students. In relation to reading, students preparing to enter a discourse community (in pre-sessional courses) and students who are already novice discourse community members (in-sessional courses) need to acquire background information relating to the functions and uses of the academic texts of their subject, including readers' purposes for engaging with its texts. They also need disciplinary subject knowledge in order to interpret the content of texts.

Some approaches to developing L2 reading argue that a theoretical basis for their activities may be found in L1 theories of reading, such as *reader response* theory, which derives from the L1 teaching of reading using literary texts. As mentioned in the previous chapter, Hirvela (2004) proposes this theory as a basis for connecting reading and writing in an L2 context. Reader response theory privileges a reader's individualized response to a text, which would inevitably be based on his/her frameworks of prior knowledge, experience of life and experience of texts. However, the previous chapter makes the point that while general life experiences may well provide a basis for processing and responding to everyday and literary texts, deriving discourses from academic texts will require a greater understanding of the knowledge and practices of the subject discourse community within which the text is located.

Thus, when addressing the reading skill in an EAP context, instruction needs to take account of background knowledge of the general academic and specific disciplinary contexts from which a text emanates in order that an appropriate discourse will emerge from the processing of the text. This involves understanding the functions of similar texts within the particular discipline community. It also includes knowledge of the communicative values and identities and purposes (*pre-textual agendas*) of writers and readers who are communicating among themselves through the written genres of that discourse community. Encouraging students to become ethnographers and text analysts in their disciplines (such as was proposed in relation to the social genre construct in the previous chapter on the writing skill) may also help them to understand the types of contextual background knowledge and specialist reader intentions needed to process subject texts in ways that are appropriate. Thus, readers who belong to a particular academic discourse community, in order to make full use of its written texts, need to understand:

- subject knowledge, including content knowledge and meta-knowledge of the genres used to communicate within the discipline
- the pre-textual purposes of regular readers and interpreters of subject texts
- vocabulary relating to discipline-specific knowledge and concepts.

Thus in processing any reading text, such as in an EAP course situation, teaching methodology and tasks need to consider the context in which the text is found and the function of the text within that context – what the text is created for. This includes identifying who the writer and audience are, and what the writer aims to communicate to that audience. Work also needs to be done on identifying and explaining content knowledge that is essential to understanding the text, as well as vocabulary (general, academic or specialist) that learners need to master in order to process the text.

2.3   Study competence for text processing

While the previous section considered knowledge that relates to or is embedded within a text, this section focuses on the readers' processing of texts for the purposes of reasoning and enquiry to achieve specific outcomes that relate to their own study purposes. In relation to this function of reading, it is salient to consider the set of academic skills that M. Waters and A. Waters (1992) and A. Waters and M. Waters (2001) term *study competence*. On the basis of studies by a number of researchers, Waters and Waters (2001) distinguish between the techniques used to process texts and the underlying study competence to which the surface processing activities relate. They explain this as: *study skills* techniques, such as the reading sub-skills of note-taking, skimming and scanning, or using a bibliography to locate information;

and *study competence*, which they say includes 'deep-level information processing strategies, relativistic attitudes to knowledge status, an information-driven approach to understanding, the ability to learn' (Waters & Waters, 2001: 377).

In encouraging the development of a reader's ability to process texts, teachers can focus on more discrete study skills tasks (such as note-taking, skimming and scanning) with the hope that they will assist in the development of an underlying study competence. However, Waters and Waters propose (2001: 378) that 'in activities for helping students to study effectively, the focus needs to be first and foremost on building up the necessary study competence', and in relation to this need they ask the question:

> What might constitute an overall approach to helping students master both study skills and [study] competence of the kind that have been identified?

In response, they suggest that, in pedagogy, the approach to processing tasks needs to be more holistic, and that problem-solving tasks (Bruner, 1975) may be an effective way of achieving this. As an illustration of this approach, Waters and Waters (1995) organize their textbook *Study Tasks in English* to have an initial focus on more discrete study skills techniques, and then in Part C, they present integrated skills units which have a study competence focus. In this section, discrete study skills activities are harnessed in the processing of larger spoken and written texts, such as an academic lecture and related reading text on the same topic. This approach is intended to mimic the types of more integrated knowledge processing that students will have to employ in an academic course setting. In the development of academic study skills in relation to reading, EAP course designers and teachers, therefore, may need to employ larger, more holistic tasks that require the exercise of a number of study skill activities in an integrated way to meet the requirements of an assigned task.

2.4   Discourse competence

While contextual knowledge and pre-textual expectations focus on the function and informational content of the text, and study skills and study competence consider the skills related to accessing and processing knowledge, *discourse competence* is concerned with the internal synthesis of knowledge and language that contributes the connectedness and comprehensibility of texts. The issue of discourse competence and its components was discussed in the previous chapter when focusing on the writing skill.

Common to the concept of discourse competence as it appears in the various communicative competence models is the idea that it relates to the appropriate arrangement of both information and language to create (and process) extended spoken or written texts. In relation to the informational element of the fusion, what is frequently emphasized is the ordering and structuring of information in ways that make it comprehensible – this aspect of discourse structuring often being referred to as *coherence*. In relation to the organization of the language system to create extended discourse, there is an emphasis on the various connective devices that combine to create extended stretches of language in ways that are comprehensible and promote coherence. This aspect of the linguistic features of discourse organization is often referred to as *cohesion*. Thus, the various proposals for what comprises discourse competence agree that it is a central component of communicative competence in a language and that it involves a number of elements, often grouped under terms such as *cohesion* and *coherence*, *reference* and *rhetorical organization*, all of which relate to creating or interpreting connected, functioning, extended units of language.

In considering discourse competence in reading tasks, a number of activities can focus on:

- the structuring of content knowledge within a text
- the procedural organization of a text in terms of more abstract-patterns – Problem- Solution, Preview-Detail
- the discourse markers that signal larger shifts of topic, rhetorical purpose
- lower-level, more specific markers of cohesion within a text.

In relation to discourse structure, reading tasks can follow a top-down structure, such as is often employed in the processing tasks, as in the approach used by Pakenham (2005).

2.5   Sub-skills competences

The different processing sub-skills that are often the focus of particular reading tasks involve particular attention to either the content or linguistic features of a text. In relation to EAP reading, Jordan (1997: 143–4) outlines the different sub-skills as:

- prediction
- skimming (reading quickly for the main idea or gist)

- scanning (reading quickly for a specific piece of information)
- distinguishing between:
  - factual and non-factual information
  - important and less important information
  - relevant and irrelevant information
  - explicit and implicit information
  - ideas and examples and opinions

- drawing inferences and conclusions
- deducing unknown words
- understanding graphic presentation (data, diagrams, etc.)
- understanding text organization and linguistic/semantic aspects, e.g.
  - relationships between and within sentences (cohesion)
  - recognizing discourse/semantic markers and their function

The exercise of each of these sub-skills relates to a particular element of content, textual or discoursal knowledge (such as described in the previous sub-sections), and in combination cumulatively contribute to a reader's comprehension of a text. Some relate to processing the meaning of the content of the text and others focus on identifying the linguistic means used to connect elements of the text. Sometimes these sub-skills are practised separately and on other occasions a number of them are combined in a reading task. The exercise of these reading sub-skills can also be considered in relation to the area of study skills and study competence. To achieve the purposes of particular study tasks, they may be employed in the processing of texts for specific purposes related to identification, retrieval and use of knowledge.

2.6 Summary

The reading of extended texts in academic contexts may be conceptualized as exercising a complex language skill that involves different types of processing and knowledge from these different (but closely related) areas of contextual knowledge, pre-textual expectations, study skills competence, discourse competence and the efficient use of the sub-skills of reading processing. Therefore, any EAP course that seeks to address the development of the reading skill in a systematic way through the staging of tasks, pedagogy and materials design needs to acknowledge and integrate elements of these areas in any reading skills activities. Also, consideration needs to be given to how the selection of texts and the development of reading skills may be integrated with other language skills. Consideration, for example, needs to be given to the integration of the knowledge-organizing systems that are shared by the two receptive skills of reading and listening. Also it is important to consider the relationship between reading skills development and writing task outcomes in an EAP course context. Section 3 provides some general principles that relate to this issue of integrating reading within the wider EAP course.

3.   Integrating reading within an EAP course

Decisions relating to the location and role of the reading skill within an EAP course depend on a variety of factors, such as whether the course is pre-sessional, in-sessional or postgraduate, and whether the course is discipline-specific or interdisciplinary.

Potentially the most comprehensive skills integration will occur in a pre-sessional, interdisciplinary EAP course whose overall aim is to prepare students for entry to undergraduate study, such as a foundation studies course. This setting will generally require a balance of the four skills of listening, speaking, reading and writing. To achieve this type of coverage within the cycle of teaching and learning of a course unit, the following organizational principles and progressions are proposed:

- establishing contextual knowledge and pre-teaching vocabulary that can be incorporated into subsequent receptive and productive skills activities
- receptive (before productive) skills, such as processing written and spoken texts before producing writing and speaking outcomes – the pre-textual purposes related to reading and listening texts will be part of the introductory focus of this phase
- a focus on content, discoursal, organizational and linguistic knowledge in written and spoken texts when focusing on the receptive skills (for example, some of the areas of 'social genre' knowledge presented in Chapter 5, Section 5, of context, epistemology, stance and content schemata could be incorporated into this stage)
- a genre-based approach to teaching the productive skills with cycles of analysis and synthesis.

These principles are sufficiently general to apply to a number of teaching and learning contexts. The internal organization of the units of an EAP curriculum that integrates multiple language skills should not, therefore, be haphazard, but should make logical and cumulative connections between the target skills and their development within the course unit. The receptive texts used in teaching the reading (and listening) skills will generally be more extensive that those that are the focus of the productive skills of writing and speaking. Yet in an integrated skills unit of this type, receptive texts and productive outcome texts may be linked by means of topic, content and vocabulary. The genre outcomes required in the productive skills focus may or may not be embedded in the reading (or listening) texts, depending on context and practicality.

In relation to higher-level EAP courses, such as in-sessional or pre-Masters courses, where there is greater potential for specification of the target needs of the students, there may be a narrower skills focus relating to the required outcomes of specific courses. For example, in such an EAP setting, it may be more important to focus on reading and writing than on listening and speaking skills. However, the same principles will still apply in such a setting. For example, it will still be important to identify the contextual knowledge and pre-textual purposes of texts and focus on receptive before productive skills. Following this cycle of teaching and learning can facilitate the training of students to be discourse analysts in the ways that they approach the literate activities of reading and writing within their particular disciplines.

4. Specific issues in the development of the reading skill

Two related issues which can be major challenges for EAP readers are those of reading speed and vocabulary knowledge.

Nation (2009) suggests that a number of factors influence reading speed 'including the purpose of the reading, and the difficulty of the text. The difficulty of the text is affected by the vocabulary, grammatical constructions, discourse, and background knowledge' (p. 63). To achieve optimal reader purpose in decoding and processing texts will require fast, extensive reading of larger stretches of text as well as the use of strategies related to intensive reading to focus on specific pieces of knowledge in order to fulfil particular types of reader purpose – a list of these types of purpose and their related sub-skills was introduced in Sections 2.4 and 2.5 of this chapter. Time-controlled tasks, related to skimming and scanning, can encourage learners to develop a range of reading strategies to improve the speed of their reading and processing of extended texts. However, timed reading does not necessarily require a strategy focus. As an activity to help develop reading speed, Nation (2009: 61–2) describes a simple timed reading task, which involves a class reading a text for a timed period then counting the number of words read and logging reading speed. He suggests that this should be repeated three times a week over several weeks until 25 texts have been read in this way.

In addressing the issue of L2 reading speed, Nuttall (1996) discusses what she terms *efficient reading*. She proposes that this involves:

- using 'resources within the text' (pp. 45, 50), such as titles, headings, blurb, biographical information, summary, table of contents, list of figures, preliminary material and index
- 'using the text effectively' (p. 48), which does not necessarily mean reading as fast as possible, but rather being flexible in terms of the reading strategies applied to a text
- 'improving reading speed' (p. 54), involving developing the relationship between both physical and mental process, such as identifying sense groups, 'each chunk [sense group] is taken by one fixation of the eye, e.g. The good old man/ raised his hand/ in a blessing' (p. 55). (Division into three sense groups would be indicative of a good reader.)

A good reader takes in the sense of a whole chunk without having to process individual words. However, the non-native speaker (NNS) reader's problem is that s/he doesn't know the language well enough to chunk words effectively into such sense groups. She suggests that developing chunking can be achieved by the frequent use of skimming activities with appropriately selected texts, such as the column reading activity suggested by Nuttall (1996: 55–6).

The second issue related to effective reading is that of vocabulary knowledge (or the lack of it). A number of research studies that have examined L1 reading suggest that (for L1 readers) lack of vocabulary knowledge can be a core reason for slow reading or problems with reading and fully understanding texts. Vellutino and Scanlon (1982), after reviewing a large number of reading studies state (p. 219):

> existing evidence is consistent with the idea that lexical development and word-decoding ability are intrinsically related. While no causal relationship can be inferred, substantial correlations between these two variables have been observed in cross-sectional and longitudinal studies using pre-school, school age and adult subjects.

Since the 1980s, a considerable amount of research relating to L2 readers has been devoted to the area of identifying what are termed *lexical thresholds*, meaning the level of vocabulary knowledge necessary to process and understand a particular text. Studies have, therefore, been performed to discover what these threshold levels are. For example, Hirsh and Nation (1992) propose that an unsimplifed text can be understood where 95% of the words of the text are understood by the reader; they suggest that this means one unknown word in every two lines of printed text. If students know the *general service list* (GSL; Bauman & Culligan, 1995), i.e. the 2,300 most commonly used words in English, corpus studies suggest that this accounts for 80% of the words that occur in most texts; however, in a printed text this would mean on average two unknown words per printed line, which means that the text is incomprehensible. By adding the *university word list* (800 words; Xue & Nation, 1984) to the GSL, some researchers, e.g. Sutarsyah, Nation and Kennedy (1994), argue that the these two types of lists (combined) provide a basis for an EAP syllabus that takes a learner to the fringe of a particular academic domain in which they wish to read. In support of this proposal, research by Cobb and Horst (2001) suggested that an intensive vocabulary learning focus on the GSL and the *academic word list* (AWL) (Coxhead, 2000) assisted students in economics to 'cross the threshold' of being able to understand and process economics texts. However, as was pointed out in Chapter 6, identifying vocabulary in terms of general lists and academic word lists doesn't necessarily provide a basis for bridging the vocabulary gap in some disciplines. The work of Hyland and Tse (2007) mentioned in Chapter 6 is relevant here. In their study, they found that the GSL and the AWL failed to account for 22% in the science corpus, which suggest that novice readers with knowledge of the two lists may still stumble on one word in five, making a text incomprehensible. Clearly the GSL and AWL lists are important, but EAP users also need to develop knowledge of a range of specialized vocabulary in their subject area that goes well beyond this. Thus, EAP students' vocabulary development needs to be based on three components – the GSL, the AWL and more subject-specific vocabulary employed in the subject area that the student aspires to join. So, how can EAP students improve their vocabulary knowledge and, as a consequence, their reading?

First and foremost, the EAP student must have regular and frequent requirements to carry out both extensive and intensive reading in order to develop a larger passive vocabulary. It is claimed that moderate L1 readers can recognize 50,000 words. These were not taught, but met in context by extensive reading. However, Hu and Nation (2000) claim that it is only possible to carry out extensive, unassisted reading if 95% to 98% of the words in the text are known to the reader, and that where more than one word in 50 is unknown, extensive reading becomes intensive reading. As a way of developing vocabulary knowledge, Schmidt and Carter (2000) argue for what they call *narrow reading*. This involves intensive reading of several texts that deal with a common subject, with a range of tasks on each text. They suggest that this has two advantages: 'readers become familiar with the topic and have much better background knowledge for future passages on the topic . . . . [and] from a vocabulary perspective, multiple exposures to recurrent words should facilitate vocabulary learning' (p. 5). In more subject-specific EAP courses, texts based around disciplinary topics need to be selected for this type of narrow reading task and vocabulary development.

In addition, the student also needs extensive reading input beyond this, along with training in a series of strategies in order to process autonomously texts containing unknown lexical items. These strategies include learning when to ignore difficult or unknown words. For many EAP students, this is difficult to do and goes against their habit of looking up every unknown word in the dictionary. Therefore, developing a tolerance for unknown words needs to be a guided activity in the class. Nuttall (1996: 64) suggests the following approach:

Before reading   Why am I going to read this? What do I want to get
                 from it?
While reading   Do I need to stop and look up the meaning of this
                 word, or can I get the gist of the text without it?
After reading   Have I got what I wanted? If not, where in the text
                 is it hidden? Can I get it by looking up any words?
                 If so, which ones?

5. The reading skill: summary

Although this chapter focused its discussion almost exclusively on the reading skill, it is acknowledged that in EAP courses and target academic contexts, reading will be closely integrated with other language skills when carrying out most assignment tasks. Section 2 reviewed the types of knowledge and skill that converge in the exercise of the reading skill. This review included discussion of the types of task and activity that focus on these areas of knowledge when teaching and assessing the reading skill. In Section 3 a pedagogic progression was proposed, placing processing before the production of written or spoken texts (receptive skills followed by productive skills). In relation to this proposed curricular progression, the chapter also encouraged the EAP teacher to consider more widely the integration of content and language knowledge along with the range of processing skills that converge when carrying out the reading skill. Section 4 considered two salient issues that relate to the process of L2 reading in academic contexts: first reading speed and ways of developing it, and second the connection between reading proficiency and vocabulary knowledge. In relation to the latter, the role of intensive reading for vocabulary development was considered, along with reader strategies for approaching unknown vocabulary items.

10
EAP and Teaching the Listening Skill

1. Introduction

A constant theme of previous chapters is the needs-driven nature of EAP courses. This characteristic is the result of institutional requirements placed on such courses to prepare students for study in higher education, usually university courses. In relation to this ongoing theme, the aim of this chapter is to consider the issue of developing the listening skill of students in order that they are able to process the types of spoken monologue and interaction that occur in higher education contexts.

Hyland (2009b: 27) identifies ten spoken academic genres that are found in higher education contexts: lectures, seminars, tutorials, peer study groups, colloquia, student presentations, office hour meetings, conference presentations, PhD defences/vivas and admission interviews. While some of these are events in which the students' oral participation is of primary importance (for example, the routine event of the office hour and the unique event of the PhD defence), others, such as the lecture, are important spoken genres which students have to process aurally in order to be able to participate successfully in their studies. While the spoken genres of tutorials and seminars may allow for some management of the spoken input through interactions and turn-taking, lectures require students to have the capacity to process extensive spoken monologues and simultaneously take notes. Developing this capacity is important, since the lecture is likely to be an important source of subject-specific knowledge. Although mediation by technologies, such as podcasting, may help students to capture and filter such extended spoken texts, the need to develop the listening skill to cope with this type of text in real time, nevertheless, remains crucial in order to participate effectively in academic courses.

This chapter is concerned with developing the listening skill in EAP courses, with a particular focus on processing extended spoken texts that are mainly monologic, such as lectures. The chapter has three sections. Section 2 discusses the types of process and knowledge that relate the exercise of the listening skill in academic contexts; Section 3 then summarizes the key elements of the listening skill that need to be developed by students preparing for academic study; and Section 4 reviews types of task that may be employed when developing the listening skill in an EAP course.

2.   Processes and knowledge that relate to listening in academic contexts

With reference to relevant research and theories, this section provides a brief overview of the types of process and knowledge related to listening, which are discussed in relation to processing spoken texts in academic contexts. The overview considers:

- the listening process and developing the listening skill
- types of knowledge that the language user draws upon in listening
- the requirements of listening to extended spoken texts, such as lectures
- the discoursal organization of extended spoken texts.

Then, against this background, the rest of the chapter will examine more closely developing academic listening skills within an EAP context.

2.1   The listening process and developing the listening skill

A preoccupation of much of the literature that relates to developing the listening skill is the relative use of top-down and bottom-up processing in understanding spoken language (Flowerdew & Miller, 2005; Lynch & Mendelsohn, 2002). Top-down processing involves an individual listening to a new input of spoken text and then deriving an interpretation by matching the input to their prior knowledge of contexts and content patterns (see Rost, 1990). On the other hand, bottom-up processing means listening to all the parts of the input, such as individual words and phrases, and assembling them in order to create an interpretation of the text. Bottom-up processing relies on separating and recognizing separate sounds, words or word combinations. In accounting for the overall operation of the listening skill, it is generally acknowledged that all listening involves some kind of interaction between these two broad interpretational processes.

In relation to teaching the listening skill to second language learners, some researchers, such as Osada (2001), claim that over-emphasis on the development of bottom-up skills in listening does not leave listeners with adequate attentional resources to construct meaning. Similarly, on the basis of a study that compared listeners at different proficiency levels, Cook and Liddicoat (2002) suggest that higher- and lower-proficiency listeners differ in the ability to process both contextual and linguistic information when comprehending request strategies. In their study they found that lower-level listeners had to concentrate more on specific details, using bottom-up processing. Because this was not such an automatic activity, they had less opportunity to think about contextual information. However, other theorists and researchers, such as Cauldwell (1996) and Field (1999, 2003), argue for a more intensive focus on bottom-up listening practice. A criticism that has been levelled against focusing mainly on top-down approaches to teaching the listening skill is that such an approach is merely 'practising comprehension (or simply testing it) rather than teaching something that might improve students' performance' (Wilson, 2003: 335). Wilson's article seems to reflect a current view in the literature that while in the past, top-down processing skills have been emphasized, there also needs to be systematic development of bottom-up listening strategies. While acknowledging this renewed emphasis on bottom-up processing, Lynch (2006: 92) proposes that:

> teachers should not regard the approaches (top-down/bottom-up) as mutually exclusive but as essentially complementary, and should create listening tasks in which language learners make conscious use of both top and bottom as they try to understand what a speaker is saying.

Furthermore, Flowerdew and Miller (2005) also suggest that a binary division of the listening process into top-down or bottom-up is somewhat simplistic, and only relates to the comprehension of content. In proposing a more complete account of listening, they suggest that, in addition to the top-down and bottom-up orientations, 'the process also encompasses individual, cultural, social, contextualized, affective, strategic, intertextual and critical dimensions' (p. 97). The affective area relates to motivation and the emotional orientation of the listener toward the text. The strategic dimension includes metacognitive processes that are being applied to monitoring and managing learning, such as in relation to a spoken text, while the intertextual element relates to assumed knowledge of other texts. A critical element involves considering the relative social relations that exist between the speaker and the listener and how these are enacted in the text.

This summary suggests that while training in the strategies of top-down meaning processing, such as contextualizing texts, orientation activities (that engage prior knowledge of the world) and tasks that require the listening for gist, are important, listening development should also focus on the decoding activities that relate to bottom-up processing, such as listening to and decoding sounds, sound patterns, words and groups of words. Furthermore, tasks also need to consider issues such as particular cultural attitudes towards texts and text-processing, intertextual knowledge, as well as monitoring and managing learning when engaged with extended spoken texts. In processing texts, learners also need to become aware of the types of social relations that frame the attitudes and behaviours that accompany and are embedded within spoken academic texts.

2.2 Types of knowledge that the language user draws upon in listening

In addition to the issue of the types of processing strategies that are employed when dealing with spoken texts, it is also important to consider the types of knowledge that are drawn upon when listening. This section briefly considers five areas of knowledge that are integrated in exercising the listening skill: *contextual* (including *pragmatic*), *semantic, syntactic, lexical* and *phonological knowledge*. In reality, this separation of knowledge related to language and content into such areas is simply for convenience, in order to analyse aspects of spoken input. However, when listening to and processing language in a real-time situation, these areas of knowledge are used more or less simultaneously.

The first type of knowledge at the top of the hierarchy is *contextual and pragmatic knowledge*. This may involve more general knowledge of the world, such as the knowledge of world events, history and politics as well as knowledge that is more local, culture- and context-specific, such as cultural practices and locally preferred ways of doing things. In an academic context, this also includes knowledge of the content of the academic subject that is the object of the lecture as well as knowledge of other texts that present this content – *intertextuality*. For example, a lecture may begin with:

'Today I am going to talk about *culture shock* . . .'

When they hear this, listeners may immediately retrieve what knowledge they may already have about culture shock, perhaps theoretical (in terms of how they may have heard this term defined before), perhaps schematic, including more abstract notions of culture and cultural difference, or perhaps experiential, in terms of the stresses that they themselves may have felt at some time in their lives when visiting or living in another culture. On hearing the term, the listener then begins a delimiting process of matching what is already known with what is being presented. They become engaged in a process of drawing on this prior knowledge and using it to construct mental models of the incoming information as it is encountered during the delivery of the lecture.

The second type of knowledge in this proposed hierarchy is *semantic knowledge,* and what follows is merely a brief discussion of two key elements that relate to listening and processing extended, monologic spoken texts of lectures. Two key terms arise in relation to semantic knowledge: *cohesion* and *coherence.* Cohesion refers to the linguistic elements that form connections between words or groups of words (phrases and sentences) in order to create units of meaning. Coherence refers to the underlying meaning relationships that are retrieved by the reader (of written texts) or hearer (of spoken texts). Cohesion is manifest in the linguistic features of texts, while coherence exists in the mind of the reader or hearer as they process a text and create a mental representation of its content. While some textbooks and courses place most emphasis on cohesive devices, drawing on Halliday and Hasan's (1976) approach, it is important to note that while coherence can be retrieved from texts through the use of cohesive devices, it can also result without the use of linguistic signalling through cohesive devices. For example, what Crombie (1985) would term a Reason Result (cause–effect) relation can be retrieved from the following two sentences simply from a juxtaposition of two propositions:

It started raining. She went inside to collect her umbrella.

Another point that Hoey (1991) makes is that much linguistic signalling of cohesion is lexical (e.g. through nouns and verbs) whereas most language textbooks tend to place emphasis on grammatical cohesion, such as conjunctions, e.g.

The reason for his reluctance to testify in the trial was that the publicity would endanger his family who were still living in Hungary. (Result Reason)

As an extension of the issues that arise in relation to cohesion and coherence, when processing extended texts, elements of syntactic knowledge also need to be considered. In particular, words signalling connections within extended texts don't always have a fixed meaning, but a listener has to apply the most salient meaning to a word when understanding it in the context in which it occurs. This can even apply to common function words, such as conjunctions, which are often taught as having one fairly fixed meaning. For example, *and* (as a co-ordinating conjunction) is a function word that is usually taught as having an *additive* meaning, in that it signals the addition of some information:

He has paid the telephone bill <u>and</u> has done the shopping.

However, *and* may be used to signal different types of relations between propositions in each of the following sentences:

He overspent on his credit card <u>and</u> had to pay an additional charge.
(Reason Result relation)

Do that again <u>and I</u> will call the police!
(Condition Consequence relation)

Clearly, the issue of developing a coherent interpretation of texts requires pedagogy also to take account of theories of coherence, to train learners in identifying relationships between propositions and to realize that meaning relations between propositions are sometimes not signalled linguistically, and that linguistic signallers will vary in function and meaning according to context.

The lower-level, more specific elements of knowledge that need to be considered include vocabulary and phonology. The issue of vocabulary knowledge in EAP courses has been considered in Chapter 6 (in relation to syllabus design) and again in Chapter 9 (in relation to the reading skill and processing reading texts). In effect, the comments made there concerning vocabulary knowledge and reading texts apply equally to listening texts. Kelly (1991), on the basis of an empirical study, proposes that lack of vocabulary knowledge is the greatest single barrier to listening comprehension with advanced learners. In relation to written texts, the notion of vocabulary knowledge thresholds is important and it would seem that the same issue applies to extended spoken texts, such as lectures.

An additional area that is crucial to the processing of all of the previously mentioned linguistic elements of a lecture or seminar is the ability to detect and process their phonological encodings. Students may be able to recognize and process the written forms of the language, but if they miss key elements of the spoken delivery of a lecture, then successful processing is not achieved. The elements of phonological knowledge, such as phonemes, stress-timing, tone groups, assimilation, elision and intonation are all important to the successful processing of spoken text.

2.3   Requirements of listening to extended spoken texts

In relation to listening in academic lectures, Flowerdew and Miller (2005: 89–90), drawing on a number of their ethnographic studies, suggest that the challenge of this context is that listening is usually integrated with a range of other processes and activities, which may include both reading handouts (or PowerPoint frames) and taking notes at the time of listening. Prior to listening, students may have been required to carry out background reading and after the lecture they may need to use the information gained to participate in a tutorial, to write an assignment and eventually to sit a written examination. Similarly, Tauroza (2001: 363–4) points out that the fundamental challenges of listening to extended discourse in academic contexts, such as lectures, tutorials and seminars are the following: language users are required to combine information coming from both visual and aural sources; students usually hear a lecture presented in a 'conversational style' rather than listen to a lecturer reading aloud from notes; and students are required to process stretches of discourse lasting 15 minutes or longer. These characteristics distinguish listening to extended mono-logues in academic contexts, such as lectures, seminars and other presentations, from other types of listening in terms both of the types of spoken input that the listener receives and the strategies that they have to employ to process that input.

In most other contexts, spoken texts are dialogic (a dialogue) rather than the extended monologue of the university lecture. The spoken text of a dialogue is fragmented, occurring in relatively short sections, and can be managed by the listener, who has the opportunity to take turns during which they can ask questions, seek clarification and pro-vide feedback to the input provider. Furthermore, meaning is mediated in dialogues by contextual clues (relating to where the dialogue takes place), and by the use of paralinguistic clues (sometimes termed *kinesics* or *body language*), such as facial expressions and gestures by both the sender and receiver of information. On the other hand, in the context of a large lecture, while the spoken language delivered by the lecturer may retain a number of the meaning-mediating elements of spoken language, such as redundancy (repetition) and speaker body language, the interactional element of turn-taking is largely removed (although some lecturers may restore this in a limited way by allowing for questions at certain points during a lecture). As a result, the quantity and density of spoken text that the student has to process is considerably greater than that of dialogue interactions, such as casual conversation. Furthermore, depending on the preparation and style of the lecturer, the spoken text of the lecture may vary from relatively formal and scripted to somewhat closer to written language in terms of the density of words and information (see Ferris & Tagg, 1996). As a result, a number of areas of difficulty arise in listening to lectures, which James (1977) suggests will relate to: decoding, that is recognizing what is said; comprehending, i.e. understanding the main and subsidiary points; taking down notes, i.e. writing down quickly, briefly and clearly the important points for future use.

Therefore, because the types of listening required in academic contexts and the related processing demands differ considerably from listening in non-academic contexts (such as conversation), the focus on listening in an EAP course needs to provide preparation for the students in coping with the types of extended spoken text that occur in the academic community. In particular, pedagogy needs to equip students with strategies to process and extract appropriate meaning from extended spoken texts, such as lectures, seminars and other monologic events.

2.4 The discoursal organization of lectures

Having considered aspects of processing and knowledge that students need to bring to the activity of exercising the listening skill in academic contexts, this section now turns to consider potential organization and types of language that may occur in lectures, referring to studies that have been undertaken in this area, considering the style or levels of formality of language employed, how lectures may be organized, and particular communicative and linguistic features that may occur in lectures.

Several research studies that have examined academic lectures in an attempt to identify the style or register of language that they employ have characterized them somewhere between formal, written language, where the lecture is scripted and basically read (perhaps interspersed with some incidental comment) and informal conversational language, where the lecturer may speak from notes, but the language formed is closer to informal spoken language in terms of the types of choices that are made and how it is delivered (see, for example, Ferris & Tagg, 1996). Although there is no published survey of the relative frequency of types of lecture style, the general consensus is that an informal, conversational style, based on notes or handouts, is probably the predominant mode of lecture presentation in English-medium contexts (Biber 2006; DeCarrico & Nattinger, 1988; Dudley-Evans & Johns, 1981; McDonough, 1978). However, what distinguishes the lecture from regular conversation is that there is very little opportunity for turn-taking and management of the communication by the other interlocutor – the students listening to the lecture. Therefore, to facilitate the communication of meaning to the hearers, despite its conversational style, the lecture has to take on some of the characteristics of an extended written text, such as having an organizational structure and indicating the sections of that structure in ways that are recognizable to the listeners in order to assist them to manage the flow of information.

To date, genre theorists have not proposed an overall schematic structure or a move structure for academic lectures. Strodt-Lopez (1991), after examining a corpus of humanities and social science lectures, found that the lectures in her sample did not exhibit the types of organizational structuring that have been proposed for many academic written genres. She states:

> The work on discourse structures and interpretive frames suggests that a lecturer should adhere to a conventional lecture structure, thereby maintaining topicality and evoking in students at least a partially pre-existing frame to reinforce the intended interpretation. This is not, however, what lecturers do. Rather, they develop topics from many angles and evoke numerous interpretive frames (Strodt-Lopez, 1991: 11)

One study that has examined an aspect of lecture organization is that of Thompson (1994), who examined a sample of 18 lecture introductions from a range of disciplines. For lecture introductions, Thompson provisionally proposes two overall functions or stages, each of which contains a series of sub-stages. The two overall functions were:

- set up lecture framework, containing possible sub-stages of: announce topic, indicate scope, outline structure; and,
- present aims, containing possible sub-stages of: show importance/ relevance of topic, relate 'new' to 'given', refer to earlier lectures.

However, Thompson proposes these functional stages of lecture introductions only as tendencies, and cautions that lecturers will display considerable variation in the use of such structures, and that listeners should not expect a linear approach to the sequencing of such functional stages, as lecturers may move back and forth between functions and subfunctions. Therefore, in dealing with the substantial content that follows the introduction to a lecture, it is the listener's capacity to recognize the local context- and content-specific structuring of the sections of the lecture that is vital for their processing and understanding of the content that is being delivered. In extended written texts, these types of section marking (which may be overt or less obvious) have been referred to as *rhetorical shifts* (see Selinker, Todd-Trimble & Trimble, 1978).

Thus in relation to recognizing the communicative purposes and rhetorical shifts that mark the organization of the body of a lecture, it is important that the listening students recognize key signals from the lecturer telling them that a section is ending or a new section is beginning, as well as the types of connections that exist between one section and the next. The listener must, therefore, notice the language elements that guide them in making these kinds of connections, language that is sometimes referred to as *metapragmatic signalling*. Some of the categories proposed in Hyland's (2005) summary of what is referred to as *metadiscourse* include types of language feature that are used to perform this function. The role of this type of language was also recognized in some of the earlier research on academic lectures, and DeCarrico and Nattinger (1988) analysed 'macro-organisers' occurring in lectures from a variety of disciplines. They set up eight main categories of 'lexical phrase', as they refer to these devices:

1. topic markers e.g. 'let me start with . . . '
2. topic shifters e.g. 'so let's turn to . . . '
3. summarizers e.g. 'to tie this up . . .'
4. exemplifiers
5. relators
6. evaluators
7. qualifiers
8. aside markers.

Another aspect of communication that takes place in lectures is interpersonal engagement in the communication from the lecturer to the audience. Flowerdew (1992) examined how lecturers' provision of definitions involve several pragmatic features relating to the lecturers' engagement with, and appealing to, the audience. In a similar vein, Strodt-Lopez (1991) examined how the telling of anecdotes and asides also were used as devices for a more personal type of communication with an audience. The problem with this is that asides and anecdotes generally step outside of the topics, schemata and vocabulary of the lecture in ways that further challenge the L2 student listener. In a lecture, the listener has to distinguish between what is more important information – and what may be less important, such as jokes, anecdotes or asides. To the non-native speaker, humour presents a problem because it relies on background knowledge and assumptions about the world that may be very culture-specific. An intense focus on attempting to decode a humorous utterance may, in fact, deflect a listener from other, more important, non-humour-related content that occurred either before or after the joke. In relation to relevance, Brown and Yule (1983) point out that the focus in lectures tends to be more on the propositional or literal meaning of the language, whereas in conversation the illocutionary meaning is more important.

Another researcher, Rounds (1987) examined how good working relationships between lecturer and audience were established in mathematics lectures. Rounds proposes that competent lecturers develop 'an atmosphere of cooperative interaction and consensus – a sense of working together to achieve a common goal' (p. 666). Rounds calls this 'elaboration', as opposed to the mere transmission of knowledge. Elaborate features of discourse included:

- naming processes
- overtly marking major points, both to evaluate and reinforce student achievement
- developing cohesion and continuity within and between classes by repetition and 'linking talk'
- explicitly organizing topics and marking topic changes
- stating the scope of the students' responsibility
- using questions in a timely fashion
- using persuasive techniques.

With the development of two corpora of academic spoken language, the *Michigan Corpus of Academic Spoken English* (MICASE) and the *British Academic Spoken English Corpus* (BASE), a number of studies have examined specific linguistic features of lectures across subject disciplines. For example, using the MICASE, Murillo (2006) examines reformulation markers in lectures, and Fortanet (2004) examines lecturer self-mention across disciplines. An example of the application of corpus research on lectures in a disciplinary subject is the work on business studies lectures by Crawford Camicciottoli (2007). Also, more directly pedagogic material that has been developed from the BASE corpus is the *Essential Academic Skills in English Project* developed by the University of Warwick (see Nesi, 2001).

2.5 Summary

This section has considered a range of elements of skill and knowledge that relate to the listening skill, with a focus on listening in academic contexts, such as lectures. Within such a section, it is not possible to examine the listening skill comprehensively including all of the elements that relate to the exercise of this skill when processing spoken texts. However, the aim has been to provide a basis for the following discussion of the teaching and learning of the listening skill in EAP courses.

3. Aspects of the listening skill to be developed in EAP contexts

The previous section reviewed research and theory that relate to a range of elements of the listening skill, elements that are salient to processing and extracting meaning from extended spoken texts, such as lectures, seminars and other monologic events in academic contexts. The review established that listening to and processing such events is multi-faceted, and involves a combination of different elements of knowledge and a range of sub-skills. The review noted Wilson's (2003) point that developing listening skills requires tasks and activities that rather than merely practising or testing listening, actively teach it. Therefore, building on this review, this section briefly discusses the key areas of listening skill development to be addressed in the teaching and learning activities of EAP courses. Section 4 will then connect each of these areas to possible tasks and activities that could be implemented in such courses.

In relation to the development of the listening skill, the brief overview presented in the previous section suggests that development of the listening skill should involve development of both processing skills and task knowledge. Processing skills may be considered within the areas of:

- the top-down processing of meaning
- the bottom-up processing of linguistic information
- the ability to monitor and manage learning when engaged with extended spoken texts, such as university lectures.

The areas of task knowledge identified in the overview include understandings of presuppositions about (and expectations of) texts, including conventionalized patterns of textual organization (genres) and intertextual knowledge, and understandings of the types of social relation that frame the attitudes and behaviours that are reflected in the language of spoken academic texts.

Top-down processing relates to establishing the context of a target text, activating prior knowledge and carrying out listening for gist activities and making inferences. In relation to the issue of the content knowledge contained within a listening text, the review in the previous section emphasized both the need for an adequate contextualization of the content as well as the pre-teaching of vocabulary. A focus on vocabulary is particularly important when developing the listening skill with students who have lower levels of language proficiency. For such students, tasks have the dual function of developing the listening skill and overall language proficiency development. However, it is also suggested that with more advanced students there may be a need for activities that require learners to take more individual responsibility for the contextualization process by retrieving and matching oral input to prior knowledge when processing and extracting meaning from texts. Therefore, tasks that involve texts that are only partially contextualized and require listening for gist to establish context may also be an important activity that forms part of a programme to develop the listening skill.

Bottom-up processing involves intensive listening to the sound elements of texts, such as phonemes, words, stress-timing and intonation patterns. It is important for learners to identify the salient elements of the linguistic trace of the spoken text, as well as understand the special discoursal meanings that particular sound elements endow the text with. For example, in English, particular stress and intonation patterns are important for understanding nuances of meaning relating to topicalization and speaker attitude. In analysing a listening text and creating bottom-up processing tasks for the EAP teaching and learning context, an important principle in relation to key spoken elements is salience to the overall message communicated. The materials designer or teacher pre-listens to the text, and identifies the phonological elements that are crucial to processing the key aspects of the meaning of the text. This could be a particular stress-timing or intonation pattern, or key phonemes that present particular difficulties for certain groups of learners. Awareness of learners' particular listening needs and analysis of listening texts for the most salient elements should guide the choices that are made in respect of a focus on bottom-up processing skills, in turn influencing the selection of practice tasks that relate to a particular listening text.

The other area of processing knowledge is development of the learner's metacognitive ability to monitor his/her processing while listening. This includes distinguishing information that is more relevant and less relevant in the lecture, such as filtering comment and humour. Goh (2008: 198–9) proposes an idealized model of metacognitive awareness related to listening activities. Based on Flavell's (1976) original theory of metacognition, the essential elements involve *personal knowledge* of one's own listening, *task knowledge* and *strategy knowledge.* In her model, in relation to each of the three elements (knowledge of self, task and strategy), Goh proposes the three strategies of *planning, monitoring* and *evaluating* and suggests that, to be effective, metacognitive training needs to be ongoing during the listening skills development of a course.

In selecting and using any extended text to develop the listening skill, it is important to be aware of the disciplinary presuppositions about content and intertextual knowledge assumed by the speaker. Possible questions for course designers and teachers who are selecting and preparing spoken texts are:

- Who are the regular listeners to this type of text?
- Why do they listen to this type of text?
- How will regular listeners expect the text to be organized and delivered?
- What subject knowledge (and related vocabulary) is needed to understand this text?
- What assumed knowledge of other texts does this text draw on in communicating its message?

Consideration also needs to be given to the types of social relations that accompany and are embedded within spoken texts such as lectures:

- What type of learning purpose does the lecture/seminar/ talk relate to?
- Is the speaker speaking to their audience as someone who is equal or inferior in knowledge to him/herself? (What elements of language and delivery indicate this?)
- How will the speaker expect the listener to process the text?
- What signals does the speaker give in relation to their expectations of listeners and listeners' processing?

In relation to the types of language and organization of language within a lecture or academic monologue, the review considers:

- the style of the language and structuring of information in lectures (including the signalling of such structuring)
- identifying relevant information
- language relating to the nature of the speaker's engagement with the audience
- elements of cohesion and coherence.

It was suggested in the previous section of this chapter that the style of the language of academic lectures is often close to informal spoken language, but that it is unlike conversation in that the normal, interactional turn-taking through which meaning is negotiated and clarified is largely absent. As a consequence, lectures, although informal in their delivery, also take on some of the characteristics of written texts in terms of a more developed arrangement and sectioning of knowledge in order to assist comprehension. Speakers will employ a range of devices that mark the different sections of a lecture, such as those that deal with different aspects of a topic or larger topic shifts. Therefore, despite the informality of the delivery, it is important that the listener is able to identify key linguistic signallers of sections or topic shifts. In the PowerPoint era, this type of sectioning of information may be indicated visually, but within visual frames there may also be further subdivisions that are only signalled through the spoken language. (Also the speaker needs to be able to notice the inconsistencies and mismatches between the visual and the spoken signalling of divisions that sometimes occur.) It is also important that the listener understand that such pragmatic signalling devices indicating section and topic marking will relate closely to overall speaker purpose, which is usually (but not always) mapped out at the beginning of the monologue.

Also in relation to the informal, conversational nature of many lectures, the issue of distinguishing between more relevant and less relevant information arises. Important elements of language to examine in relation to relevance include: the use of conversational devices to direct attention, signallers of attitude toward content knowledge, such as evaluation of information, emphasis on certain points or emphasizing relevance, exemplifying and digression. As mentioned in the previous section, digression may involve the introduction of humour, which often relies on cultural knowledge and attitudes. Therefore, the listener needs to be able to assess the overall relevance of the humour to the lecture and whether it contributes to the development of its meaning or is an 'aside' that is of less importance. Closely related to the area of relevance is language that signals speaker–audience engagement.

The review in the previous section also proposed that when considering lectures and their internal organization, cohesion and coherence are important aspects that need to be addressed when assisting students to process extended spoken texts. Students need to understand the role of the key cohesive devices in texts, such as conjunction, reference, ellipsis and substitution. Pedagogy also needs to take account of theories of coherence. For example, students need to recognize that meaning relations between propositions that lead to a coherent interpretation of a text are sometimes not signalled linguistically. Listening tasks, therefore, need to include a focus on the different types of semantic relationship that exist in texts, including those signalled by grammatical or lexical cohesive devices as well as those that are retrieved simply through the arrangement of propositions. Listening tasks, therefore, need take account of all of the types of meaning relations that lead to the retrieval of a coherent interpretation of a listening text.

EAP course developers and teachers, therefore, need to consider these different elements of processing and knowledge in relation to the preparation and staging of listening tasks that relate to extended listening texts.

4. Teaching listening: developing processing and task knowledge in an EAP context

Having identified a variety of aspects of the listening skill that relate to the processing of extended, oral academic texts, (for example, when listening to lectures) and the range of knowledge areas that converge in such texts, this section of the chapter provides some discussion about the types of task and activity that can be employed in relation to each of these elements of the listening skill. These aspects of listening are grouped in two areas: elements that relate to processing knowledge and elements that relate to task (and text) knowledge.

4.1 Top-down processing of meaning

The first of the strategy areas relates to developing top-down approaches to processing meaning. For example, Salehzadeh (2006: 8–9) lists strategies that can assist students in the development of top-down processing, grouping these into activities that take place before and after the lecture. Activities that can be employed before the lecture include reviewing previous lectures that lead up to and connect with the lecture and reflecting on these connections. Another pre-lecture strategy is to read the assigned texts that relate to the particular lecture and list predictions about its content, create questions about the lecture and make a list of terms from the reading material that appear to be central to the lecture. Where possible, she suggests discussing the lecture with classmates as part of the predictive, anticipatory process.

A strategy that students can use during the lecture involves close listening to the introduction of the lecture and mapping a framework (from the introduction), which can then become the basis for note-taking and structuring the information that they receive. Hyland (2009b: 99) says that

> listeners must create a mental map of the organization of the lecture as a 'sequential-hierarchic network structure' (Givón, 1995: 64) in which information is not only received linearly but where topics and sub-topics are structured and connections made.

This predictive framework also becomes a basis for listening for cues that signal topics and mark sections, which may involve language cues but also may involve body language, such as gesture and facial expressions.

Strategies that students can apply after the lecture include highlighting the main ideas in their notes, writing brief summaries of the main ideas immediately after the lecture (while the information is fresh) and further reading of the assigned material. Further discussion of the lecture is also suggested as another post-lecture strategy, either with peers or academic staff in tutorials or during 'office' hours.

In relation to top-down processing, another element that needs to be considered is the possibility that L1 students may employ regularized, default schemata in the processing and comprehension of lecture material. This appeared to be confirmed in a study by Allison and Tauroza (1995), investigating an earlier proposal by Olsen and Huckin (1990) that in some disciplines, such as engineering, lectures tend to be organized around recursive Problem-Solution structures that are familiar to L1 students of the discipline and frame their comprehension of lecture content. This research suggests that, where appropriate, identifying and pre-teaching such schematic knowledge will benefit students' processing and comprehension of lectures. (Possible frameworks for structuring lectures are considered in the next sub-section that deals with task and text knowledge.)

Also, in deciding the relative salience of the informational elements of lectures, students need to be sensitized to language devices that draw attention to the importance of more salient pieces of information. In relation to this, Lynch (2004) identifies a category of words, which he terms *importance markers* 'with which lecturers underline and emphasise points in their argument' (p. 39). He categorizes these into: noun phrases that relate to the content, such as 'the central problem'; direct appeals to the audience, such as 'it's important to bear in mind that. . .' and personalizing, 'My point is . . .' (p. 39).

Similarly, in a study that examined monologic texts (such as lectures) from the MICASE corpus, Simpson (2004) examined the use of formulaic language and found 'a wide range of functional categories, including a number of discourse-organizing functions, such as summarizing, temporal sequencing, focusing and meta-discourse, as well as categories related to interactional functions, such as explaining or demonstrating, giving instructions or advice, eliciting feedback, and asking questions (p. 51). The category of functional expressions that relate to discourse organizing was the largest classificatory group among Simpson's findings; however, she also found a considerable degree of overlap with formulaic expressions used for both discourse-organizing and interaction (p. 53).

In an EAP setting, a focus on spoken language in lectures that highlights relevance of information could involve tasks that require post-listening analysis of lecture scripts for instances of the high-frequency expressions that Simpson identifies as well as for the expressions that Lynch terms 'importance markers', and consideration of their local, functional roles in the target texts of a course. This type of consciousness-raising will help to sensitize students to the importance of the use of this type of expression.

4.2 Bottom-up processing of spoken language

In an EAP course, as well as focusing on listening strategies for the top-down processing of meaning, it is also suggested that students be provided with opportunities to practise bottom-up processing of micro-elements of phonology. For example, using audio or video extracts of lectures, such a focus could include such aspects of speaking as: *contractions, linking, assimilation, reduction, false starts* and such stylistic elements as *colloquialisms* and *slang*. In terms of the staging of this focus on bottom-up processing, Goh (2008: 207) suggests:

> While this type of practice is clearly needed, there is a potential risk of learning becoming decontextualized and some teachers returning to drills involving sound discrimination. One way to address this is

to integrate perception activities with normal listening activities as in the post-listening perception activity. After learners have completed a comprehension or communication task based on a listening text, they revisit the text to focus on phonological features of words in context.

Goh's suggestion for a pedagogic focus on bottom-up processing as a *post-listening* perception activity may be more appropriate for classes of higher-level learners whose work on the lecture texts proceeds from a larger knowledge (and experience) base and, with such learners, the post-text task may be useful as a 'mopping up' activity. However, with lower-level learners, it may be helpful to identify and practise bottom-up elements *before* listening to the whole text, and then also follow-up with post-text activities so that the learners are sufficiently scaffolded in this area. The types of elements of a bottom-up focus may include:

- *contractions* – llistening, reading and pencil-analysing transcripts of video segments of lectures to draw attention to this feature. Salehzadeh (2006: 35) points out that students are often taught to notice contractions with subject pronouns, but that the MICASE corpus also shows evidence of contractions of modal verbs after nouns, a feature that tends to be overlooked, and she provides the examples of:

  how many *people'll* want to leave

  this *one'll* be zero

  two'd be enough for our purposes

- *linking, assimilation, reduction* – closely related to contractions is the feature of *linking* spoken language in which proficient speakers connect sounds and slide words together, such as vowels linked to following consonant sounds, e.g. *see_that, right_up* particularly when such words are unstressed and follow more strongly stressed words, as in:

  But *you'll* **see_that** *another trend* **right_up** *this end of the chart shows . . .*

- An extension of linking is that of *assimilation* – where two sounds are blended to make a third sound which, in running speech, may be unrecognizable to a listening non-native speaker, such as the connection made between the first two words in the following example:

What'you'll make of this, I'm not sure . . . in spoken language sounds' like

Whachill make . . .

- *Reduction* – refers to the disappearance of sounds in words in running speech. For example:

  Finally I want to summarize what it is I have been saying here . . .

  *Finally, I **wanna** summarize **wodidiz** I've been . . .*

- *Ellipsis* – refers the omission of repeated parts of verb groups or whole parts of sentences if the speaker feels that their repetition is unnecessary:

  How this situation impacted on Chrysler is evident in Table 2 . . . where you can see the declining sales in those particular markets . . . especially the Gulf States.

  . . . Toyota? The situation is the reverse . . . as you can see in Table 3.

  Attention to context and co-text (text that occurs before and after the ellipsis) is necessary to retrieve this type of linguistic information.

- *false starts* – more common in unplanned conversation than in lectures where more planning has preceded speaking. However, with asides or spontaneous examples and explanations there will be more false starts as the lecturer begins to speak more casually. Students should be directed to notice pauses and body language that accompany false starts. With this type of feature, video rather than audio texts are important.

- *colloquialisms and slang* – according to the preparation and presentation of the speaker, the language used in lectures will vary from formal to informal and this may vary across disciplines (Ferris & Tagg, 1996). The use of colloquialisms and even slang may be among the least accessible elements to non-native speaker students. While occasional use may be less problematic, the repeated use of favourite idioms by a speaker can inhibit comprehension, as in a business studies lecture:

> *With the repatriation of profits by foreign investors, citizens increas-*
> *ingly took a* **NIMBY** *view of any proposal for a new project that came*
> *along. . . . I think it is fair to say that in this* **neck of the woods**, *the*
> *government has lost some its appetite for this type of project – given*
> *the attitude of its constituency.*

With the occasional use of idiomatic expressions, the surrounding context can help the listener retrieve the meaning. However, with repeated use by a speaker, students need to develop managing strategies. For example, early in a course, students need to note and check the meaning of favoured idioms that are repeatedly used by one speaker.

- *unfamiliar* terms – in the pre-lecture preparation, reading ahead and identifying and checking the meaning of key terms in the related readings may help learners with this. Students should be trained not to focus excessively on one unknown word that they hear (and should not be reaching for dictionaries in a lecture, which may be unfruitful anyway in the case of words with multiple meanings). Such words encountered in-lecture should be listed for checking later. Students also need to realize that their repeated use within a context may assist in processing their meaning.

4.3   The ability to monitor and manage listening and information processing

When engaged with extended spoken texts, such as university lectures, students need to be encouraged to employ internalized (metacognitive) strategies towards lectures. An example of this is the 'personal strategy inventory' that Salehzadeh (2006: 8–9) proposes. This includes activities before, during and after class and an overall strategy for monitoring one's progress. Similarly, Lynch (2004) also encourages the development of such metacognitive information-processing strategies in order to manage listening to and processing extended text. He terms these *macrostrategies*, and they include 'predicting, monitoring, responding, clarifying, inferencing, evaluating' (pp. 16, 91). One post-task, reflective strategy that could be used in training contexts, such as EAP classes that regularly practise listening skills, could be to require students to keep a brief post-task journal where they record their progress in listening tasks and note the areas that they need to improve on.

4.4   Genre knowledge

In the previous section, in relation to the top-down processing of meaning, mention was made of research relating to the use of schematic knowledge to process lectures, such as Problem-Solution structures. In considering the types of schematic structures that may occur in lectures, Salehzadeh (2006: 74–8) proposes eight possible macro-patterns for lecture organization. According to the brief taxonomy that she provides, lectures may be *information-driven, Problem-Solution, comparative, thesis/ point-driven, cause and effect, data versus theory, sequential, classification/ description*. For each of the eight patterns, Salehzaheh provides a brief description of the organizational principle to which it relates. In EAP courses that focus on developing knowledge about the spoken lecture genre, the preparation for listening may involve raising awareness of the macro-pattern as part of predictive activities that aid the processing of the lecture. In conjunction with the structuring of knowledge in a lecture, Lynch (2004: 19–22) draws students' attention to what he terms *signposting* and practises this activity by first getting students to listen to a lecture segment and fill in a grid where some of the instances of signposting are provided, and as a post-listening task, provides a transcript and gets the students to read and underline instances of signposting.

In an EAP course, listening practice tasks with audio- and video-recorded lectures need to encourage students to become familiar with recurrent, conventionalized organization and language elements that relate to lectures. Some of this type of schematic knowledge is described under the previous point relating to the positioning of the speaker, and some relates to organizational patterns that are used for the structuring of knowledge that are described under the next point. Pre-set tasks that involve following a top-down sequence for the recognition and processing of knowledge conveyed in practice task lectures may help the EAP student to develop and enrich the schematic knowledge that they hold about lectures. Such tasks could involve listening to and analysing lecture introductions for the types of organizational patterns and associated language that Thompson (1994) proposes.

4.5   Social and attitudinal positioning of speakers

Students need to understand culturally driven assumptions about the nature of knowledge and approaches to its communication. In relation to cultural differences that distinguish lectures in different national or cultural contexts, Salehzadeh (2006: 13–15, 21, 23) contrasts characteristics of North American university lectures, such as the provisional nature of knowledge communicated, the notion of questioning or challenging a speaker and opportunities for lecturer–student interactions, with the more authoritative delivery of knowledge and lecturer-dominant roles that may have been experienced by students in other cultures. In relation to writing, Swales and Feak (2004: 42) propose the notion of the *positioning* of writers in relation to their knowledge and to their audience. A similar approach could be taken to examining the positioning of lecturers towards both the content knowledge that they present and towards their student audience in terms of the lecturer's communicative stance and the listeners' expected roles. Part of a focus on this type of knowledge may involve examining lecture transcripts for examples of the types of *interactional metadiscourse* that Hyland (2005: 42) proposes. Similarly, the interactional formulaic expressions that Simpson (2004) identifies in the MICASE corpus could also help to provide a basis for doing this type of analysis.

5. The listening skill: conclusion

In EAP course units, listening to texts and related tasks will be integrated with activities and outcomes that involve the other skills of speaking, reading and writing. Nevertheless, as this chapter indicates, attention needs to be given to processing skills and textual (and discoursal) knowledge in order to develop students' capacity to cope with the listening requirements of academic contexts, such as university courses. Furthermore, in the development of different aspects of the listening skill, the directionality of processing (top-down, bottom-up) needs to be considered, along with a range of other influencing factors, such as those identified by Flowerdew and Miller (2005).

11
EAP and Teaching the Speaking Skill: Teaching Critical Thinking

1. Introduction

This chapter addresses two further areas of skills development in EAP courses: first the speaking skill in relation to EAP students and their future study needs, and second, the area of critical thinking (CT) skills.

In courses that aim to cover the four skills (of listening, speaking, reading and writing), speaking tends to receive the least formal attention in the classroom. It is often assessed on the basis of the presentation of a prepared talk, leading a seminar or participation in a formal class debate. However, it is important to consider the actual types of speaking that EAP students will be required to perform when participating in discipline-specific courses, and how the EAP course can provide preparation for those types of speaking requirement. Robinson *et al.* (2001: 348) state: 'most needs analyses of ESL students in academic environments have established the importance of interactive, holistic speaking tasks, such as small group oral discussion'. In support of this idea, a number of survey studies that include the views of non-native speaker (hereafter NNS) undergraduate students (Ferris & Tagg, 1996; Johns, 1981; Mason, 1994; Ostler, 1980) show that students self-report concerns about their language proficiency levels, including their capacity to cope with academic listening and speaking tasks. More recent studies of NNS graduate students (Kim, 2006; Lee, 2009) also report similar concerns.

The study by Ferris and Tagg (1996) suggests that course requirements in relation to oral speaking and listening skills vary across disciplines. Business courses, for example, appear to have higher expectations in relation to students' ability to lead discussions, participate in debates and carry out assignment tasks that require interactions with native speakers. A follow-up study by Ferris (1998) of expectations in relation to the performance of NNS students suggests that most of the academic teaching staff surveyed believed that NNS students enrolled in under-graduate courses would benefit from further training and practice in the exercise of oral/aural skills in relation to course tasks.

This focus on speaking begins by considering theoretical approaches to the types of knowledge and skill that are brought to bear in oral com-munication with reference to academic contexts. Consideration is then given to the specific types of oral communication expected of students in academic courses. These categories are based on Jordon's (1997) tax-onomy and those identified in the surveys of Ferris and Tagg (1996) and Ferris (1998). In each case, suggestions are made concerning the ways in which EAP courses can prepare students for each of these aspects of oral participation. Finally, some brief suggestions are provided about how speaking activities may be incorporated within EAP courses, specifically in relation to the need to incorporate tasks that promote interactivity on a regular and ongoing basis and in relation to the development of oral presentation skills.

2.   Oral communication: elements of process and knowledge and their development

This section first reviews theoretical perspectives on the speaking skill, including the cognitive and physical elements of the speaking process as well as the types of knowledge drawn upon in oral communication. The section then briefly considers how these approaches to process and knowledge may inform instruction in the speaking skill in an EAP class setting.

In relation to the cognitive and physical process of speech production, this section draws on the proposal of the cognitive psychologist Levelt (1989) that spoken messages are, in fact, planned and implemented in terms of a hierarchical structure that involves: *conceptualizing, formulat-ing, articulating* and *monitoring*. 'Conceptualizing' is purpose-driven, pre-verbal planning that involves *procedural knowledge* (about how to arrange information) and *declarative* knowledge (relating to the con-tent of the message). Levelt proposes that conceptualizing involves realizing an overall communicative goal through sub-goals, around which knowledge is appropriately organized. 'Formulating' involves translating a 'conceptual structure into a linguistic structure' (p. 11). This stage involves first the selection and arrangement of words that grammatically encode the meaning of the pre-planned message, and secondly the phonological encoding of the message by retrieving the appropriate phonetic features for the grammatical and lexical elements of the encoded message. The encoded message or 'internal speech' is temporarily stored in an *articulatory buffer zone*. What then follows is 'articulating' the message, which involves activating the motor organs or 'the respiratory, the laryngeal and the supralaryngeal systems' (p. 12). During and after the articulating stage, 'monitoring' may take place, which involves avoiding errors or repairing any errors that may occur. Monitoring may involve work on the temporarily stored internal speech or post-production repairing of errors noticed by the speaker in their output.

In order to account for the types of knowledge that are drawn upon in speech production, this section refers to a recent model of communicative competence proposed by Martínez-Flor, Usó-Juan and Alcón-Soler (2006: 147). The model proposes *discourse competence* as central to exercising the speaking skill, which is supported by four subsuming competences of *linguistic competence, pragmatic competence, intercultural competence* and *strategic competence*. Discourse competence is at the core of the abilities that the language user draws upon in producing spoken output and 'involves the speaker's ability to use a variety of discourse features to achieve a unified spoken text given a particular purpose and the situational context where it is produced' (p. 147). Linguistic competence involves knowledge of the systems of the language. Such systemic knowledge involves grammar, vocabulary and phonology in order to produce utterances that are sufficiently accurate to achieve the speaker's purpose. Pragmatic competence relates to a speaker's 'knowledge of the function or illocutionary force implied in the utterance that they intend to produce as well as the contextual factors that affect the appropriacy of the utterance' (p. 149). Intercultural competence describes the speaker's knowledge of the culturally governed, non-verbal factors that relate to the use of language in a given context. Such factors may include the use (or avoidance) of silence, body language and issues related to turn-taking in interactions. The final subsidiary competence that supports discourse competence in spoken language is that of strategic competence. This involves the language user's learning and communication strategies, such as the use of redundancy. Communication strategies could include devices that help to overcome knowledge gaps that result from deficiencies in other areas of language knowledge.

Thus, the frameworks of Levelt's (1989) processing model (that accounts for the process) and the communicative competence model by Martínez-Flor, Usó-Juan and Alcón-Soler (2006) (that accounts for knowledge) posit speaking as a complex activity. This activity involves the integration of cognitive, psycho-motor and interpersonal processes in the exercise of the skill, and draws on a range of knowledge elements, such as those proposed in the communicative competence model.

In relation to the types of complex, oral task required in academic contexts, it is proposed that speakers need to automate the stages of the process and the application of the knowledge elements because of the large cognitive attentional resources required to focus on each one consciously during communication (see Bygate, 1998). Bygate (1996, 1998, 2001, 2006) argues that repetition of tasks is an important way to routinize and improve their performance. He proposes that during the process of repeating and revisiting tasks, the novice speaker's attentional resources change. Initially, the main focus of their attention will be on 'the content of what they want to say, and on finding as quickly as possible the words that will express the meanings' (Bygate, 2006: 170). However, as a task is repeated and the content becomes more familiar, the speaker's attention will shift more to the form and accuracy of the language that is used to convey the content:

> If learners then *repeat* a speech activity, or at least significant elements of the activity, this will lead them to have to allocate less attention to the content, and enable them to allocate more attention to how the content is expressed, than they did first time around. That is, on repetition their attention would be expected to shift from the content, to the form, with the result that grammatical details are gradually integrated into the whole. (Bygate, 2006: 170)

This developmental effect from repetition is reported in a number of studies that have examined the classroom practice of routinized oral activities (see Bygate, 2001; Bygate & Samuda, 2005; Hall, 1993; Morita, 2000). In an EAP context, Lynch and Maclean (2000) report a preliminary study that monitored two students from a group that performed a *poster carousel task*. The task involved students converting a research article into a conference poster, which they then had to present to multiple 'visitors' – other members of the class – who spent three minutes with each presenter. The findings from this study also showed some evidence of the speakers shifting the focus of their output from content to aspects of accuracy as they had the opportunity to present their posters several times to different peers. As well as recording and analysing the output of two participants, Lynch and Maclean also interviewed the same two students, who self-reported a shift in their conscious focus from the content to the form and accuracy of their presentation.

Thus, theory and empirical research on the speaking skill along with the findings of survey research that relate to target needs analyses appear to indicate first the need to identify the types of speaking routine that EAP students will encounter in academic contexts, and second, to provide opportunities for developmental practice of such routines in order to allow for the schematization of the types of process and knowledge required.

3.   Types of oral communication in academic settings

In identifying the repertoire of speaking routines, tasks and genres that students need to participate in, in a university setting, Jordan (1997: 193) identifies the following:

- asking questions in lectures
- participation in seminars (tutorials), discussions
- making oral presentations, and answering audience questions or responding to audience comments
- verbalizing data, and giving oral instructions, in seminars/workshops/laboratories.

Ferris and Tagg (1996) identify a similar range of activities, including: class participation, small group work, working with peers, oral presentations, leading discussions, debates and group assignments.

3.1   Speaking in lectures: questions or comments

For some time, educational psychologists have seen value in student-generated questions as a way in which learners elaborate on and deepen their understanding of new material (see, for example, King, 1992). A corpus study of American university lectures by Csomay (2007) provides empirical data that support the idea of the increasingly participatory nature of university lectures, with the teacher taking 44% of turns across the corpus compared with 56% of turns taken by students. The difference is that student turns tended to be very brief with an average of 30 words. Thus it seems that student turns in classes or lectures, although frequent, are relatively short, for example in the form of a comment or question. In an earlier case study conducted at another American university, Tapper (1996) found that in lectures the type of exchange that occurred most frequently was a two-part exchange of a student question followed by a teacher response. This pattern is similar to the adjacency pairs of normal conversation, but Tapper found that in her study NNS students did not participate and her data came from the participation of NS students.

In relation to the types of questioning carried out by students in lectures, McKenna (1987: 197) reports four main types of questions:

1. Clarification
   a. Repeat information
   b. Additional information
2. Interpretation check
   a. Rephrasing information
   b. Illustrating given information
3. Digression
4. Challenge

However, McKenna points out that most of the questions asked by native speakers were not for the purpose of clarification or explanation, but rather to contribute to the discourse by commenting, adding something or challenging. Despite this finding, she suggests that NNS still need to be given help in developing the skills to seek clarification or understanding in lectures. This recommendation is supported strongly by Kim (2006), who surveyed East Asian graduate students in US universities (taking subjects other than science and engineering) and found that 65% reported that they 'were *always* or *frequently* expected to ask instructors questions during class' (p. 483). Finding that the 'whole-class discussion was the most common academic speaking task in graduate courses, and that students reported it to be one of the most challenging classroom activities' (p. 487), Kim strongly recommends that EAP classes prepare students for this activity by providing opportunities to participate in whole-class discussions. Similarly, Northcott's (2001) ethnographic study of interactivity in lectures in the MBA programme at the University of Edinburgh underlines the importance of oral participation by graduate students, particularly in an MBA course, but notes the difficulties that NNS students face in interpreting subtle references by lecturers (and by native-speaker students) to UK academic cultural knowledge, intertextual knowledge and humour that is culturally bound.

In the recommendations following her study, McKenna (1987) proposed that specific training in this skill needs to be carried out by getting students to analyse the language of lectures and, in particular, the type of lecturer–student exchanges that take place. In effect there are two areas of knowledge that EAP students need to develop here: fluency, accuracy and appropriateness in question-forming; and pragmatic (contextual) knowledge about how to ask a question in a lecture or group setting – how to manage the type of turn-taking that is appropriate. In relation to the pragmatic or contextual dimension, it would appear that the use of video- and not just audio-text may be important for teaching this skill. Video-recordings may facilitate analysis and discussion of the verbal and non-verbal elements of interactivity in lectures.

3.2 Interacting in groups, tutorials or seminars

The second type of oral academic communication that Jordan (1997) listed is participation in seminars or group discussions. Generally, seminars aim to provide opportunities to ask questions, to refine understandings and to gain new information. In seminars, the teacher's role is usually to guide the discussion, which for the most part should be carried out by the students themselves. Seminars can take a variety of forms. In a study by Furneaux *et al.* (1991) that examined the different types of seminar and the types of participation expected of students, they identified four types of seminar and a variety of roles that students were expected to play in each seminar type:

- student group work, such as a problem-solving exercise
- nominated students go over prepared answers to case studies
- discussion of material previously assigned for reading by a whole group
- presentation – class members reporting on a reading or research students reporting on their progress.

Furneaux *et al.* (1991) also recommend that part of the bridging role that EAP teachers can perform is to identify the types of seminars common in receiving departments (departments that EAP students aim to enter) and to prepare students for the types of task and expectations of such seminars.

Lynch and Anderson (1992) suggest that the types of difficulty faced by NNS students when participating in seminars include:

- the publicness of the performance
- the need to think on your feet
- the requirement to call up relevant subject knowledge
- the need to present logically ordered arguments
- the fact that your contribution is being assessed.

They emphasize that students face assessment of both the presentation of seminars and also of their *participation* in seminars, even if they are not the principal presenter. To prepare students, they propose the teaching of seminar skills and specifically the oral language related to presentation and language related to participation. Therefore, as Furneaux *et al.* (1991) suggest, it seems that the EAP classroom also needs to anticipate some of these challenges and begin skills development in these areas in terms of some of the oral tasks and practice activities that are introduced.

Jordan (1997: 198–9) suggests that some of sub-skills that relate to participation in a seminar include: *indicating non-comprehension, asking for clarification, questioning* and *disagreeing*. He includes two lists of communicative functions that potentially relate to seminar participation, i.e. those of Tomlins (1993) and Price (1977). Common to both lists are the functions of: *agreeing, disagreeing, expressing an opinion, expressing criticism, making a suggestion, giving an example, giving a reason*. Part of assessed participation may also be the requirement to formulate appropriate questions at the end of a presentation. Lynch and Anderson (1992) also offer some advice about how this may be done, focusing on functions for: indicating that you have a question that you wish to ask; avoiding an answer; and asking a follow-up question (pp. 24–5).

However, Basturkmen (2002: 234) suggests that pedagogic preparation for seminars may also need to go beyond this approach. She notes that where published textbooks offer advice about language for participation in discussions in academic contexts, they tend to focus on unitary functions, such as expressing agreement, disagreement, or requesting clarification or expressing an opinion. However, she suggests that 'this is a view of ideas as existing *a priori*, something a speaker presents rather than something that emerges through interaction' (p. 234). On the other hand, the need to 'think on your feet', as Lynch and Anderson express it, relates to the activity of speakers working together to negotiate and co-construct meaning in an interactive environment. It also suggests that any EAP class preparation for this type of activity needs to take account of the nature of the types of interactions that are likely to occur among seminar participants. In her study of student-to-student interactions in UK university seminars, Basturkmen (2002) examined the types of exchange structure that were common, structures within which ideas were formed. She noted that about 67% of the interactions followed a simple IRF sequence (interaction, response, feedback), but approximately 33% of the interactions, where an interlocutor was dissatisfied with the initial response, followed an IFR/IF(R) structure (initiation, response, feedback that includes a second initiation, second response, second feedback).

Thus, while not discounting the value of teaching the types of functional language used in participatory discussion in seminars, Basturkmen, on the basis of her study, also recommends a complementary focus on the *process* of negotiating and constructing meaning through these types of common exchange structure. As preparation, sequences of discussion could be presented and deconstructed to raise awareness of the negotiation of meaning. She also suggests that in relation to this sub-skill of speaking, EAP course objectives could specify *interlocutor skills* as well as speaker skills, with suggested objectives, such as: 'learners will be able to engage in extended exchanges until a satisfactory outcome is achieved' and 'learners will be able to modify and refine ideas in light of feedback from interlocutors' (p. 140).

3.3   Oral presentations

As well as being audience participants in academic group discussions, students also have to prepare and present academic oral presentations that relate to the content of their course. This type of assessed oral academic activity is becoming increasingly common across a range of disciplines. Within the context of a Canadian university, Zappa-Hollman (2007) carried out an ethnographic study that examined both the role and functions of oral presentations in a range of disciplines, with a particular focus on the experiences of NNS students. In relation to views of both academic staff and students about oral academic presentations (APs), Zappa-Hollman reports:

> The instructors' views on the role of APs were echoed by NES and NNES students, who saw the activity as an opportunity to refine their presentation skills and to rigorously organize their ideas in order to better prepare themselves as future professionals. In addition to this, NNES students also acknowledged another function of APs: the opportunity to practise speaking English. (2007: 469)

However, Zappa-Hollman's study shows that oral presentations also present a particular set of challenges for NNS students in relation to both the preparation and use of oral language when carrying out this type of task in an academic context. In relation to preparation time, the NNS informants in her study took on average 30% longer to prepare an oral presentation than NS students. In terms of the type of language of oral presentations, using 'extemporaneous talk' in an academic context was also identified as a particular area of difficulty for NNS students, specifically when they tried, in making their presentation, to match the NS students' style of speaking from a set of notes and PowerPoint frames, rather than reading a script. This self-reported lack of ability to use extemporaneous talk relates to students feeling that they are unable to 'appear smart' in front of NS student peers. For example, when verbalizing complex concepts (in unplanned situations), they often had to resort to simple language forms and overused vocabulary. However, it was managing the question and answer session after the presentation that was identified as the greatest challenge, as this involves comprehending and responding to unexpected questions and unanticipated viewpoints and orientations towards the subject matter that they have just presented. Also in relation to the speed of delivery of oral presentations by NNS students, a study by Hincks (2010) reports that fluent Swedish speakers of English are, on average, 23% slower when using English than when delivering their presentations in their L1.

Pedagogical advice and materials that relate to academic oral presentations tend to focus on the organization of content, use of language and issues of delivery, such as engaging the audience, kinesics (body language) and handling the question/answer section. For example, in relation to the organization of the language and content of a presentation, Reinhart (2002) considers the language requirements of speeches in relation to different types of communicative purpose. She concentrates on four types of communicative purpose: *describing an object, explaining a process or procedure, defining a concept,* and *describing a problem-solution.* To this one perhaps might reasonably add (for academic settings) the presentation and interpretation of data and the presentation of a discursive argument or case. Reinhart relates the types of communicative purpose to patterns for the internal, cognitive organization for the speech. For example, if the communicative purpose of the speech is to describe an object, she proposes that the internal pattern of the speech may be: spatial, general to specific, or from the most important to the least important part. Reinhart then considers types of linguistic structures that are commonly used to fulfil certain types of communicative purpose. For example, in relation to a presentation that describes a process, she proposes a range of features that relate to the linking of propositions and choice of aspect of verbs (2002: 68).

In relation to interactivity in presentations, Anderson, Maclean and Lynch (2004) focus on the use of the visual elements of communication, body language and how to manage the question and answer session, by suggesting ways of responding to different types of question or comment. This type of pedagogic focus is also important as the academic oral presentation is increasingly becoming a multi-modal genre, and the relation between the multi-modal elements and the presenter's language needs to be carefully examined and managed.

While in an EAP context, a pedagogic focus on academic oral presentations will tend to be on fundamental features that are common to presentations in different disciplinary contexts, it is also important for students to understand that presentations in disciplinary academic contexts will involve appropriating the characteristics and values that relate to the subject discipline in which they occur. This issue is explored in Morton's (2009) study of the oral presentations of architecture students and, in particular, the practices that the students employ to facilitate intended readings of their design by an audience. She suggests that a competence in the use of these practices is 'not necessarily intuitive', but rather is acquired by engagement with and participation in the context subject discipline (p. 218). While the focus on oral presentations in EAP courses (pre-sessional and in-sessional) may be on the fundamentals of language and delivery, students need to be aware that it will be important to overlay these with the particular skills, identities and orientations that typically occur in oral presentations in their particular subject areas.

3.4   Verbalizing data

The final type of oral communication in Jordan's list is verbalizing (describing) data or giving oral instructions. Talking about data or findings has been identified as important in many courses. Jordan (1997) points out that many EAP students reach the point where reading and writing about data, especially numerical data, presents little difficulty; however, verbalizing about numerical data, for example when the data is part of an oral presentation, can be challenging. Jordan suggests that practice needs to be given in the areas of: different ways of expressing numbers (ordinal, cardinal, fractions, formulae, equations, measures) and graphical presentation of data (graphs, tables, histograms, diagrams, charts, plans, maps).

3.5   Non-verbal elements of academic communication

Robinson *et al.* (2001) make the point that the non-verbal aspects of communication, and especially those that relate to academic discussion, is an area of research that has been largely ignored by EAP researchers.

For example, drawing on research from other domains, they make the following points about eye contact (what they refer to as *gaze*) in academic communication:

- Functions of gaze include
  - regulating the flow of conversation through floor-taking signals
  - monitoring feedback
  - influencing audience evaluation
  - expressing emotions

- In Euro-American culture, listeners who gaze more are judged as being more positive (truthful, mature) and speakers who gaze less as more negative (defensive, unconfident).

Robinson *et al.* (2001) in their study found a synthetic, skills-based approach to teaching aspects of non-verbal communication to be more effective than an holistic task-based approach. They also found that acquiring these aspects of communicative ability are a long-term enterprise and are not readily acquired in the short-term.

3.6   Summary: implications of the literature and research on speaking

This review of a number of landmark studies that have examined the speaking skill indicate the need for students in EAP classes to have opportunities to develop this skill in order to be able to perform a range of routines and tasks in academic contexts. There appears to be some evidence that repetition of a speaking activity assists students in internalizing task and content knowledge and, thereby, allows them to focus on the accuracy of their linguistic output. In relation to interactive skills, students need practice in question-forming and other aspects of turn-taking in order to participate effectively in the larger group contexts of lectures as well as in smaller group, tutorial discussions. The review also suggests that extended oral presentations should receive a strong focus in EAP courses and that students should have regular opportunities to develop this skill. As part of this focus, students need to develop awareness of types of procedural knowledge that relate to the presentation of different types of content. In relation to presentations, it seems that for many disciplines students need practice in presenting and discussing numerical data. Also the post-presentation stage of managing questions and providing further extemporaneous discussion of elements of the presentation also needs to be anticipated and worked on.

4.   Incorporating oral skills development into EAP courses: practical issues

The development of the capacity to interact in academic contexts, such as asking questions and making comments in larger lectures as well as more intensive engagement in smaller group discussions, such as seminars and tutorials, has emerged as an important part of the repertoire of oral skills needed by EAP students. The recent retrospective case studies of graduate students by Kim (2006) and Lee (2009) insist that this development of interactivity is essential for EAP courses. However, the prior educational contexts and learning experiences of students will often not have included (or placed any value on) an interactive dimension. Therefore, EAP teachers need to encourage students' regular oral participation in class in order to prepare them for future disciplinary discourses that will assume this interactive capacity. This preparation may begin in small ways and be part of an ongoing, gradual, acculturative process. For example, teachers can incorporate interactivity in their day to day teaching methodology, in both whole-class events and regular small group tasks that require student to student interaction and reporting back to the class.

While the review in the previous section has indicated that students need training in the planning and delivery of effective oral presentations, one practical problem is that individual oral presentations within an EAP class are time-consuming, and much of the time the audience is passive. For this reason, oral presentations are sometimes only included as summative assessments at the end of courses. A possible way of incorporating this type of task on a more regular basis into an EAP course could be mini-oral presentations that can be presented in groups and peer-rated. Teachers can monitor and collate peer feedback. Such smaller group presentations could be a way of helping students to prepare for a larger oral presentation that is a summative assessment task.

In working on the group of skills related to oral presentations, the review of the previous section has indicated that students need to view and analyse video models of presentations, which they can then use as a basis for their own planning. Reinhart's top-down approach to deconstructing the language and content elements of oral presentations can be an example. In addition, video examples can also provide a basis for examining the contextual, multi-modal and interactive elements of oral presentations. It appears that the development of skills in this area requires specific training over quite a period of time, so it seems that this type of training needs to be regular and ongoing.

Finally, in many disciplines, students need to be able to present and discuss quantitative (and qualitative) data. Reporting of data and explanation of a process, which are the communicative purposes of writing tasks, can also be the basis of oral assignments that are woven in with and support writing assignments. As well as writing an essay using an assigned set of data, students can be required to prepare and deliver small oral presentations to groups, fulfilling the same communicative purpose and using the same data set as that employed in the writing task.

5.   Critical thinking and its development

In the final section of Chapter 1, I addressed the debate about whether EAP courses should be accommodationist or critical in terms of their orientation towards the academic world and their preparation of students for participation in academic courses. In that section I questioned the value of aligning with either polarized position in relation to this issue, and proposed that elements of both need to characterize approaches to EAP instruction. An adjunct debate is that which relates to the development of *critical thinking* (hereafter CT). Because CT is commonly identified as an important academic skill, I include some further discussion here, although much of the position that I have taken in relation to this issue has been laid out in Chapter 8 in relation to the developmental stages proposed for academic writers, along with the concomitant discussion about appropriate methodology for the teaching of academic writing. In that chapter, the genre-based approach to writing envisages a *cognitive apprenticeship* approach to the development of CT, such as is proposed by Collins, Brown and Newman (1989). However, since Chapter 8 largely avoids any developed discussion of the debate about the overt teaching of CT, this section addresses the issue.

A central aim of many courses and textbooks (for both L1 and L2 learners) is to develop the skill of CT. However, what is meant by the term and how it is employed have been described in different ways. According to Atkinson (1997), attempts to define CT have generally fallen within two approaches:

- the application of logic to argument – this approach sees critical thinking as a well-defined, rational, transparent teachable set of behaviours – although when pressed, most of those who advocate their teaching have difficulty in defining them (p. 74).

- social practice – an organic part of the culture, which may be a culturally based behaviour. This behaviour is tacit and learned in a largely unconscious way. Teaching academic 'thinking behaviours' overtly is not transferred into other contexts. (p. 72)

The two different approaches to CT give rise to two different approaches to its teaching, which Atkinson terms the *teachable skills* approach which draws on the logical argument approach to critical thinking (p. 77), and the *cognitive apprenticeship* approach, drawing on a social practice approach to critical thinking. (pp. 87–8)

5.1 The teachable skills approach

Traditionally, writing and rhetoric courses have promoted the teaching of CT through writing as a set of fairly abstract, cognitive skills that are not specifically bound to a context. It was thought that the training of writers in the use of a set of generalizable CT skills may be transferred later into disciplinary contexts. An example of the *teachable skills* approach is proposed by Cottrell (1999: 189–96), who presents advice about critical thinking when reading and writing as a set of abstract steps to follow. In relation to reading academic texts, she proposes the steps:

- identify the line of reasoning
- critically evaluate the line of reasoning
- question surface appearances
- identify evidence in the text
- evaluate the evidence
- identify the writer's conclusions
- evaluate whether the evidence supports the conclusions.

In relation to writing, Cottrell advises:

- be clear about your conclusions
- have a clear line of reasoning
- use evidence to support your reasoning
- evaluate your own writing through critical reading.

Focusing more on contextual issues, Thomson (2009: 3) sees CT as *critical questioning* that can be applied to our own and others' work when reading. For example, to compare and understand the ideological viewpoint of texts, she proposes that students ask the following questions:

- Who is the author?
- Are they male or female?
- What are their ethnic origins, their social and political backgrounds?
- What kind of information is useful and/or important to find out about the author?
- In what kind of publication does the work appear?
- What kind of perspective is the author taking in relation to the subject matter?
- What kind of language is used in the publication?
- How reliable is the evidence or supporting information used to substantiate the main points being made?

Although the object knowledge that is the focus of these two writers is different, they both largely reflect the teachable skills approach to critical thinking. The first encourages students to focus on the rhetorical organization of texts, particularly in relation to their staging of an overt argument, while the second principally encourages students to consider authors, their positioning and other contextual issues that may influence the meaning of a text. While they differ in their focus, problems arise in relation to their assumptions about the nature of academic writing and disciplinarity and about students' capacity to make the types of evaluative judgements that both sets of advice are proposing.

First, in relation to the assumptions made about academic writing, much of the advice about critical thinking in this approach relates to the analysis or structuring of an overt, persuasive argument in a text, often about a common issue (such as an environmental problem). The problem with such advice is that although much academic writing does relate to the development and presentation of a case (an argument in a wide sense), the types of general rhetorical purpose involved rarely include overt, persuasive argument. Rather, developing a case in much academic writing involves the marshalling of a range of textual resources and intermeshing rhetorical purposes within an extended piece of writing (see Bruce, 2010). Therefore, writer orientation and the range of textual resources used in the development of a complex case will differ widely in the writing of different disciplines.

The second difficulty that arises relates to the levels of assumed students' background knowledge about any particular text. For example, in order to identify an author's perspective in relation to subject matter (in a disciplinary context), students already need to have a considerable amount of epistemological knowledge about the subject within which the text occurs as well as a considerable amount of prior knowledge of the particular type of texts of the discipline. They need these types of knowledge in order to carry out a critical reading of a text 'within [the particular] field's accepted standards of judgement' (Swales & Feak, 2004: 180). While at one level the steps that Cottrell proposes in relation to reading or writing texts appear systematic and reasonable, they largely ignore the issue that for students to make these types of evaluative judgement about texts, they need to be able to understand the influences of the disciplinary discourses that both surround the text and manifest directly and indirectly through the text.

The teachable skills approach to CT has been challenged by a number of theorists and researchers reviewed by Ramanathan and Kaplan (1996a), who conclude that 'the transfer and general applicability of critical thinking/reasoning skills [across domains] is at best a debatable one' and that the incorporation of CT into writing 'is situated and context/discipline-dependent' (p. 242). This is a view that resonates with the later 'academic literacies' views on the discipline-specificity of knowledge and skills that relate to academic writing. Thus, the principal difficulty with the teachable skills approach is that it does not problematize sufficiently the notion of the expert audience of a particular discourse community, an audience that is the actual consumer of academic writing generated within that community. For example, Ramanathan and Kaplan suggest that

> A publishable manuscript in the social sciences, for instance, often includes certain sectioning conventions, such as a review of prior research, methods, results, and discussion. On a more essential level, a manuscript must reveal certain characteristics, have an *ethos* (in the broadest sense) conforming to the standards of the discourse community (1996b: 30).

5.2 The cognitive apprenticeship approach

The cognitive apprenticeship approach to critical thinking is based on the idea that the students begin as novices in a new academic or discourse community and that they need to learn its practices (including the practice of critical thinking) in the same way that trade apprentices are trained by master tradesmen or people who are qualified experts in their field. In his article, Atkinson (1997: 88) proposes that a social practice approach to critical thinking could be realized in teaching and learning by means of the proposal by Collins, Brown and Newman (1989) that involves three stages of *modelling, coaching* and *fading*, based on the traditional master–apprentice roles in vocational training:

> In this sequence of activities, the apprentice repeatedly observes the master executing (or modeling) the target process, which usually involves some different but interrelated subskills. The apprentice then attempts to execute the process with guidance and help from the master (i.e., coaching). A key aspect of coaching is the provision of scaffolding, which is the support, in the form of reminders and help, that the apprentice requires to approximate the execution of the entire composite of skills. Once the learner has a grasp of the target skill, the master reduces (or fades) his participation, providing only limited hints, refinements, and feedback to the learner, who practices by successively approximating the smooth execution of the whole skill. (Collins, Brown & Newman, 1989: 456)

In Chapter 8, I proposed that for students who aim to join a particular discourse community, the exercise of critical thinking skills is an integral part of their exercise of their discourse competence in relation to the reading and writing of academic texts. In many ways relating the three stages of the cognitive apprenticeship approach to CT (modelling, coaching and fading) is closely related to the four stages of the genre-based approach to the teaching of writing, such as proposed by Hammond *et al.* (1992: 17):

> Stage 1 – building the context or field of the topic or text-type
> Stage 2 – modelling the genre under focus
> Stage 3 – joint construction of the genre
> Stage 4 – independent construction of the genre.

It is proposed here (and in Chapter 8) that discipline-situated CT is inextricably bound to the processing and creation of written and spoken texts within the constraints of the discourses and practices of an academic discipline. Thus, the development of critical thinking skills closely relates to students' development and exercise of discourse competence in English – their ability to process and create written and spoken texts appropriate to a particular discourse community. For example, academic writing textbooks frequently relate critical thinking skills to critique writing. However, as stated previously in this chapter, it is important to acknowledge that critique writing within a discipline requires the writer to 'express evaluative comments within a field's accepted standards of judgement' (Swales & Feak, 2004: 180) on someone else's work. Thus, part of a student's academic development consists of identifying and understanding their field's accepted standards of judgement and the social and linguistic conventions used for expressing this type of judgement. This involves understanding the nature of knowledge as it is conceived within a particular field of study, and attitudes towards that knowledge, particularly in respect of its validation (how new knowledge is proven), in other words, its epistemology. To gain this kind of understanding, it is necessary for a student to read regularly the literature of their field and, importantly, to understand the research methods of the field.

To conclude, the position taken here and reflected in the approaches to teaching academic writing in Chapter 8 is that it is problematic to teach CT in isolation from discipline-specific, contextual knowledge and the discoursal and textual contexts through which such knowledge is communicated. Critical thinking is more than just arranging warrants and proofs in argumentation, such as in oral debate and persuasive writing. Rather, it is embedded in the identities and practices of a subject discourse community, displaying attributes that stem from the particular epistemology and practices that surround the creation and communication of knowledge within that community. Uncovering and acquiring the CT of such an academic community is inextricably bound up with its literate practices and, therefore, is part of the process of gaining a discourse competence in relation to its particular texts and communicative forms.

12
EAP and Assessment

1. Introduction

While general ELT courses aim to teach and assess language proficiency across a wide range of activities and tasks, EAP courses tend to focus more specifically on language outcomes that relate to higher education contexts. Therefore, the sampling of teaching and learning tasks for assessment in EAP courses will tend to include the types of language outcome described in the previous four chapters. It follows, therefore, that the principles that constrain the design of the EAP syllabuses and courses (that focus on these types of academic language as learning outcomes) will also relate to the assessment of those outcomes. For example, in Chapter 4 (Section 2), it was proposed that an EAP syllabus should include:

- a focus on procedural as well as declarative knowledge
- a holistic rather than an atomistic approach to the framing of objectives
- a focus on top-down processing (as a balance to the bottom-up approaches of most second language learning)
- an analytic syllabus organized around larger units of language that are deconstructed and reconstructed in systematic ways

In continuing to consider these principles in relation to assessment, this chapter discusses some key aspects of the assessment of teaching and learning in EAP courses (note that in this chapter I use the terms *assessment* and *testing* interchangeably; while some writers draw a distinction between the two terms, none is made here). However, what is presented here is not a comprehensive overview of EAP course assessment (which would require a separate volume); rather this chapter aims to provide a brief review of some key concepts and principles that relate to language testing with particular reference to EAP courses and a discussion of performance testing in relation to speaking and writing tasks in EAP contexts.

The chapter begins by reviewing some core concepts that relate to the design and implementation of language assessment. On the basis of this review, Section 3 will discuss assessment of the productive skills of writing and speaking within an EAP context, and will consider how the syllabus design principles presented in Chapter 4, Section 2, can relate to the design of assessment.

2. Key concepts in language testing

This section briefly reviews some key concepts of language testing including operationalizing tasks for tests, the test-criterion relationship, types of language test, types of measurement of test outcomes and the concepts of validity and reliability in relation to language testing. In reviewing each of these concepts, reference will be made to the design and use of tests in EAP courses.

2.1 Operationalizing EAP tasks for assessment

Because language is a highly complex phenomenon, the activities of teaching and assessing language (including all of its constituent elements) need to be able to account for this complexity. For example, in EAP courses, holistic tasks related to processing and creating extended spoken or written texts will involve the language learner drawing upon a wide range of skills and types of knowledge. The need to test each of these task elements requires teachers to use frameworks and approaches that will identify and measure the different components of language outputs in ways that are realistic and fair.

Bachman (1990) defines a test as 'a measurement instrument designed to elicit a specific example of an individual's behavior' (p. 20). Thus, a language test may involve any type of task that requires a learner to process or use language in a way that shows either some kind of understanding that is measurable (as in the case of listening or reading tests), or a productive language outcome that is measurable (as in the case of speaking or writing tests). Therefore, it is necessary to consider the issue of operationalizing language for assessment, which means describing the use of language in ways that are measurable.

Models of communicative competence, such as those of Bachman (1990: 87) and the Council of Europe (2001), are an attempt to provide operational descriptions of language that identify all of its component parts in a comprehensive way, as a possible basis for measurement. In Bachman's model, for example, processing and creating extended texts relates mostly to the area of *organizational competence*, which includes the areas of *textual competence* (including *cohesion* and *rhetorical organization*) and *grammatical competence* (including *vocabulary, syntax, morphology, phonemes and graphemes*). Such models provide a starting point for identifying the component areas of knowledge that need to be considered in the assessment of a complex language task in an EAP context, such as listening to and processing a lecture, or writing an extended academic essay. However, when considering language outcomes that involve extended texts from which discourses can be derived, it must be acknowledged that the outcome as a whole is greater than the sum of its constituent parts. That is, while operational definitions for the purpose of assessment need to be able to account for the different knowledge components employed in tasks (such as those identified in communicative competence models), they also need to be able to acknowledge an individual's capacity to *integrate* these different areas of knowledge in language use. Such an operationalization, therefore, requires recourse to theories of text and discourse that can account for the regularized integration and organization of such knowledge components within a piece of text and its discoursal context.

Previous chapters (Chapter 4 addressing syllabus design and Chapter 8 dealing with academic writing) have discussed ways of operationalizing these types of knowledge in an integrative way. Therefore, as an extension of this discussion, it is proposed here that because language learning in the EAP context requires an integrative syllabus and course, it also needs integrative, holistic assessments. Such an approach to assessment is a crucial element in course design in order to avoid the negative washback effects that would result from using types of test that do not support the principles that underpin the EAP syllabus, materials and pedagogy presented in Chapter 4, Section 2. Approaches to holistic assessment are included in Section 3 of this chapter, which discusses EAP performance tests of speaking and writing.

2.2   The test/criterion relationship

It is also important to establish the intended meaning or significance of measurements gained from language testing. Language testing is about getting a learner to use language in a particular way, and then, on the basis of the learner's performance, making inferences about how well that the learner would use the same language in a real-world context. In testing theory, the use of language in the real-world context is known as the *criterion* (McNamara, 2000: 7–8).

In general English language teaching that has the broad aim of overall proficiency development, relating the criterion (proficiency in real-world contexts) to teaching, learning and assessment will tend to be done incrementally by focusing on different areas of knowledge and performance individually as a way of managing the complexity of the process. For example, in a course unit for elementary learners, a unit related to meals and transactions about food may involve learning and using relevant unitary functions, such as offering, accepting, refusing, requesting and thanking. (The same unit may have previously involved some preparatory learning of food vocabulary.) However, in relation to EAP courses, identifying the criterion involves operationalizing the use of language in academic contexts, an activity that can be multi-faceted and constantly changing. Such language uses could involve listening to lectures and making notes, reading textbooks and source materials in order to extract knowledge, knowledge that is then synthesized and presented in an extended essay or an oral seminar presentation. In Chapter 4, it was proposed that the framing of EAP course objectives involves drawing upon theories of text or discourse to develop objectives that are systematic, teachable, learnable and also assessable. Thus, in an EAP situation, outcomes of objectives could involve tasks such as listening to and processing a recorded lecture, participating in a seminar, or reading an article and making notes. The purpose of eliciting examples of students' performance of such tasks in tests is to indicate how a person may perform the same (or similar) task in a real-world university situation, which is the criterion.

Thus, the construction of any type of language test will be influenced by the test designer's theoretical understanding of the nature of language, which may draw upon elements of a model, such as Bachman's model of communicative competence, as well as a theory of text or discourse, such as genre theory. It will also be influenced by his/her understanding of the relationship between a test performance and the criterion. Therefore, important questions to ask about any test task or item are:

- What is the criterion?
- Does the type of task allow the tester to make inferences about the learner's performance in relation to the criterion?

- Does the inference (made in terms of the criterion) provide some kind of realistic feedback to a stakeholder in the teaching/learning process?

2.3   Types of language test

McNamara (2000: 5–7) essentially classifies language tests according to method of testing, which he describes as either *paper and pencil tests* or *performance tests,* and purpose of the test, which may be to measure previous learning (*achievement tests*) or to predict capacity for future language use (*proficiency tests*).

In relation to the *method* of testing, paper and pencil tests can be employed to test separate aspects of linguistic knowledge, such as morphology, syntax, grammar and vocabulary. They are also used to test elements of listening and reading comprehension with some kind of written task. Test items in such tests are often in a fixed response format, such as multiple-choice, true/false, short answer, or some kind of gap fill. Sometimes this type of test can be marked by a machine. The advantages of such tests are they are easy to administer and score, but the problem is that they are not effective in testing the productive skills of speaking and writing (McNamara, 2000: 5).

Performance tests differ from paper and pencil tests in that these are tests where language skills are tested by having the test-taker use language to communicate in some way. Performance tests tend to be used to assess speaking and writing. A test may involve the test taker producing an extended piece of speaking or writing, which is then rated in relation to pre-established criteria (McNamara, 2000: 6). Performance tests of the productive skills are particularly important in the EAP context, and these are the focus of the next section of this chapter.

The other way in which language tests can be categorized is according to the purpose for testing, the two types being achievement tests and proficiency tests. An *achievement* test is any type of measurement of the language that has been learned, usually in the classroom situation. Achievement tests are usually built into the process of instruction. They can vary greatly to reflect the type of language that has been learned in the classroom and the way that it has been learned. They may occur at the end of a unit of learning or at the end of a course. Therefore, achievement tests are retrospective in that they measure what has been learned as the result of teaching. Proficiency tests, on the other hand, look forward to the future situation of language use without necessarily any reference to past teaching. The future 'real-life' language use (in unspecified situations) is the criterion (p. 7). Generally, testing in EAP courses will be retrospective achievement testing that aims to test teaching and learning regularly during a course and at the end of the course. The primary role of such tests is to provide feedback about what has been taught and learned during a course and not necessarily to provide a future prediction of performance, such as the future use of language in a university course.

2.4 Types of measurement of outcomes of tests

Approaches to measuring the outcomes of testing can be broadly categorized in terms of two approaches: *norm-referenced measurement* and *criterion-referenced measurement*. Norm-referenced measurement adopts a framework of comparison between the individuals taking a test for understanding the significance of any one score. Each score is seen in relation to the other scores, particularly in relation to its frequency – i.e. in relation to the number of other people who received the same score. In most fields, norm-referenced measurement assumes that scores will fit within a *normal distribution* – that is a high number of scores will be grouped around the average or mean and the lowest number of scores will be at the top and bottom ends of the distribution.

Criterion-referenced measurement (see Hughes, 2003: 19–22; McNamara, 2000: 64) does not use a comparison between individuals as the frame of reference. Rather, individuals are rated against prose descriptions of satisfactory performance at a given level. In this way performance goals can be set for individuals who can reach these goals at their own rate. In EAP tests of speaking and writing, it is suggested that the regular use of criterion-referenced assessment (such as the analytic marking of essays or oral performance; see Section 3) provides developmental feedback that is more useful to students than norm-referenced scores that merely rank test-takers.

2.5 Validity and reliability

Two other key concepts that need to be considering in planning and implementing any type of language testing are those of *validity* and *reliability* Validity in language testing refers to whether a test actually measures what it claims to be measuring. For example, to test a course unit that has the aim of teaching the oral language of shopping interactions (such as enquiring about an item, asking the price, signalling the intention to buy), it will be appropriate to use a speaking test that has a task that involves a role play, such as a customer communicating with a shop assistant when buying something. The task is valid, since the role play involves the oral use of the same language which would be used in a real shopping transaction. A less valid test, however, would be to require the test-taker to write a shopping dialogue.

Validity often needs to be considered when selecting types of testing items that will be used in any test. A valid selection will depend on the object knowledge and the learner skill that is being examined in the test. Generally, test items are divided into those that are used either in *direct testing* or in *indirect testing*.

Direct testing is asking the student to perform the skill that is the object of the test, and is generally easier to carry out when testing the productive skills of speaking and writing. For example, testing essay writing by getting students to write an essay is an example of direct testing. Testing speaking in the context of oral presentation skills by asking students to prepare and deliver a short oral presentation is direct testing. Reading and listening, on the other hand, are less amenable to direct testing. With these skills, testing usually involves performing the skill and then providing a written response that shows how successfully the skill has been employed.

Indirect tests measure the underlying, separate content knowledge and language components that are integrated in actual language use. Such underlying components may include grammar, vocabulary and syntax. An example of the indirect testing of writing is an earlier version of the TOEFL test of writing, which used to be a multiple choice test of vocabulary, grammar and syntax. This indirect testing of writing is justified by the claim that knowledge of these elements correlates with ability to write a piece of text. Generally, it would now be considered that a multiple-choice test of linguistic knowledge does not completely operationalize the writing skill and, therefore, is not a valid test of writing.

Reliability refers to the consistency of measurement that a test provides when it is used on more than one occasion. Hughes (2003: 94) proposes guidelines for ensuring validity and reliability, advising:

- set tasks which can be reliably scored
- restrict candidates choice of tasks or give no choice of tasks to ensure comparability
- (in writing texts) ensure that the tasks elicit a sufficiently long sample of written text and,
- create appropriate rating scales for scoring.

After developing a test that relates both to the context of learning and content of the course, it is then important to plan the scoring of a text either by developing a schedule of answers for short items or a marking guide (set of criteria) for larger tasks.

3.   Performance tests in EAP contexts: testing speaking and writing

In this section, I briefly discuss performance testing of the speaking and writing skills and some of the key issues that need to be considered in planning this type of test. In relation to both skills, I advocate the use of performance tests based on genres combined with the use of analytic scoring as a way of comprehensively assessing the different elements of academic tasks. In Chapter 8 it was proposed that the genre-based approach to teaching and learning the writing skill involves deconstructing and practising elements of a target genre (category of texts) as a basis for creating new examples of the same genre. As an extension of this approach to teaching and learning, a sample of the same target genre is then elicited in a performance test. *Analytic scoring* involves assigning scores to a number of aspects of a student's output (such as the elements of knowledge of an oral presentation or an academic essay). The overall score is then derived from the sum of the component scores allocated to the different elements of the language output. (References to examples of analytic scoring are provided in each of the following sub-sections on speaking and writing.) However, in order to ensure construct validity in this approach to assessment, care needs to be taken over the operationalization of a test task, such as the genre elements identified for separate attention in the analytic scoring, along with the weightings of scores assigned to each of the task elements.

Hughes (2003) suggests that the advantages of analytic scoring are that it requires the even development of sub-skills, in that scorers are required to look at a range of aspects of the speaker's or writer's performance. While scoring in this way is more time-consuming than providing a grade based on overall impression (holistic scoring), it is proposed that an analytic approach provides more developmental feedback for students, and complements a genre-based approach to pedagogy by focusing on a range of task elements.

3.1   How should the speaking skill be tested?

Achievement testing should be carried out in relation to clearly articulated and understood teaching and learning objectives. Therefore, a speaking test that is valid should elicit a sample of speaking for assessment that reflects the teaching and learning objectives and related activities of the course unit that it assesses. The test measurement should then provide a basis for feedback about a student's achievement in relation to the teaching and learning objectives of the course. However, providing useful feedback to test-takers about a performance achievement test requires the salient elements of the target output, such as an oral presentation, to be transparent and identifiable for the purposes of both pedagogy and assessment.

In Chapter 11, which focused on the aspects of the speaking skill to be developed in EAP courses, a range of academic speaking activities were identified, including asking questions in lectures, participation in seminars or tutorial discussions, making oral presentations (including answering audience questions or responding to audience comments), verbalizing data, and giving oral instructions in seminars/workshops/laboratories (Jordan, 1997: 193). Chapter 11 also reviewed research that indicates value in repeated practice of these types of routine spoken activity in order to automatize aspects of task performance. The research findings appear to suggest that the teaching of oral skills (related to these tasks) should be by means of a modified, task-based approach. As an extension of this approach to pedagogy, it is argued here that the most appropriate assessment of academic speaking activities is performance testing of a representative sample of the tasks that have been presented and practised in class. As part of this approach, it is also proposed that analytic scoring should be carried out on the basis of pre-established criteria that relate to elements that are most salient to the fulfilment of the task. In this way, the aim is for the speaking test to be a formative, developmental exercise that provides feedback that supports and reinforces the learning process.

3.2   Operationalizing the speaking skill for assessment

In developing speaking tests, such as tests of the types of academic speaking activity identified in Chapter 11, it is first necessary to consider the range of elements or components of the speaking skill that a target activity may draw upon. To identify elements of the content, its organization and aspects of the delivery of the spoken message, Bygate (1987) offers a taxonomy that groups task features into those relate to informational skills, interactional skills, texts, topics and vocabulary. For example, the content elicited by a particular speaking test task may be judged in terms of the amount of information that is successfully conveyed, the relevance of the information that is conveyed and the social appropriateness of the information that is conveyed. In relation to the actual sounds of the language that the speaker produces in

English, this may include such elements of phonology as pronunciation, stress timing and intonation.

However, when considering the assessable elements of a speaking outcome, it is important to identify those aspects of an oral performance that are most salient to the fulfilment of the particular task, and to establish weightings that reflect this importance in any measurement that is carried out. An example of a genre-focused approach to teaching and assessing an oral presentation is offered by Reinhart (2002: 59–84) in relation to presentations that explain a process. This particular teaching and learning unit offers a top-down approach to deconstructing and practising the organizational, linguistic and paralinguistic features of the presentation of a process, including elements that relate to:

- introductions – opening with rhetorical questions, providing background information, such as the definition of the process, the purpose of the process, other important definitions, equipment and material used in the process, the people involved in the process, the number of steps in the process
- staging of the process – sequential steps, use of 'linking' words, use of 'let's' to include the audience, use of the informational present, choice of the active or passive voice, use of imperatives to explain how to carry out a task, use of modal in instructions, non-use of modals in explanations.

After the assessable elements (and their relative importance) are identified, the next step is to establish performance criteria that provide a basis for making evaluative judgements about each of the task elements. For example, the salient elements that relate to the delivery of a monologic, oral presentation will differ from those that relate to participation in a seminar discussion. In the case of the oral presentation, it is likely that the schematic organization of content and its delivery in ways that are informationally accessible and comprehensible to an audience will provide parameters for identifying and selecting the most salient assessment criteria.

In the case of the example of Reinhart's unit, she offers an analytic, criterion-referenced assessment schedule entitled a *Process Speech Evaluation form* (Reinhart, 2002: 80–1), which requires scoring of the individual components that relate to the oral presentation of topic, introduction, process (organization), transitions, grammar, pace, eye contact, gestures, loudness, interaction with the audience, use of equipment, pronunciation, and other comments. In relation to each of these elements, descriptors are provided to guide the assessor. However, in relation to assessing participation in a seminar discussion, performance elements related to the communication of meaning in oral interactions and the management of turn-taking will clearly be salient elements that relate to the fulfilment of the task, such as developing a line of questioning, responding to questions, making suggestions and reformulating and elaborating responses, and body language related to effective interactional engagement.

3.3   How should the writing skill be tested?

While academic courses increasingly use oral assignments and require active, oral participation, it is likely that for most students, writing will still be the productive skill that is most important for their participation in academic courses. Chapter 8 included a discussion of methodology and curriculum in relation to the teaching of the writing skill in an academic context, a discussion that advocated a genre-based approach to the teaching of academic writing. This approach also has implications for writing assessment. As was proposed in relation to the assessment of speaking, it is proposed here that writing should also be assessed by means of a direct, performance test, an idea that is supported by Hughes' (2003: 83) assertion that no satisfactory way of testing writing indirectly has yet been devised. However while setting a whole writing task may seem relatively uncomplicated, the issue of the assessment of an extended piece of writing is complex because of the many types of knowledge that are employed in any writing task. The assessment of an extended piece of writing needs to account for an integration of contextual and content knowledge, organizational knowledge and linguistic knowledge.

As Hyland (2004: 163) points out, an important argument for using a genre-based approach to teaching and assessing writing is that it provides an integrative approach to the different types of knowledge involved, and enables the establishment of criteria for the evaluation of a writing outcome that are transparent. The extended discussion in Chapter 8 supports the use of genre constructs for classifying and analysing whole texts for the purpose of the teaching of academic writing; however, it also acknowledges that this is still an area which has a variety of competing theories and approaches, many of which refer to common areas of knowledge while they often use different terminologies, which can lead to confusion. Therefore, when assessing (like teaching) writing, it is important to identify the salient elements of the underlying genre constructs in order to establish assessment criteria that are appropriate and transparent.

3.4   Operationalizing writing for assessment

As I pointed out in Chapter 5, Section 5, the categorization of texts in terms of genre tends to operate at two levels:

- texts identified in terms of a clearly recognized social purpose, such as newspaper editorials, letters to the editor, news reports, novels, and research articles in academic journals
- texts (or segments of texts) identified in terms a single type of communicative or rhetorical purpose, such as narrative, exposition, argument.

There and in other chapters in this book, I have responded to this problem with the social genre and cognitive genre model. In relation to planning the assessment of writing, a similar approach to the categorization of writing outcomes is adopted by Hughes (2003: 84), who calls cognitive genres (relating to a single communicative purpose) *operations* and social genres *types of texts*. Thus, it is important to decide whether a piece of writing elicited by a test task will focus on a cognitive genre or the production of a social genre. This decision has to be taken by means of a close examination of the focus of the teaching and learning objectives employed in a particular context and the type of genre construct that they relate to.

The next step is to consider how the elements of genre knowledge that should be included in the piece of writing can be described and measured. In using a genre-based approach, this again suggests that an analytic approach to scoring will be adopted. An example of an analytic scoring guide for writing may be found in Hughes (2003: 101–2), which contains graded descriptors under the five areas of grammar, vocabulary, mechanics, fluency and form (organization). In relation to a larger piece of writing, the social genre of an investigative report project, Hyland (2004: 176) offers a similar analytic scoring guide with graded descriptors under the three areas of format and content, organization and coherence, sentence construction and vocabulary. In relation to the assessment of a smaller cognitive genre (text type) writing segment, I have proposed a scoring guide that relates to the scoring of the Report cognitive genre, a segment of writing that is primarily concerned with the presentation of data that is non-chronological (Bruce, 2008a: 149).

This guide requires analytic scoring of three broad areas: task response (structuring of ideas), discourse organization (overall textual organization, paragraph sequencing, cohesion) and vocabulary and sentence structure.

Thus, in designing a writing assessment (as with speaking), it is important to identify the context of learning within which a test occurs. The aims and objectives of the language unit or course book chapter being tested should be clearly understood and should guide the choices that are made in developing both the test and the approach to its scoring. Thus the writing task of the test should mirror the types of writing outcomes that have been practised in the course, which in the case of a genre-based course will have involved the explicit identification of, deconstruction and practice of the component knowledge types. Once the genre focus of the text task has been established, it will be possible to identify the separate knowledge components that have to be considered and to establish the criteria in an analytic marking guide for making assessment judgements.

4. Conclusion

In this chapter, genre-based instruction, performance testing (of speaking and writing) and the analytic scoring of productive tasks are all proposed with the aim of developing the discourse competence of EAP students. While this approach to testing and scoring is more time-consuming than other approaches, it provides the type of developmental feedback required in order that students develop discourse competence. This chapter has been included to advocate this approach to testing, for the reason that the washback effect of testing is powerful; testing can either support or undermine learning, despite the types of methodological choices made in syllabus design, materials development and pedagogy. The four principles that were proposed in Chapter 4 to underpin EAP course development and pedagogy are worth spelling out once more at the end of our discussion of assessment:

- a focus on procedural as well as declarative knowledge
- a holistic rather than an atomistic approach to the framing of objectives
- a focus on top-down (as well as bottom-up) processing
- an analytic syllabus organized around larger units of language that are deconstructed and reconstructed in systematic ways.

It is important that these principles not be undermined by negative washback from the forms of testing that are employed in EAP courses. Therefore, to support the ongoing development of discourse competence, it is proposed that testing of the productive skills should be by means of eliciting whole-task, genre-based outcomes that are evaluated by using analytic scoring.

References

Adam, C. & Artemeva, N. (2002). Writing instruction in English for academic purposes (EAP) classes: Introducing second language learners to the academic community. In A. M. Johns (ed.), *Genre in the Classroom: Multiple Perspectives*. Mahwah, NJ: Lawrence Erlbaum Associates, pp. 179–96.

Adam, J.-M. (1985). Quels types de textes? *Le Français dans le Monde, 192*: 39–43.

Adam, J.-M. (1992). *Les Textes: Types et propotypes*. Paris: Nathan.

Alexander, O., Argent, S. & Spencer, J. (2008). *EAP Essentials: A Teacher's Guide to Principles and Practice*. Reading, England: Garnet.

Allison, D. & Benesch, S. (1994). Comments on Sarah Benesch's 'ESL, Ideology, and the Politics of Pragmatism'. *TESOL Quarterly, 28*(3): 618–24.

Allison, D. & Tauroza, S. (1995). The effect of discourse organisation on lecture comprehension. *English for Specific Purposes, 14*(2): 157–73.

Anderson, K., Maclean, J. & Lynch, T. (2004). *Study Speaking: A Course in Spoken English for Academic Purposes* (2nd edn). Cambridge: Cambridge University Press.

Artemeva, N. (2008). Toward a unified social theory of genre learning. *Journal of Business and Technical Communication, 22*(2): 160–85.

Atkinson, D. (1997). A critical approach to critical thinking in TESOL. *TESOL Quarterly, 31*(1): 71–94.

Bachman, L. F. (1990). *Fundamental Considerations in Language Testing*. Oxford: Oxford University Press.

Badger, R. & White, G. (2000). A process genre approach to teaching writing. *ELT Journal, 54*(2): 153–60.

Bakhtin, M. M. (1986). *Speech Genres and Other Late Essays* (Trans. V. W. McGee). Austin, TX: University of Texas Press.

BALEAP (2008). *Competency Framework for Teachers of English for Academic Purposes [CFTEAP]*. Retrieved from http://www.baleap.org.uk/teap/teap-competency-framework.pdf.

Barron, C. (2003). Problem-solving and EAP: Themes and issues in a collaborative teaching venture. *English for Specific Purposes, 22*(3): 297–314.

Barsalou, L. W. (1992). Frames, concepts and conceptual fields. In A. Lehrer & E. Feder Kittay (eds.), *Frames, Fields and Contrasts: New Essays in Semantic and Lexical Organization*. Hillsdale, NJ: Lawrence Erlbaum Associates, pp. 21–74.

Basturkmen, H. (2002). Negotiating meaning in seminar-type discussion and EAP. *English for Specific Purposes, 21*(3): 233–42.

Bauman, J. & Culligan, B. (1995). The general service list. From http://www.auburn.edu/~nunnath/engl6240/wlistgen.html

Benesch, S. (1993). ESL, ideology, and the politics of pragmatism. *TESOL Quarterly, 27*(4): 705–17.

Benesch, S. (2001). *Critical English for Academic Purposes: Theory, Politics, and Practice*. Mahwah, NJ: Lawrence Erlbaum.

Benson, P. (2001). *Teaching and Researching Autonomy in Language Learning.* Harlow: Longman.

Bhatia, V. K. (1993). *Analysing Genre: Language Use in Professional Settings.* Harlow: Longman.

Bhatia, V. K. (1998). Generic conflicts in academic discourse. In T. Dudley-Evans & I. Fortanet Gomez (eds.), *Genre Studies in English for Academic Purposes.* Castello de la Plana: Publ. de la Univ. Jaume, pp. 15–28.

Bhatia, V. K. (2002). Applied genre analysis: Analytical advances and pedagogical problems. In A. M. Johns (ed.), *Genre in the Classroom: Multiple Perspectives.* Mahwah, NJ: Lawrence Erlbaum Associates, pp. 279–83.

Bhatia, V. K. (2004). *Worlds of Written Discourse.* New York: Continuum.

Biber, D. (1989). A typology of English texts. *Linguistics, 27*(1): 3–44.

Biber, D. (2006). *University Language: A Corpus-based Study of Spoken and Written Registers.* Amsterdam: John Benjamins.

Biber, D. & Finegan, E. (1989). Styles of stance in English: Lexical and grammatical marking of evidentiality and affect. *Text, 9*(1): 93–124.

Biber, D., Conrad, S. A. & Reppen, R. (1998). *Corpus Linguistics: Investigating Language Structure and Use.* Cambridge: Cambridge University Press.

Bizzell, P. (1993). Review: Patricia Bizzell's response. *Rhetoric Society Quarterly, 23*(1): 50–2.

Bloor, M. (1998). Variations in the methods sections of research articles across disciplines: The case of fast and slow text. In P. Thompson (ed.), *Issues in EAP Writing, Research and Instruction.* Reading, England: CALS, University of Reading, pp. 84–106.

Blue, G. (1988). Individualising academic writing tuition. In P. C. Robinson (ed.), *Academic Writing: Process and Product.* London: Modern English Publications and The British Council, pp. 95–9.

Borg, E. (2003). Key concepts in ELT: Discourse community. *ELT Journal, 57*(4): 398–400.

Braine, G. (1989). Writing in science and technology: An analysis of assignments from ten undergraduate courses. *English for Specific Purposes, 8*(1): 3–15.

Braine, G. (1995). Writing in the natural sciences and engineering. In D. Dewhurst Belcher & G. Braine (eds.), *Academic Writing in a Second Language: Essays on Research and Pedagogy.* Norwood, NJ: Ablex Publishing Corporation, pp. 113–34.

Brett, P. (1994). A genre analysis of sociology articles. *English for Specific Purposes, 13*(1): 47–59.

Brown, G. & Yule, G. (1983). *Discourse Analysis.* Cambridge: Cambridge University Press.

Bruce, I. (2003). Cognitive Genre Prototype Modelling and its Implications for the Teaching of Academic Writing to Learners of English as a Second Language. Unpublished PhD dissertation, University of Waikato, New Zealand.

Bruce, I. (2005). Syllabus design for general EAP writing courses: A cognitive approach. *Journal of English for Academic Purposes, 4*(3): 239–56.

Bruce, I. (2006). Opportunities to develop discourse competence in writing: an analysis of New Zealand English curriculum documents. *New Zealand Journal of Educational Studies, 41*(2): 205–22.

Bruce, I. (2007). Defining academic genres: An approach for writing course design. In O. Alexander (ed.), *New Approaches to Materials Development for*

Language Learning. Proceedings of the 2005 joint BALEAP/SATEFL conference. Oxford: Peter Lang, pp. 103–16.

Bruce, I. (2008a). *Academic Writing and Genre: A Systematic Analysis.* London: Continuum.

Bruce, I. (2008b). Cognitive genre structures in Methods sections of research articles: A corpus study. *Journal of English for Academic Purposes, 7*(1): 38–54.

Bruce, I. (2009). Results sections in sociology and organic chemistry articles: A genre analysis. *English for Specific Purposes, 28*(2): 105–24.

Bruce, I. (2010). Textual and discoursal resources used in the essay genre in sociology and English. *Journal of English for Academic Purposes, 9*(3): 153–66.

Bruffee, K. A. (1995). *Collaborative Learning: Higher Education, Interdependence, and the Authority of Knowledge.* Baltimore: Johns Hopkins University Press.

Bruner, J. S. (1975). Beyond the information given. In J. Entwhistle & D. Hounsell (eds.), *How Students Learn.* Lancaster: Institute for Post-Compulsory Education, Lancaster University, pp. 105–16.

Bush, D. (1995). Writing at university: What faculty require. *EA Journal, 13*(2): 16–28.

Butt, D., Fahey, R., Feez, S., Spinks, S. & Yallop, C. (2000). *Using Functional Grammar: An Explorer's Guide.* (2nd edn). Sydney: National Centre for English Language Teaching and Research.

Bygate, M. (1987). *Speaking.* Oxford: Oxford University Press.

Bygate, M. (1996). Effects of task repetition: Appraising learners' performances on tasks. In D. Willis & J. Willis (eds.), *Challenge and Change in Language Teaching.* London: Heinemann, pp. 136–46.

Bygate, M. (1998). Theoretical perspectives on speaking. *Annual Review of Applied Linguistics, 18*: 20–42.

Bygate, M. (2001). Effects of task repetition on the structure and control of language. In M. Bygate, P. Skehan & M. Swain (eds.), *Task-based Learning: Language Teaching, Learning and Assessment.* London: Longman, pp. 23–48.

Bygate, M. (2006). Areas of research that influence L2 speaking instruction. In E. Usó-Juan and A. Martínez-Flor (eds.), *Current Trends in the Development and Teaching of the Four Language Skills.* (Studies on Language Acquisition series). Berlin: Walter de Gruyter, pp. 159–86.

Bygate, M., & Samuda, V. (2005). Oral second language abilities as expertise. In R. Ellis (ed.), *Planning and Task Performance in a Second Language.* Amsterdam: Benjamins, pp. 37–74.

Canagarajah, A. S. (2002). *Critical Academic Writing and Multilingual Students.* Ann Arbor, MI: University of Michigan Press.

Canale, M. (1983). On some dimensions of language proficiency. In J. R. Oller Jr (ed.), *Issues in Language Testing Research.* Rowley, MA: Newbury House, pp. 333–42.

Canseco, G. & Byrd, P. (1989). Writing required in graduate courses in business administration. *TESOL Quarterly, 23*(2): 305–16.

Cauldwell, R. T. (1996). Direct encounters with fast speech on CD-audio to teach listening. *System, 24*(4): 521–8.

Celce-Murcia, M., Dörnyei, Z. & Thurrell, S. (1995). Communicative competence: A pedagogically motivated model with content specifications. *Issues in Applied Linguistics, 6*(2): 5–35.

Charles, M. (2003). 'This mystery ...': A corpus-based study of the use of nouns to construct stance in theses from two contrasting disciplines. *Journal of English for Academic Purposes, 2*(4): 313–26.

Christie, F. (1990). *Literacy for a Changing World.* Hawthorn, Victoria: Australian Council for Educational Research.

Cobb, T. (1997). Is there any measurable learning from hands-on concordancing? *System, 25*(3): 301–15.

Cobb, T. & Horst, M. (2001). Reading academic English: Carrying learners across the lexical threshold. In J. Flowerdew & M. Peacock (eds.), *Research Perspectives on English for Academic Purposes.* Cambridge: Cambridge University Press, pp. 315–29.

Coffey, B. (1984). ESP – English for Specific Purposes. *Language Teaching, 17*(1): 2–16.

Cohen, L., Manion, L. & Morrison, K. (2007). *Research Methods in Education* (6th edn). London: Routledge.

Collins, A., Brown, J. S. & Newman, S. F. (1989). Cognitive apprenticeship: Teaching the crafts of reading, writing and mathematics. In R. Glaser & L. B. Resnick (eds.), *Knowing, Learning and Instruction.* Hillsdale, NJ: Lawrence Erlbaum Associates, pp. 453–94.

Connor, U. & Mauranen, A. (1999). Linguistic analysis of grant proposals: European Union research grants. *English for Specific Purposes, 18*(1): 47–62.

Cook, M. & Liddicoat, A. (2002). The development of comprehension in inter-language pragmatics: The case of request strategies in English. *Australian Review of Applied Linguistics, 25*(1): 19–39.

Cottrell, S. (1999). *The Study Skills Handbook.* Basingstoke: Palgrave Macmillan.

Council of Europe. (2001). *Common European Framework of Reference for Languages: Learning, Teaching, Assessment.* Cambridge: Press Syndicate of the University of Cambridge.

Coxhead, A. (2000). A new academic word list. *TESOL Quarterly, 34*(2): 213–38.

Coxhead, A. & Nation, P. (2001). The specialised vocabulary of English for academic purposes. In J. Flowerdew & M. Peacock (eds.), *Research Perspectives on English for Academic Purposes.* Cambridge: Cambridge University Press, pp. 252–67.

Crawford Camiciottoli, B. (2007). *Language of Business Study Lectures: A Corpus-assisted Analysis.* Amsterdam: John Benjamins.

Crombie, W. (1985). *Process and Relation in Discourse and Language Learning.* Oxford: Oxford University Press.

Csomay, E. (2007). A corpus-based look at linguistic variation in classroom inter-action: Teacher talk versus student talk in American university classes. *Journal of English for Academic Purposes, 6*(4): 336–55.

DeCarrico, J. & Nattinger, J. R. (1988). Lexical phrases for the comprehension of academic lectures. *English for Specific Purposes, 7*(2): 91–102.

Derewianka, B. (1990). *Exploring How Texts Work.* Sydney: Primary English Teaching Association.

Devitt, A. J. (2004). *Writing Genres.* Carbondale, IL: Southern Illinois University Press.

Dijk, T. A. van (1980). *Macrostructures: An Interdisciplinary Study of Global Structures in Discourse, Interaction, and Cognition.* Hillsdale, NJ: Lawrence Erlbaum Associates.

Dudley-Evans, A. (1986). Genre analysis: An investigation of the introductions and discussion sections of MSc dissertations. In M. Coulthard (ed.), *Talking about Text*. Birmingham: University of Birmingham Press, pp. 128–45.

Dudley-Evans, A. (1993). Variation in communication patterns between discourse communities: The case of highway engineering and plant biology. In G. M. Blue (ed.), *Language, Learning and Success: Studying through English*. (British Council ELT Review series). London: Longman, Macmillan, Prentice Hall, pp. 141–7.

Dudley-Evans, T. (1989). An outline of the value of genre analysis in LSP work. In C. Lauren & M. Nordman (eds.), *Special Language: From Humans Thinking to Thinking Machines*. Clevedon: Multilingual Matters, pp. 72–9.

Dudley-Evans, T. (1994). Genre analysis: An approach to text analysis in ESP. In M. Coulthard (ed.), *Advances in Written Text Analysis*. London: Routledge, pp. 219–28.

Dudley-Evans, A. & Johns, T. A. (1981). *A Team Teaching Approach to Lecture Comprehension for Overseas Students in the Teaching of Listening Comprehension*. London: The British Council.

Dudley-Evans, T. & St John, M. J. (1998). *Developments in English for Specific Purposes: A Multi-disciplinary Approach*. Cambridge: Cambridge University Press.

Duff, P. A. (2002). The discursive co-construction of knowledge, identity, and difference: An ethnography of communication in the high school mainstream. *Applied Linguistics, 23*(3): 289–322.

Dunmore, D. (1989). Using contextual clues to infer word meaning: An evaluation of current exercise types. *Reading in a Foreign Language, 6*(1): 337–47.

Eblen, C. (1983). Writing across-the-curriculum: A survey of a university faculty's views and classroom practices. *Research in the Teaching of English, 17*(4): 343–8.

Eggins, S. (1994). *An Introduction to Systemic Functional Linguistics*. London: Pinter.

Eggins, S. (1996). *An Introduction to Systemic Functional Linguistics* (2nd edn). London: Continuum.

Elbow, P. (1981). *Writing with Power: Techniques for Mastering the Writing Process*. New York: Oxford University Press.

Ellis, G. D. & Sinclair, B. (1989). *Learning to Learn English: A Course in Learner Training*. Cambridge: Cambridge University Press.

Elton, L. (2008). Academic writing and tacit knowledge. Paper presented at the Centre for Excellence in Enquiry-Based learning (CEEBL), University of Manchester, 20 February.

Emig, J. A. (1971). *The Composing Processes of Twelfth Graders*. Urbana, ILL: National Council of Teachers of English.

Feez, S. (2002). Heritage and innovation in second language education. In A. M. Johns (ed.), *Genre in the Classroom: Multiple Perspectives*. Mahwah, NJ: Lawrence Erlbaum Associates, pp. 43–69.

Ferris, D. (1998). Students' views of academic aural/oral skills: A comparative needs analysis. *TESOL Quarterly, 32*(2): 289–318.

Ferris, D. & Tagg, T. (1996). Academic oral communication needs of EAP learners: What subject-matter instructors actually require. *TESOL Quarterly, 30*(1): 31–58.

Field, J. (1999). 'Bottom-up' and 'top-down'. *ELT Journal, 53*(4): 338–9.

Field, J. (2003). Promoting perception: Lexical segmentation in L2 listening. *ELT Journal, 57*(4): 325–34.

Flavell, J. H. (1976). Metacognitive aspects of problem solving. In L. B. Resnick (ed.), *The Nature of Intelligence*. Hillsdale, NJ: Lawrence Erlbaum Associates, pp. 231–5.

Flower, L. & Hayes, J. R. (1981). A cognitive process theory of writing. *College Composition and Communication, 32*(4): 365–87.

Flowerdew, J. (1992). Definitions in science lectures. *Applied Linguistics, 13*(2): 202–21.

Flowerdew, J. (2002). Corpus-based analyses in EAP. In J. Flowerdew (ed.) *Academic Discourse*. London: Longman.

Flowerdew, J. & Miller, L. (2005). *Second Language Listening: Theory and Practice*. Cambridge: Cambridge University Press.

Flowerdew, J. A. & Peacock, M. (2001). *Research Perspectives on English for Academic Purposes*. Cambridge: Cambridge University Press.

Flowerdew, L. (2005). An integration of corpus-based and genre-based approaches to text analysis in EAP/ESP: Countering criticisms against corpus-based methodologies. *English for Specific Purposes, 24*(3): 321–32.

Fortanet, I. (2004). The use of 'we' in university lectures: reference and function. *English for Specific Purposes, 23*(1): 45–66.

Foucault, M. (1977). *Discipline and Punish: The Birth of the Prison* (Trans. A. Sheridan). London: Penguin.

Foucault, M. (1980). Power and strategies. In C. Gordon (ed.), *Power/Knowledge: Selected Interviews and Other Writings, 1972–1977*. New York: Pantheon Books.

Fowler, A. (1982). *Kinds of Literature: An Introduction to the Theory of Genres and Modes*. Cambridge, MA: Harvard University Press.

Freedman, A. & Medway, P. (1994). *Learning and Teaching Genre*. Portsmouth, NH: Boynton/Cook Publishers.

Freire, P. (1979). *Reading and Writing Reality: Explorations into Adult Education*. New Delhi: Vishwa Yuvak Kendra.

Freire, P. (1994). *Pedagogy of Hope: Reliving Pedagogy of the Oppressed* (Trans. A. M. A. Freire & P. Freire). New York: Continuum.

Furneaux, C., Locke, C., Robinson, P. & Tonkyn, A. (1991). Talking heads and shifting bottoms: The ethnography of academic seminars. In P. Adams, B. Heaton & P. Howarth (eds.), *Socio-cultural Issues in English for Academic Purposes*. London: Macmillan Education, pp. 74–87.

Geertz, C. (1973). Thick description: Towards an interpretive theory of culture. In C. Geertz (ed.), *The Interpretation of Cultures*. New York: Basic Books.

Givón, T. (1995). Coherence in text vs. coherence in mind. In M. Gernsbacher & T. Givón (eds.), *Coherence in Spontaneous Text*. Amsterdam: John Benjamins, pp. 59–116.

Goh, C. (2008). Metacognitive instruction for second language listening development: Theory, practice and research implications. *RELC Journal, 39*(2): 188–213.

Goodman, K. S. (1967). Reading: A psycholinguistic guessing game. *Journal of the Reading Specialist, 4*: 126–35.

Gough. P. B. (1972). One second of reading. *Visible Language, 6*(4): 291–20.

Grabe, W. (2002). Narrative and expository macro-genres. In A. M. Johns (ed.), *Genre in the Classroom: Multiple Perspectives*. Mahwah, NJ: Lawrence Erlbaum Associates, pp. 249–67.

Grabe, W. & Stoller, F. L. (2002). *Teaching and Researching Reading*. Harlow: Longman.

Gumperz, J. J. (1972). Introduction. In J. J. Gumperz & D. Hymes (eds.), *Directions in Sociolinguistics*. New York: Holt, Rinehart and Winston, pp. 1–25.

Hale, G., Taylor, C., Bridgeman, B., Carson, J., Kroll, B. & Kantor, R. (1996). *A Study of Writing Tasks Assigned in Academic Degree Programs*. Princeton, NJ: Educational Testing Service.

Hall, J. K. (1993). The role of oral practices in the accomplishment of our everyday lives: The sociocultural dimension of interaction with implications for the learning of another language. *Applied Linguistics, 14*(2): 145–66.

Halliday, M. A. K. & Hasan, R. (1976). *Cohesion in English*. London: Longman.

Hammond, J., Burns, A., Joyce, H., Brosnan, D. & Gerot, L. (1992). *English for Social Purposes: A Handbook for Teachers of Adult Literacy*. Sydney: National Centre for English Language Teaching and Research.

Hasan, R. (1978). Text in the systemic functional mode. In W. Dressler (ed.), *Current Trends in Text Linguistics*. Berlin: Walter de Gruyter, pp. 51–72.

Hasan, R. (1989). The identity of a text. In M. A. K. Halliday & R. Hasan (eds.), *Language, Text and Context*. Oxford: Oxford University Press, pp. 97–118.

Hincks, R. (2010). Speaking rate and information content in English lingua franca oral presentations. *English for Specific Purposes, 29*(1): 4–18.

Hirsh, D. & Nation, P. (1992). What vocabulary size is needed to read unsimplified texts for pleasure? *Reading in a Foreign Language, 8*(2): 689–96.

Hirvela, A. (2004). *Connecting Reading and Writing in Second Language Writing Instruction*. Ann Arbor: University of Michigan Press.

Hoey, M. (1979). *Signalling in Discourse* (Discourse Analysis Monograph No. 6). Birmingham: English Language Research, University of Birmingham.

Hoey, M. (1983). *On the Surface of Discourse*. London: George Allen & Unwin.

Hoey, M. (1991). *Patterns in Lexis in Text*. Oxford: Oxford University Press.

Hoey, M. (1994). Signalling in discourse: A functional analysis of a common discourse pattern in spoken and written English. In M. Coulthard (ed.), *Advances in Written Text Analysis*. London: Routledge, pp. 26–45.

Hoey, M. (2001). *Textual Interaction: An Introduction to Written Discourse Analysis*. London: Routledge.

Hopkins, A. & Dudley-Evans, T. (1988). A genre-based investigation of the discussion section in articles and dissertations. *English for Specific Purposes, 7*: 113–22.

Horowitz, D. M. (1986). What professors actually require: Academic tasks for the ESL classroom. *TESOL Quarterly, 20*(3): 445–62.

Hu, M. & Nation, I. S. P. (2000). Unknown vocabulary density and reading-comprehension. *Reading in a Foreign Language, 13*(1): 403–30.

Hughes, A. (2003). *Testing for Language Teachers* (2nd edn). Cambridge: Cambridge University Press.

Hutchinson, T. & Waters, A. (1987). *English for Specific Purposes: A Learning-centred approach*. Cambridge: Cambridge University Press.

Hyland, K. (1999). Academic attribution: citation and the construction of disciplinary knowledge. *Applied Linguistics, 20*(3): 341–67.

Hyland, K. (1996). Talking to the academy: Forms of hedging in science research articles. *Written Communication, 13*(2): 251–81.

Hyland, K. (2001). Bringing in the reader: Addressee features in academic articles. *Written Communication, 18*(4): 549–74.

Hyland, K. (2002a). Directives: Argument and engagement in academic writing. *Applied Linguistics, 23*(2): 215–39.

Hyland, K. (2002b). Specificity revisited: how far should we go now? *English for Specific Purposes, 21*(4): 385–95.

Hyland, K. (2003). Genre-based pedagogies: A social response to process. *Journal of Second Language Writing, 12*(1): 17–29.

Hyland, K. (2004). *Genre and Second Language Writing.* Ann Arbor, MI: University of Michigan Press.

Hyland, K. (2005). *Metadiscourse: Exploring Interaction in Writing.* London: Continuum.

Hyland, K. (2006). *English for Academic Purposes: An Advanced Resource Book.* Abingdon: Routledge.

Hyland, K. (2009a). Different strokes for different folks: Research evidence for specificity in EAP. Paper presented at the BALEAP Biennial Conference: English for Specific Academic Purposes, University of Reading, April, 5, 2009.

Hyland, K. (2009b). *Academic Discourse: English in a Global Context.* London: Continuum.

Hyland, K. & Hamp-Lyons, L. (2002). EAP: Issues and directions. *Journal of English for Academic Purposes, 1*(1): 1–12.

Hyland, K. & Tse, P. (2007). Is there an 'academic vocabulary'? *TESOL Quarterly, 41*(2): 235–53.

Hymes, D. (1972). Models of the interaction of language and of social life. In J. J. Gumperz & D. Hymes (eds.), *Directions in Sociolinguistics.* New York: Holt, Rinehart and Winston, pp. 35–71.

Hyon, S. (1996). Genre in three traditions: Implications for ESL. *TESOL Quarterly, 30*(4): 693–722.

James, K. (1977). Note-taking in lectures: Problems and strategies. In A. P. Cowie & J. B. Heaton (eds.), *English for Academic Purposes.* University of Reading: BAAL/SELMOUS.

Johns, A. M. (1981). Necessary English: A faculty survey. *TESOL Quarterly, 15*(1): 51–7.

Johns, A. M. (1997). *Text, Role, and Context: Developing Academic Literacies.* Cambridge: Cambridge University Press.

Johns, A. M. (2001). The future is with us: Preparing diverse students for the challenges of university texts and cultures. In M. A. Hewings (ed.), *Academic Writing in Context: Implications and Applications. Papers in honour of Tony Dudley-Evans.* Birmingham: University of Birmingham Press, pp. 30–42.

Johns, A. M. (ed.) (2002). *Genre in the Classroom: Multiple Perspectives.* Mahwah, NJ: Lawrence Erlbaum Associates.

Johnston, M. (1987). Understanding learner language. In D. Nunan (ed.), *Applying Second Language Acquisition Research.* Adelaide, Australia: National Curriculum Research Center, pp. 5–44.

Jordan, R. R. (1989). English for academic purposes (EAP). *Language Teaching, 22*(3): 150–64.

Jordan, R. R. (1997). *English for Academic Purposes: A Guide and Resource Book for Teachers*. Cambridge: Cambridge University Press.

Just, M. A. & Carpenter, P. A. (1980). A theory of reading: From eye fixations to comprehension. *Psychological Review, 87*(4): 329–54.

Just, M. A. & Carpenter, P. A. (1986). *The Psychology of Reading and Language Comprehension*. Boston: Allyn and Bacon.

Kanoksilapatham, B. (2005). Rhetorical structure of biochemistry research articles. *English for Specific Purposes, 24*(3): 269–92.

Kanoksilapathan, B. (2007). Rhetorical moves in biochemistry research articles. In D. Biber, U. Connor & T. A. Upton (eds.), *Discourse on the Move: Using Corpus Analysis to Describe Discourse Structure*. (Studies in Corpus Linguistics 28). Amsterdam: John Benjamins, pp. 73–119.

Kelly, R. (1991). The Graeco-Latin vocabulary of formal English: Some pedagogical implications. *RELC Journal, 22*: 69–83.

Kim, S. (2006). Academic oral communication needs of East Asian international graduate students in non-science and non-engineering fields. *English for Specific Purposes, 25*(4): 479–89.

Kincheloe, J. L. (2008). *Critical Pedagogy Primer* (2nd edn). New York: Lang.

King, A. (1992). Facilitating elaborative learning through guided student-generated questioning. *Educational Psychologist, 27*(1): 111–26.

Knapp, P. & Watkins, M. (1994). *Context – Text – Grammar: Teaching the Genres and Grammar of School Writing in Infants and Primary Classrooms*. Broadway, NSW, Australia: Text Productions.

Knapp, P. & Watkins, M. (2005). *Genre, Text, Grammar: Technologies for Teaching and Assessing Writing*. Sydney: University of New South Wales Press.

Kroll, B. (1979). A Survey of the writing needs of foreign and American college freshmen. *ELT Journal, 23*(3): 219–27.

Lackstrom, J., Selinker, L. & Trimble, L. (1973). Technical rhetorical principles and grammatical choice. *TESOL Quarterly, 7*(2): 127–36.

Lankshear, C. A. & McLaren, P. M. (eds.) (1993). *Critical Literacy: Politics, Praxis, and the Postmodern*. Albany, NY: State University of New York Press.

Lave, J. & Wenger, E. (1991). *Situated Learning: Legitimate Peripheral Participation*. Cambridge: Cambridge University Press.

Lea, M. R. (2005). 'Communities of practice' in higher education: Useful heuristic or educational model? In D. Barton & K. Tusting (eds.), *Beyond Communities of Practice: Language, Power and Social Context*. Cambridge: Cambridge University Press, pp. 180–97.

Lea, M. R. & Street, B. (1999). Writing as academic literacies: Understanding textual practices in higher education. In C. N. Candlin & K. Hyland (eds.), *Writing: Texts, Processes and Practices*. London: Longman, pp. 62–81.

Lea, M. R. & Street, B. V. (1998). Student writing in higher education: An academic literacies approach. *Studies in Higher Education, 23*(2): 157–72.

Lee, G. (2009). Speaking up: Six Korean students' oral participation in class discussions in US graduate seminars. *English for Specific Purposes, 28*(3): 142–56.

Levelt, W. J. M. (1989). *Speaking: From Intention to Articulation*. Cambridge, MA: MIT Press.

Lindemann, S. & Mauranen, A. (2001). 'It's just real messy': The occurrence and function of *just* in a corpus of academic speech. *English for Specific Purposes, 20* (Supplement 1): 459–75.

Lynch, T. (2004). *Study Listening: A Course in Listening to Lectures and Note-taking* (2nd edn). Cambridge: Cambridge University Press.

Lynch, T. (2006). Academic listening: Marrying top and bottom. In E. Usó Juan & A. Martínez Flor (eds.), *Current Trends in the Development and Teaching of the Four Language Skills*. Berlin: de Gruyter, pp. 91–110.

Lynch, T. & Anderson, K. (1992). *Study Seaking: A Course in Spoken English for Academic Purposes*. Cambridge: Cambridge University Press.

Lynch, T. & Maclean, J. (2000). Exploring the benefits of task repetition and recycling for classroom language learning. *Language Teaching Research, 4*(3): 221–50.

Lynch, T. & Mendelsohn, D. (2002). Listening. In N. Schmitt (ed.), *Introduction to Applied Linguistics*. London: Arnold, pp. 193–210.

Macken, M., Kalantzis, M., Kress, G., Martin, J. R., Cope, W. & Rothery, J. (1989). *A Genre-based Approach to Teaching Writing, Years 3–6. Book 4: The Theory and Practice of Genre-based Writing*. Sydney: Directorate of Studies, NSW Department of Education in association with the Literacy and Education Research Network.

Macken-Horarik, M. (2002). 'Something to shoot for': A systemic functional approach to teaching genre in secondary school science. In A. M. Johns (ed.), *Genre in the Classroom: Multiple Perspectives*. Mahwah, NJ: Lawrence Erlbaum Associates, pp. 17–42.

Martin, J. R. (1986). Intervening in the process of writing development. In C. Painter & J. R. Martin (eds.), *Writing to Mean: Teaching Genres across the Curriculum*. Applied Linguistics Association of Australia, pp. 11–43.

Martin, J. R. (1989). *Exploring and Challenging Social Reality*. Oxford: Oxford University Press.

Martin, J. R. (1992). *English Text: System and Structure*. Philadelphia: John Benjamins.

Martin, J. R. (1994). Macro-genres: The ecology of the page. *Network, 21*: 29–52.

Martin, J. R. (1995). Text and clause: Fractal resonance. *Text, 15*: 5–42.

Martin, J. R. (1997). Analysing genre: Functional parameters. In F. Christie & J. R. Martin (eds.), *Genre and Institutions: Social Processes in the Workplace and School*. London: Cassell, pp. 3–39.

Martin, J. R. (2000). Design and practice: Enacting functional linguistics. *Annual Review of Applied Linguistics, 20*(1): 116–26.

Martínez-Flor, A., Usó-Juan, E. & Alcón-Soler, E. (2006). Towards acquiring communicative competence through speaking. In E. Usó-Juan & A. Martínez-Flor (eds.), *Current Trends in the Development and Teaching of the Four Language Skills* (Studies on Language Acquisition series) Berlin: Walter de Gruyter, pp. 139–57.

Mason, A. (1994). By dint of: Student and lecturer perceptions of lecture comprehension strategies in first-term graduate study. In J. Flowerdew (ed.), *Academic Listening: Research Perspectives*. Cambridge: Cambridge University Press.

McDonough, J. (1978). *Sociology* (Listening to Lectures series). Oxford: Oxford University Press.

McKenna, E. (1987). Preparing foreign students to enter discourse communities in the U.S. *English for Specific Purposes, 6*(3): 187–202.

McNamara, T. F. (2000). *Language Testing*. Oxford: Oxford University Press.

Miller, C. R. (1984). Genre as social action. *Quarterly Journal of Speech, 70*(2): 151–67.

Moore, T. & Morton, J. (1999). Authenticity in the IELTS Academic Module Writing Test: A comparative study of Task 2 items and university assignments. In *IELTS Research Reports 2*. Canberra: IELTS Australia, pp. 64–106.

Moore, T. & Morton, J. (2005). Dimensions of difference: A comparison of university writing and IELTS writing. *Journal of English for Academic Purposes, 4*(1): 43–66.

Morita, N. (2000). Discourse socialization through oral classroom activities in a TESL graduate program. *TESOL Quarterly, 34*(2): 279–310.

Morton, J. (2009). Genre and disciplinary competence: A case study of contextualisation in an academic speech genre. *English for Specific Purposes, 28*(4): 217–29.

Murillo, S. (2006). The role of reformulation markers in academic lectures. In A. Hornero, M. Luzon & S. Muillo (eds.), *Corpus Linguistics: Applications for the Study of English*. Switzerland: Peter Lang, pp. 353–64.

Murray, D. M. (1982). *Learning by Teaching: Selected Articles on Writing and Teaching*. Montclair, NJ: Boynton/Cook.

Nation, I. S. P. (1990). *Teaching and Learning Vocabulary* (rev. edn). Boston, MA: Heinle & Heinle.

Nation, I. S. P. (2009). *Teaching ESL/EFL Reading and Writing*. New York: Routledge.

Nesi, H. (2001). EASE: A multimedia materials development project. In K. Cameron (ed.), *CALL – The Challenge of Change*. Exeter: Elm Bank Publications, pp. 286–91.

Northcott, J. (2001). Towards an ethnography of the MBA classroom: a consideration of the role of interactive lecturing styles within the context of one MBA programme. *English for Specific Purposes, 20*(1): 15–37.

Nunan, D. (1998). Teaching grammar in context. *ELT Journal, 52*(2): 101–9.

Nuttall, C. E. (1996). *Teaching Reading Skills in a Foreign Language* (rev. edn). Oxford: Heinemann.

Nwogu, K. N. (1991). Structure of science popularizations: A genre-analysis approach to the schema of popularized medical texts. *English for Specific Purposes, 10*(2): 111–23.

Nystrand, M. (1982). *What Writers Know: The Language, Process, and Structure of Written Discourse*. New York: Academic Press.

Olsen, L. A. & Huckin, T. H. (1990). Point-driven understanding in engineering lecture comprehension. *English for Specific Purposes, 9*(1): 33–47.

Osada, N. (2001). What strategy do less proficient learners employ in listening comprehension? A reappraisal of bottom-up and top-down processing. *Journal of Pan-Pacific Association of Applied Linguistics, 5*(1): 73–90.

Ostler, S. E. (1980). A Survey of academic needs for advanced ESL. *TESOL Quarterly, 14*(4): 489–502.

Pakenham, K. S. (2005). *Making Connections: A Strategic Approach to Academic Reading* (2nd edn). Cambridge: Cambridge University Press.

Paltridge, B. (2000). *Making Sense of Discourse Analysis*. Gold Coast, Australia: Antipodean Educational Enterprises.

Paltridge, B. (2001). *Genre and the Language Learning Classroom*. Ann Arbor, MI: University of Michigan Press.

Paltridge, B. (2002). Genre, text type and the English for academic purposes (EAP) classroom. In A. M. Johns (ed.), *Genre in the Classroom: Multiple Perspectives*. Mahwah, NJ: Lawrence Erlbaum Associates, pp. 73–90.

Peacock, M. & Flowerdew, J. (eds.) (2001). *Research Perspectives on English for Academic Purposes*. Cambridge: Cambridge University Press.

Pearson-Casanave, C. P. & Hubbard, P. (1992). The writing assignments and writing problems of doctoral students: Faculty perceptions, pedagogical issues, and needed research. *English for Specific Purposes, 11*(1): 33–49.

Pearson-Casanave, C. P. & Li, X. M. (2008). *Learning the Literacy Practices of Graduate School: Insiders' Reflections on Academic Enculturation*. Ann Arbor, MI: University of Michigan Press.

Pennycook, A. (1997). Vulgar pragmatism, critical pragmatism, and EAP. *English for Specific Purposes, 16*(4): 253–69.

Pennycook, A. (1999). Introduction: Critical approaches to TESOL. *TESOL Quarterly, 33*(3): 329–48.

Perelman, C. & Olbrechts-Tyteca, L. (1969). *The New Rhetoric: A Treatise on Argumentation*. Notre Dame, IN: University of Notre Dame Press.

Pica, T. (1985). The selective impact of classroom instruction on second language acquisition. *Applied Linguistics 6*(3): 214–22.

Pienemann, M. & Johnston, M. (1987). Factors influencing the development of language proficiency. In D. Nunan (ed.), *Applying Second Language Acquisition Research*. Adelaide, Australia: National Curriculum Research Center, pp. 45–142.

Pilegaard, M. & Frandsen, F. (1996). Text type. In J. Verschueren, J.-O. Ostman, J. Blommaert & C. C. Bulcaen (eds.), *Handbook of Pragmatics*. Amsterdam: John Benjamins, pp. 1–13.

Price, J. E. (1977). Study skills – with special reference to seminar strategies and one aspect of academic writing. In S. Holden (ed.), *English for Specific Purposes*. London: Modern English Publications.

Prior, P. A. (1998). *Writing/Disciplinarity: A Sociohistoric Account of Literate Activity in the Academy*. Mahwah, NJ: Lawrence Erlbaum Associates.

Ramanathan, V. & Kaplan, R. B. (1996a). Some problematic 'channels' in the teaching of critical thinking in current L1 composition textbooks: Implications for L2 student-writers. *Issues in Applied Linguistics, 7*(2): 225–49.

Ramanathan, V. & Kaplan, R. B. (1996b). Audience and voice in current L1 composition texts: Some implications for ESL student writers. *Journal of Second Language Writing, 5*(1): 21–34.

Rayner, K. & Pollatsek, A. (1995). *The Psychology of Reading*. Hillsdale, NJ: Lawrence Erlbaum Associates.

Reinhart, S. M. (2002). *Giving Academic Presentations*. Ann Arbor, MI: University of Michigan Press.

Richards, J. C. & Schmidt, R. W. (2002). *Longman Dictionary of Language Teaching and Applied Linguistics* (3rd edn). New York: Longman.

Robinson, P., Strong, G., Whittle, J. & Nobe, S. (2001). The development of EAP oral discussion ability. In J. Flowerdew & M. Peacock (eds.), *Research Perspectives on English for Academic Purposes*. Cambridge: Cambridge University Press, pp. 347–59.

Rost, M. (1990). *Listening in Language Learning*. London: Longman.

Rounds, P. L. (1987). Characterizing successful classroom discourse for NNS teaching assistant training. *TESOL Quarterly, 21*(4): 643–71.

Rumelhart, D. E. (1977). Towards an interactive model of reading. In S. Dornic (ed.), *Attention and Performance VI: Proceedings of the Sixth International*

222 *References*

Symposium on Attention and Performance, Stockholm, Sweden, July 28–August 1, 1975. Hillsdale, NJ: Lawrence Erlbaum Associates, pp. 573–603.

Salager-Meyer, F. (1994). Hedges and textual communicative function in medical English written discourse. *English for Specific Purposes, 13*(2): 149–70.

Salehzadeh, J. (2006). *Academic Listening Strategies: A Guide to Understanding Lectures.* Ann Arbor, MI: University of Michigan Press.

Santos, T. (1992). Ideology in composition: L1 and ESL. *Journal of Second Language Writing, 1*(1): 1–15.

Santos, T. (2001). The place of politics in second language writing. In T. Silva & P. K. Matsuda (eds.), *On Second Language Writing.* Mahwah, NJ: Lawrence Erlbaum Associates, pp. 173–90.

Saville-Troike, M. (1989). *The Ethnography of Communication: An Introduction* (2nd edn). Oxford: Blackwell.

Schmidt, N. & Carter, R. (2000). The lexical advantages of narrow reading for second language learners. *TESOL Journal, 9*(1): 4–9.

Schryer, C. F. (1993). Records as genre. *Written Communication, 10*(2): 200–34.

Selinker, L., Todd-Trimble, M. & Trimble, L. (1978). Rhetorical function-shifts in EST discourse. *TESOL Quarterly, 12*(3): 311–20.

Silva, T (1990). Second language composition instruction: Developments, issues and directions in ESL. In B. Kroll (ed.), *Second Language Writing: Research Insights for the Classroom.* Cambridge: Cambridge University Press, pp. 11–23.

Simpson, R. C. (2004). Stylistic features of academic speech. The role of formulaic expressions. In U. Connor & T. A. Upton (eds.), *Discourse in the Professions.* Amsterdam: John Benjamins, pp. 37–63.

Skehan, P. (1996). A framework for the implementation of task-based instruction. *Applied Linguistics, 17*(1): 38–62.

Sloan, D. & Porter, E. (2009). The management of English language support in postgraduate business education: The CEM model (contextualization, embedding, mapping). *The International Journal of Management Education, 7*(2): 51–8.

Smart, G. (1998). Mapping conceptual worlds: Using interpretive ethnography to explore knowledge-making in a professional community. *Journal of Business Communication, 35*(1): 111–27.

Stahl, S. A. & Fairbanks, M. M. (1986). The effects of vocabulary instruction: A model-based meta-analysis. *Review of Educational Research, 56*(1): 72–110.

Strodt-Lopez, B. (1991). Tying it all in: Asides in university lectures. *Applied Linguistics, 12*(2): 117–40.

Sutarsyah, C., Nation, P. & Kennedy, G. (1994). How useful is EAP vocabulary for ESP? A corpus based case study. *RELC Journal, 25*: 34–50.

Swales, J. (1981). *Aspects of Article Introductions,* Aston Research Report No. 1. Birmingham: The University of Aston, Language Studies Unit.

Swales, J. (1988). Discourse communities, genres and English as an international language. *World Englishes, 7*(2): 211–20.

Swales, J. M. (1990). *Genre Analysis: English in Academic and Research Settings.* Cambridge: Cambridge University Press.

Swales, J. M. (1998). *Other Floors, Other Voices: A Textography of a Small University Building.* Mahwah, NJ: Lawrence Erlbaum Associates.

Swales, J. M. (2002). On models in applied discourse analysis. In C. N. Candlin (ed.), *Research and Practice in Professional Discourse.* Hong Kong: City University of Hong Kong Press, pp. 61–77.

Swales, J. M. (2004). *Research Genres: Explorations and Applications*. Cambridge: Cambridge University Press.

Swales, J. M. & Feak, C. B. (2004). *Academic Writing for Graduate Students: Essential Tasks and Skills* (2nd edn). Ann Arbor, MI: University of Michigan Press.

Tapper, J. (1996). Exchange patterns in the oral discourse of international students in university classrooms. *Discourse Processes, 22*(1): 25–55.

Tauroza, S. (2001). Second language lecture comprehension in naturalistic controlled conditions. In J. Flowerdew & M. Peacock (eds.), *Research Perspectives on English for Academic Purposes*. Cambridge: Cambridge University Press, pp. 360–74.

Thompson, S. (1994). Frameworks and contexts: A genre-based approach to analysing lecture introductions. *English for Specific Purposes, 13*(2): 171–86.

Thomson, A. (2009). *Critical Reasoning: A Practical Introduction* (3rd edn). London: Routledge.

Tomlins, J. (1993). Principles and Design of Materials for Academic Discusssion. Unpublished dissertation for MEd TESOL, University of Manchester, England.

Tribble, C. (2002). Corpora and corpus analysis: New windows on academic writing. In J. Flowerdew (ed.), *Academic Discourse*. London: Longman, Pearson Education, pp. 131–49.

UCLES (2006). *IELTS Handbook 2006*. Cambridge: University of Cambridge Local Examinations Syndicate.

UCLES (2009). *IELTS Guide for Stakeholders* [brochure] from http://www.ielts.org/pdf/IELTSGuideforStakeholders2009.pdf

Vellutino, F. R. & Scanlon, D. M. (1982). Verbal processing in poor and normal readers. In C. J. Brainerd & M. Pressley (eds.), *Verbal Processes in Children*. New York: Springer-Verlag, pp. 189–264.

Ventola, E. (1984). Orientation to social semiotics in foreign language teaching. *Applied Linguistics, 5*(3): 275–86.

Verhoeven, L. T. & de Jong, J. H. A. L. (1992). *The Construct of Language Proficiency: Applications of Psychological Models to Language Assessment*. Amsterdam: John Benjamins.

Virtanen, T. (1992). Issues of text typology: Narrative – a 'basic' type of text? *Text – Interdisciplinary Journal for the Study of Discourse, 12*(2): 293–310.

Waters, A. & Waters, M. (2001). Designing tasks for developing study competence and study skills in English. In J. Flowerdew & M. Peacock (eds.), *Research Perspectives on English for Academic Purposes*. Cambridge: Cambridge University Press, pp. 375–89.

Waters, M. & Waters, A. (1992). Study skills and study competence: Getting the priorities right. *ELT Journal, 46*(3): 264–73.

Waters, M. & Waters, A. (1995). *Study Tasks in English*. Cambridge: Cambridge University Press.

Wenger, E. (1998). *Communities of Practice: Learning, Meaning, and Identity*. Cambridge: Cambridge University Press.

Werlich, E. (1976). *A Text Grammar of English*. Heidelberg: Quelle and Meyer.

Widdowson, H. G. (1983). *Learning Purpose and Language Use*. Oxford: Oxford University Press.

Widdowson, H. G. (1990). *Aspects of Language Teaching*. Oxford: Oxford University Press.

Widdowson, H. G. (1998). Communication and community: The pragmatics of ESP. *English for Specific Purposes, 17*(1): 3–14.

Widdowson, H. G. (2000). On the limitations of linguistics applied. *Applied Linguistics, 21*(1): 32–5.

Widdowson, H. G. (2004). *Text, Context, Pretext: Critical Issues in Discourse Analysis.* Malden, MA: Blackwell.

Wilkins, D. A. (1976). *Notional Syllabuses: A Taxonomy and its Relevance to Foreign Language Curriculum Development.* London: Oxford University Press.

Williams, I. A. (1999). Results sections of medical research articles: Analysis of rhetorical categories for pedagogical purposes. *English for Specific Purposes, 18*(4): 347–66.

Wilson, M. (2003). Discovery listening: Improving perceptual processing. *ELT Journal, 57*(4): 335–43.

Xue, G. & Nation, I. S. P. (1984). A university word list. *Language Learning and Communication, 3*: 215–29.

Yakhontova, T. (2002). 'Selling' or 'telling'? The issue of cultural variation in research genres. In J. Flowerdew (ed.), *Academic Discourse.* London: Pearson Education. pp. 216–32.

Yang, R. & Allison, D. (2003). Research articles in applied linguistics: Moving from results to conclusions. *English for Specific Purposes, 22*(4): 365–85.

Zappa-Hollman, S. (2007). Academic presentations across post-secondary contexts: The discourse socialization of non-native English speakers. *The Canadian Modern Language Review/La Revue canadienne des langues vivantes, 63*(4): 455–85.

Index

academic word list (AWL) (Coxhead, 2001) 69, 96–7, 151, 213
academic literacies movement (Lea & Street, 1998) 8, 25, 128, 218
accommodationist pedagogy: *see* EAP pedagogy
achievement tests: *see* test
analytic scoring: *see* scoring
analytic syllabus: *see* syllabus

bottom-up processing 54, 57, 64, 114, 142, 155–7, 165–6, 171–2, 208; *see also* top-down processing
bridging courses 6, 132
British Academic Spoken English Corpus (BASE Corpus) 164

capacity: *see* competence and capacity (Widdowson, 1983)
CEM model (Sloan & Porter, 2009) 72, 222
cognitive apprenticeship (Collins, Brown & Newman, 1989) 190–1, 193–4, 213
cognitive genre (Bruce 2005, 2008a) 47, 56, 77–8, 81, 84–90, 93, 131–8, 207, 211–12; *see also* social genre
Common European Framework of Reference for Languages 120, 213
communicative competence 41, 46, 116, 119–21, 146, 179–80, 198–9, 212, 219
communities of practice (Lave & Wenger, 1991) 16, 20–4, 218, 223
competence: *see* competence and capacity (Widdowson, 1983)
competence and capacity (Widdowson, 1983) 4–5, 8, 42, 45–6, 49, 54–5, 58, 132
Competency Framework for Teachers of English for Academic Purposes (BALEAP, 2008) 27, 103–4, 210

componential analysis 98–9
concordance: *see* corpus
concordancing 99, 213
corpus 33–5, 75, 96–9, 137, 151, 162, 164–5, 171–2, 176, 181
    word list 33, 137
    concordance 33–4, 99, 137
criterion-referenced measurement: *see* measurement
critical competence 121–2, 128–9
critical EAP pedagogy (Benesch, 1993): *see* EAP pedagogy
critical ethnographic study 13
critical literacy (Lankshear & McLaren, 1993) 123, 128, 218
critical pedagogy (Kincheloe, 2008) 10, 12, 128, 218
critical thinking 110–12, 128, 177, 179, 181, 183, 185, 187, 189, 190–5, 213, 221

declarative knowledge: *see* knowledge
dialogic (Bakhtin, 1986) 80, 93, 116
direct test/testing: *see* test
discourse community/communities (Nystrand, 1982) 13, 14, 16, 18–20, 23–4, 26, 30, 44, 107–8, 110, 117–18, 121–2, 126–7, 129, 143–4, 193–5, 211, 219, 222; *see also* place discourse communities (Swales, 1998)
discourse competence 12–13, 41, 46, 59–60, 66–7, 83, 91, 107, 115, 119–22, 124, 129, 132, 139, 141, 145–7, 179, 194–5, 208–9, 211
discourse pattern (Hoey, 1983) 56, 65, 77, 86, 89, 90–1, 133, 216
discursive competence (Bhatia, 2004) 46, 120–2

EAP pedagogy
    accommodationist pedagogy 10, 12, 14, 190

EAP pedagogy – *continued*
  critical EAP pedagogy (Benesch,
    1993)   11, 12–13
English for Specific Purposes   4, 19,
  31, 80, 105, 125
ethnography of communication
  17–18, 29, 214, 222

gestalt(s)   56, 87, 133, 137
general service list (GSL) (Bauman &
  Culligan, 2005)   96–7, 151, 210

holistic scoring: *see* scoring

IELTS   42, 44, 69, 116, 220, 123
indirect test/testing: *see* test
in-sessional   7–9, 40, 42–3, 48, 66,
  68–9, 97, 111, 132, 135, 148–9,
  187; *see also* pre-sessional
interpropositional relations   84, 87,
  133, 135, 137

kinesics (body language)   160, 186
knowledge
  declarative knowledge   54–5, 59,
    63–4, 74, 114, 178, 196, 208
  procedural knowledge   8, 42, 49,
    54–6, 64, 178, 188

legitimate peripheral participation
  (Lave & Wenger, 1991)   21, 218;
    see also communities of practice
lexical thresholds   115, 151, 159,
  213

measurement
  criterion-referenced measurement
    201
  norm-referenced measurement
    201
metacognition (Flavell, 1976)   167,
  174, 215
metadiscourse (Hyland, 2005)   48,
  80, 84, 86, 90, 93–5, 100, 108,
  127, 136, 138–9, 163, 176, 217
Michigan Corpus of Spoken Academic
  English (MICASE)   34, 164,
  171–2, 176
moves and steps (Swales, 1990)   31,
  80, 136, 139, 218

narrow angle courses and wide angle
  courses (Widdowson, 1983)   4–6,
  45–6, 55, 132
narrow reading (Schmidt & Carter,
  2000)   152, 222
needs analysis (Hutchinson & Waters,
  1987)   7, 9, 11, 13, 15–16, 35–9,
  41, 45, 60, 65, 68, 71, 107, 111,
  113, 214
  present situation analysis   38–41,
    111
  target situation analysis   9, 13,
    15–16, 27, 35, 38–9, 42–4, 60,
    68, 71, 107, 111
New Rhetoric/Rhetorical Genre
  Studies   19, 32, 125, 221
nominalist-realist debate   25–6
norm-referenced measurement:
    see measurement

ontology   24–5, 74

paper and pencil test: *see* test
pedagogic transfer   67, 71, 78, 82
performance-based assessment   116
performance test: *see* test
place discourse communities (Swales,
  1998)   20
present situation analysis: *see* needs
  analysis
pre-sessional course   8, 43, 48;
    see also in-sessional course
pre-textual knowledge (Widdowson,
  2004)   141
Preview-Detail discourse pattern
  (Hoey, 1983)   56, 65, 146
Problem-Solution (Hoey, 1983)   89,
  146, 175, 186; *see also*
  Preview-Detail discourse pattern
procedural knowledge: *see*
  knowledge
proficiency test: *see* test

reader response theory (Hirvela, 2004)
  126, 143
reliability: *see* test
rights analysis   11, 13
Rhetorical Genre Studies: *see*
  New Rhetoric

schematic structure 30, 55–6, 65, 80,
    138–9, 162
scoring
    analytic scoring 203–4, 207–9
    holistic scoring 203
situated learning (Lave & Wenger,
    1991) 21–2, 218
social genre (Bruce, 2005, 2008a) 47,
    77, 80–1, 84, 86, 89–90, 93, 131–2,
    136–7, 139, 144, 148, 207; *see also*
    cognitive genre
speech communities (Gumperz, 1972)
    16–17, 23
stabilized-for-now (Schryer, 1993) 32
stance 26, 34, 78, 80, 93, 138, 148,
    176, 211, 213
syllabus
    analytic syllabus 54, 58–9, 114,
        130–1, 196, 208
    synthetic syllabus 58
    task-based syllabus 59
    text-based syllabus 59
    process syllabus 59
syllabus objectives
    atomistic objectives 46, 54–5,
        58–9, 63, 114, 196, 208
    holistic objectives 54–5, 59, 63,
        66, 196, 208
study competence (Waters & Waters,
    1992) 140–1, 144–5, 147, 223
synthetic syllabus 58; *see also*
    analytic syllabus

Systemic Functional Linguistics 30,
    80, 123, 125, 214

target situation analysis: *see* needs
    analysis
test
    achievement test 200–1, 203–4
    direct test 202, 206
    indirect test 202
    paper and pencil test 200
    performance test 197–8, 200,
        203–4, 206, 208
    proficiency test 116, 200
    reliability 197, 201–2
    validity 197, 201–3
    washback 114, 198, 208–9
TOEFL (Test of English as a Foreign
    Language) 44, 69, 116, 202
top-down processing 64, 114, 142,
    155–6, 165–6, 169–71, 175–6,
    196, 208, 220; *see also* bottom-up
    processing

university word list (Xue & Nation,
    1984) 97, 151, 224

validity: *see* test

washback: *see* test
wide angle course 4–6, 45–6, 55,
    132; *see also* narrow angle course
word list: *see* corpus
word networks 98–100